Prentice-Hall Educational
Administration Series
WILLIAM AMMENTORP, *Consulting Editor*

Educational System Planning
ROGER A. KAUFMAN

Development of Information Systems for Education
KHATEEB M. HUSSAIN

Understanding Communities
JAMES A. CONWAY, ROBERT E. JENNINGS,
AND MIKE M. MILSTEIN

Educational and Organizational Leadership in Elementary Schools
THOMAS J. SERGIOVANNI AND DAVID L. ELLIOTT

Policymaking in American Public Education
JOHN T. THOMPSON

Educational and
Leadership in

Organizational

Elementary Schools

Thomas J. Sergiovanni
University of Illinois, Urbana-Champaign

David L. Elliott
Studies in Education, Berkeley, California

PRENTICE-HALL, INC., ENGLEWOOD CLIFFS, N. J.

Library of Congress Cataloging in Publication Data

SERGIOVANNI, THOMAS J.
    Educational and organizational leadership in elementary schools.

(Prentice-Hall educational administration series)
    Includes bibliographical references.
    1. Elementary school administration. I. Elliott,
    David L. II. Title.
LB2822.5.S4   372.1'2   74-28247
ISBN 0-13-240689-6

Educational and Organizational Leadership in Elementary Schools

Thomas J. Sergiovanni and David L. Elliott

© 1975 by
Prentice-Hall, Inc., Englewood Cliffs, N. J.

10   9   8   7   6   5   4

Prentice-Hall International, Inc., *London*
Prentice-Hall of Australia, Pty. Ltd., *Sydney*
Prentice-Hall of Canada, Ltd., *Toronto*
Prentice-Hall of India Private Limited, *New Delhi*
Prentice-Hall of Japan, Inc., *Tokyo*

Contents

Preface

THIS IS A BOOK FOR principals, supervisors, advisors, master teachers, heads, house masters, and others interested in educational and organizational leadership in elementary schools. For convenience, we refer in the text to the *principal*, though it should be understood that he holds no monopoly on leadership. In recent years, the emphasis seems to have shifted from educational leadership to organizational leadership for principals. That is, principals are prepared knowing less about educational program matters and more about organizational matters that relate to leadership behavior, communication, decision making and morale. His university training emphasizes collective bargaining, the management of conflict, PPBS and other planning models, theories of decision making, and the politics of education. Some feel as we do—that perhaps we have gone overboard in emphasizing the principal's organizational skills. Others would have us shift the emphasis entirely away from organizational leadership, often proposing that the American principal adopt more of the characteristics of the British head—emphasizing strong educational leadership and insisting on conformity to his image as to how the school should function educationally. Should the principal be a manager or an educational leader? This really is a silly argument that proposes a fallacious dichotomy. Of course, both educational and organizational leadership are important. In this book we advocate knowledgeable and visionary principals with respect to educational program matters and competent principals with respect to such organizational matters as staff growth and development and building commitment to the school and its programs.

An assumption basic to the book is that the elementary school is a unique kind of educational institution with a distinct character, mission, and philosophy that, in turn, require the expression of a unique value and operational orientation from its principals and supervisors. Further, school size is such that the typical elementary school principal or supervisor operates in a more familiar setting (primary group) than do administrators in the senior high or central office. He finds himself closer to students, teachers, teaching, curriculum, and parents than do his counterparts—who often are forced to delegate these functions in favor of more pressing organizational demands. Moreover, since the elementary school serves very young students with special kinds of needs, this "child's world" requires a more personal, low-keyed style of administration and leadership than the sophistication in management and organization advocated by recent writers.

We believe that the principal should be a leader who can face up to and *capitalize* on the uniqueness and importance of the elementary school in our society. Educational and organizational leadership is expressed in three ways —through human resource development, educational program development, and community development. Behavioral science principles, as they apply to administration and supervision, and humanistic psychology are the origins of the human resource development thrust. Educational philosophy and knowledge about children, learning, and teaching are the origins of educational program development thrust. Community development, as an expression of educational leadership, has its origins in the extended school concept and the articulation of interdependent school–community linkages.

This book emerged from a long and continuous dialogue with a number of colleagues at the University of Illinois who are interested in children and in elementary education. This dialogue forced me, as an applied social scientist interested in administration, to answer some questions about the role of the elementary school principal. The questions were persistent—indeed sometimes annoying—and rarely easy to dismiss. Are principals actually functional? Why do organizational scientists, theorists, and management experts seem to push so hard for professionalizing administration as a discipline separate from education? Why are schools so bureaucratic? Have administrators abandoned all hopes of being effective educational leaders? Why do schools as organizations and not children as human beings seem so important to school administrators? In summary, is educational leadership dead for elementary school principals and supervisors? We try to answer these questions, though in the final analysis they can only be answered by the action of those professionals who work in the elementary schools as practitioners.

An experiential approach is used throughout much of the book. The activities utilize information the reader contributes to build concepts and to illustrate practices. Groups of people working on the activities together— either in college classrooms or on the job—will greatly enhance the utility of the book as a staff development tool.

David Elliott, a specialist in child development, early childhood education, and curriculum evaluation, assumed responsibility for the development of Part V, "Getting to the Heart of Curriculum Matters." We both appreciate the help Leslie Weston gave us in the initial stages of the book's development. Jane Morpurgo, Richard Lanagan, Ted Manolakes, and Robert J. Starratt are some of several friends and colleagues who contributed much to my thinking regarding the principal's role as an educational leader. Starratt's ideas are particularly basic to Chapter 4.

David Elliott shares with me the hope that in some small way we have contributed to rediscovering the human possibilities that the elementary school has to offer.

Thomas J. Sergiovanni

I

The Principalship:
Benchmarks
and Bearings

1

The Elementary
School in Society

ELEMENTARY SCHOOL PRINCIPALS are in a position to exert a powerful influence on the state of schooling and school administration in this country. They represent the largest group of line administrators presently functioning in schools. Moreover, since elementary school children are at a relatively formative age, teachers and principals are in a position to assume an important role in determining the kinds of human beings these young people will be in later school years and in adult life. These are formative years, not only in determining basic intellect, but in developing *humanness.*

Despite the importance of the elementary school principalship as a force that could shape American education, the potential has not been realized. We have no intention of criticizing elementary school principals or of disparaging elementary education. By and large, principals know what needs to be done, but have been unable to get it done. The power potential is there, but elementary school principals have been kept relatively powerless in spite of their numbers. Further, elementary education is still considered by many in positions of influence in and out of the schools as largely "women's work of small import."

We believe that the elementary school can come of age as an institution with promise to dramatically change American education. Much will depend on the kind of leadership which present and future elementary school principals elect to give. One of our purposes in this book is to help principals get this important job done. We are concerned with leadership, but not the old-fashioned techniques borrowed from our colleagues in secondary education and general administration. We propose a new kind of leadership with a grass-roots origin. More about this later. In this chapter, we develop a perspective on the elementary school, its purpose, importance, and unique role. In the next chapter, we examine two studies which describe the present form of the elementary school principalship.

Some Perspectives on Elementary Education

The current solution to the problems we are facing (for example, rapid change, expanding technology, urbanization, polarized society, and increased interpersonal and personal tensions) seems to be to promote a greater effort toward increasing the schools' capacity to give children more education in less time. "Let's apply American know-how to make the schools more productive than they are presently"—this seems to be the prevailing attitude.

There is a relationship between the kind of know-how that is used to solve a problem and the solution to the problem. That is, means and ends are not readily separated when effects on people, especially young people, are involved. Certain kinds of ends, particularly those difficult to quantify—such as problem-solving skills, creativity, love, and sensitivity—are not readily achieved with young people unless the organization of the elementary school encourages and nurtures these ideals as part of its culture, and the adults in the school express them in their work. The culture and form of a school should emerge from the functions and goals which it seeks, but it is just as likely that the functions and goals which the school achieves will follow its culture and form. For example, if a school wishes to prepare young people in such a way that passivity, order, and uniformity are encouraged and imagination, problem solving, and flexibility are discouraged, then the school should organize itself and its curriculum in a fashion which emphasizes rules, regulations, schedules, heavily prescribed programs arranged in rigid steps, and a system of close control and supervision. A school organized and operated in that manner will get passivity, order, and uniformity, but not imagination, problem solving, and flexibility—regardless of what it claims its goals to be.[1]

---

[1] See, for example, Herald Hage, "An Axiomatic Theory of Organizations," *Administrative Science Quarterly*, Vol. 10, No. 3 (December 1965), pp. 289–320; and Amitai Etzioni, *A Comparative Analysis of Complex Organizations* (New York: Free Press, 1961). Additional consideration is given to these concepts in Chapter 3 as we discuss manifest and latent school goals.

Perhaps we need to look less at what people say the goals of elementary schools should be and more at how the schools work to achieve these goals. In the past decade or two, the emphasis has been on the development of new and better (that is, more sophisticated and structured) curricula, more specific instructional goals, the utilization of modern technology to help improve the delivery of education to young people, the invention of ingenious structural arrangements which group youngsters in more efficient patterns for receiving instruction, and highly developed patterns of staff utilization which more efficiently use the specialized talents of teachers. These efforts to help children in elementary schools seem to consider everything except the children themselves. Most of the changes which have been proposed in recent years have focused too much on altering arrangements and materials, and not enough on altering the culture of the school. This culture is expressed in the way teachers and administrators behave toward each other and toward children and in the assumptions which are the antecedents to this behavior. Further, we have not demonstrated that we are concerned with goals and purposes in the broader sense. Of course, we have been concerned about what Johnny ought to know, but we have not been concerned enough with the kind of person he ought to become.

The major problems facing society and the schools are basically people problems which will be better understood and served as the school increases its capacity for humanness.[2] Rhetoric such as this is widely accepted and used, but little change results from it. The real task ahead of us is to close the gap between what we believe and what we do as teachers and administrators in elementary schools. Appropriate action will take hard work by committed and courageous people, and it is our hope that this book will sharpen the philosophy and perspective of its readers and will provide them with the know-how they need to make a real difference.

This is a child-centered book, but it is more than that. It is a people-centered book which concentrates on the concerns and needs of parents, teachers, and administrators as well as children. We maintain that humanism is not something we can give to children, but is a condition which should be cultivated and nurtured in the school by all of its participants.

---

[2] Some readers will naturally wonder whether the intent is to trade off academic, intellectual, and skill goals with which elementary schools have been traditionally concerned in order to provide more emphasis to human goals. Quite the contrary, for the two kinds of goals are interdependent. With respect to "freedom to learn," for example, the work of Pablo Freire in Latin America and of informal-education advocates in England and in the United States seems to show convincingly that feeling free to learn is an important facilitator to learning itself. Combs has been pointing out the interdependent nature of knowledge and personal meanings with respect to this knowledge for what seems like generations: Arthur W. Combs, *Educational Accountability Beyond Behavioral Objectives* (Washington, D.C.: Association for Supervision and Curriculum Development, National Education Association, 1972), pp. 17–33. See also David Nyberg, *Tough and Tender Learning* (New York: National Press Books, 1971), p. 127.

The Elementary School
as a Unique Institution

Uniqueness is something which most members of organizations and institutions prize, for each likes to think that his purposes and mission are special and important. Few formal institutions in our society, however, can rival the elementary school, and particularly the extended elementary school concept, in importance. The extended elementary school concept is one which includes in the elementary school's responsibility for education the period from the child's conception to his formal entry into kindergarten. This extension is accomplished by developing linkages between school and home which increase the family's capacity for parenthood.[3]

IMPORTANCE IN SOCIETY

When considered together, the extended elementary school concept and the formal elementary school program are in contact with youngsters at the most crucial time in their development. Bloom's classic work on the development of educational capacity provides a convincing argument for this view.

> By about four, 50 percent of the variation in intelligence at age 17 is accounted for . . . in terms of intelligence measured at age 17; from conception to age four, the individual develops 50 percent of his mature intelligence; from ages four to eight he develops 30 percent, and from ages eight to 17, the remaining 20 percent. . . . We would expect the variations in the environments to have relatively little effect on the IQ after age eight, but would expect such variation to have marked effect on the IQ before that age, with the greatest effect likely to take place between the ages of about one to five.[4]

The early years of formal schooling, kindergarten through grade 3, are important for capitalizing on whatever intellectual capacities individual children have. It is during these years that the ability to work independently, to develop and refine verbal and written skills, to acquire an intrinsic interest in and love of learning, and to develop skills of problem solving and inquiry become pronounced. Not to be overlooked is self-concept development, the ability to work with others, and the ability to come to know and love success in school. These formative years largely determine who will and will not suc-

[3] Examples of school-home linkages in the extended elementary school include health and education programs for pregnant mothers, child-care programs, home visitation programs, toy exchange libraries, day-care centers, and nursery school programs. We examine these concepts and ideas more systematically in Chapter 13 as we consider school and community relationships.

[4] Benjamin S. Bloom, *Stability and Change in Human Characteristics* (New York: John Wiley and Sons, 1964), p. 68.

ceed in later life both in and out of school, as students and more importantly as human beings.

In a recent report, the Education Commission of the States speaks of early education as an investment. The investment argument should not be overdone, but it can be useful to elementary school principals as they work with those deeply skeptical of increased costs for elementary education in general and for the extended elementary school concept in particular.

> To the extent that an educational program for young children contributes to their success as students and citizens, it will significantly reduce subsequent remedial, counseling and even penal and welfare costs. There are no definitive statistics on how much a state might save in the long term by investing in early childhood education. And there is not yet enough experience to analyze precisely the relationship of early training to prevention of later problems.
>
> But it is clear that a relationship exists. Failure in the initial years of formal education can be closely tied to the high percentage of drop-outs in the public schools. It costs approximately twice as much to retain a child in a mentally retarded or remedial classroom as in a regular classroom. Once in a special class, he usually remains there at least eight years. And yet, for example, over half the Spanish-surnamed and Negro children in mentally retarded classrooms in California have the ability to be in regular classrooms and have been misclassified because they lacked early training in English and the basic skills demanded by the public schools. It costs per year, on a national average, $4,070 to detain a juvenile, $1,898 to keep an individual in a state penitentiary, and about $1,000 for an individual on welfare.[5]

AN INFORMAL-FORMAL ORGANIZATION

Elementary schools, like most institutions in our society, share many characteristics of formal organizations. Hierarchy, rules, status systems, and a division of labor are not unknown to elementary schools in the United States. One cannot help but wonder whether such attributes of formal bureaucratic organization need to be so omnipresent. After all, the typical elementary school is relatively small, having less than 500 pupils on the average and about 18 full-time teachers.[6] The small size of typical elementary schools permits them to approximate an informal or semiformal organization if the principal is willing.

Smaller faculties and facilities permit a primary-group orientation to dominate the activities of the elementary school. Simply put, people are closer

[5] *Early Childhood Development Alternatives for Program Implementation in the States.* A report of the Education Commission of the States (Denver, June 1971), pp. 13–14.

[6] Only about 2 percent of the 2,200 principals surveyed by the Department of Elementary School Principals in 1968 reported enrollments in excess of 700 pupils with 38 percent reporting enrollments of less than 400. *The Elementary School Principalship in 1968. . . . A Research Study* (Washington, D.C.: Department of Elementary School Principals, National Education Association, 1968), p. 67.

to each other as people. Principals are closer to teachers, students, and parents and relate to them less as role incumbents and more as people. True, there are many dangers in moving in this direction, for a feeling of intimacy in and of itself is not necessarily a building block of an effective organization.[7] We are not, however, referring to a social club setting, but to an informal organization which is committed to pulling together, sharing, and hard work on behalf of young people.

An elementary school so organized would deemphasize rules, regulations, routines, standardization, job descriptions, hierarchy, formal authority, status systems, and schedules. The emphasis would be on the work to be done, the goals to be accomplished and the *joy* of accomplishing this work. It is important that we think of these dimensions not in terms of either/or (that is, either rigid rules and regulations or none), but rather in terms of emphasis and the extent to which organizational dimensions are consistent with elementary school goals and purposes. A certain amount of formal organization can be helpful and even supportive of elementary school goals, providing that the organization becomes increasingly flexible as the focus shifts from operating the school efficiently to living and working with children. Organizational efficiency is important, but must not be achieved at the expense of human values.

More obvious aspects which differentiate the elementary school from other kinds of schools are the very young children which they serve and a faculty which is largely female, more satisfied with the job, more stable in terms of turnover, and less inclined to be specialized in terms of preparation and interest.[8] Further, evidence from the Teacher Characteristics Study suggests that attitudes of elementary school teachers toward pupils, administrators, fellow teachers, and nonacademic staff are more favorable than similar attitudes of secondary school teachers. This same study revealed that educational viewpoints of secondary school teachers were of a more traditional or learner-centered nature, while those of elementary school teachers seemed more permissive or child-centered.[9]

Parents of elementary school children seem more interested in what is going on in the school and express a greater willingness to support the school with their time, effort, and talents. In general, parents would like to be more

---

[7] Halpin finds, for example, that elementary schools described as open and those described as closed both exhibit high intimacy: Andrew Halpin, *Theory and Research in Administration* (New York: Macmillan, 1967), pp. 150–151.

[8] See, for example, Ward S. Mason, *The Beginning Teacher: Status and Career Orientations* (Washington, D.C.: U.S. Department of Health, Education and Welfare, 1961), pp. 81–83; W. W. Charters, Jr., "Some 'Obvious' Facts About the Teaching Career," *Educational Administration Quarterly*, Vol. 3, No. 2 (1967), 183–193; Francis Trusty and Thomas J. Sergiovanni, "Perceived Need Deficiencies of Teachers and Administrators: A Proposal for Restructuring Teacher Roles," *Educational Administration Quarterly*, Vol. 2, No. 1 (1966), 168–181.

[9] David G. Ryans, *Characteristics of Teachers* (Washington, D.C.: American Council on Education, 1960), p. 385.

involved and would like to contribute more to the school if they knew how or could be made more welcome. Very young children do not differentiate between learning at home and learning at school. This suggests a need for better integration of educational opportunities and settings both in and out of school. Parents can help the school in this important work.

With this in mind, it should be obvious that the orientation of the elementary school principal must also be unique. He should not continue to look to his counterparts in the junior high, senior high, superintendent's chair, or central office for models of administration, supervision, and program development. Rather, he needs to find his models in the uniqueness of his school and its links with its tasks and goals, its children, its faculty, and its community. If he is successful, perhaps his counterparts will model themselves after him. His leadership efforts need to be less concerned with educational administration in a managerial sense and more concerned with educational and community leadership and development. To this end, successful elementary school principals seek opportunities to work first-hand with children, teachers, and parents as people and to see the problems they face. Ineffective principals often seem to view children, teachers, and parents as the enemy and work to insulate themselves from them. Insulation takes the form of overemphasizing protocol, procedures, rules and regulations, status systems, lines of authority, established ways of doing things, schedules, standardizations, and other manifestations of too formal and overly bureaucratic organizations. Soon children, teachers, and parents learn that insulation and defense are patterns that they too must adopt in order to survive. Indeed, survival—making it through the system—supersedes all else.[10] This is a pattern which needs to be avoided, or, if presently in effect in a given school, needs to be broken. This book should help, for it provides value and action bases for principals interested in educational and community leadership and development.

In the next chapter, we describe the present status of the elementary school principal, inventory some of the major problems he feels he faces, provide some clues to the characteristics effective principals have in common, and present the basic plan for the remainder of the book.

---

[10] See, for example, Ellen Lurie, *How to Change the Schools: A Parents' Action Handbook on How to Fight the System* (New York: Random House, 1970).

2

The Principalship: Two Studies

In 1968, the Department of Elementary School Principals of the National Education Association conducted a status study of the elementary school principalship. This study represented the fourth of its kind (previous reports were made in 1928, 1948, and 1958). The 1968 study showed only minor differences from the one conducted in 1958 which suggests a strand of stability in the principalship role. On this basis, one can assume that a similar study, if conducted today, would reveal information much like that obtained in 1968. A representative sample of persons with responsibility for individual elementary schools—2,318 principals—participated in the survey. Some estimates place the total number of persons with this responsibility at between 40 and 50 thousand. Of the group surveyed, approximately 4 percent listed themselves as "head teacher," 15 percent as "teaching principal," 69 percent as "principal," and 13 percent as "supervising principal." The data we summarize from this survey [1] will refer to all of the participants

---

[1] Unless otherwise indicated, all the information summarized in this section is abstracted from *The Elementary School Principalship in 1968. . . . A Research Study* (Washington, D.C.: Department of Elementary School Principals, National Education Association, 1968).

10

unless otherwise stated. When subgroupings are referred to, "teaching principal" will refer to head teachers and teaching principals, and "supervising principal" will refer to the remainder of the sample.

Characteristics of Principals

In 1928, 55 percent of the principals were women. This percentage decreased to 41 percent in 1948, to 38 percent in 1958, and was only 22 percent in 1968. Seventy-one percent of the male supervising principals were under 50 years of age (median age 43), while 77 percent of the female supervising principals were 50 years or older (median age 56). Sixteen percent of the male supervisory principals were under 35 as compared with 2 percent of their female counterparts. These statistics are particularly interesting when one considers that in the 1969–1970 school year only 15.4 percent of the teachers in public elementary schools were men.[2]

Sixty percent of the principals held positions as elementary school teachers just prior to assuming the principalship. Ten percent were assistant principals of elementary schools, and 18 percent came from the secondary school system, with the remaining 12 percent coming from an assortment of roles including central office and graduate school. Sixty-seven out of 100 male supervisory principals were appointed before age 35, and 61 out of 100 females were appointed between ages 35 and 49.

When asked why they chose the principalship, 20 percent indicated that they preferred administration and supervision over classroom teaching, 17 percent indicated that they needed a larger income, 30 percent considered the principalship to be especially important, and 30 percent were encouraged to take the principalship by the superintendent's office. Fifty-six percent of the female supervisory principals (as opposed to 16 percent of the men) took the principalship because they were encouraged to do so by the superintendent's office. This statistic is of interest in light of a recent study of the principalship discussed later in this chapter which found that most effective principals had intended to teach, but were encouraged to become principals by their superiors.[3] Eighty percent of the principals indicated that they certainly or probably would become a principal again as opposed to only 7 percent who indicated that they certainly or probably would not. Of the total sample, 5 percent were principals of schools with less than 100 students, 33 percent had 100 to 399 students, 39 percent had 400 to 699, 17 percent had 700 to 999, and 6 percent had 1,000 or more students. The median school size was 490 students.

---

[2] Mildred Bledenkapp and Jacob Goering, "How Masculine Are Male Teachers?" *Phi Delta Kappan,* Vol. 53, No. 2 (1971), 115.

[3] Gerald Becker et al., *Elementary School Principals and Their Schools* (Eugene: University of Oregon, Center for the Advanced Study of Educational Administration, 1971), p. 2.

Sex was not a factor in determining the distribution of principals among schools of various sizes.

The number of principals surveyed with master's or higher degrees has risen from 16 percent in 1928, 67 percent in 1948, and 82 percent in 1958, to 90 percent in 1968. The major area of undergraduate study for principals in the 1968 survey was social studies (40 percent). Physical education majors accounted for 3 percent of the principals. Majors in graduate school were elementary school administration (47 percent), secondary school administration (4 percent), general school administration (20 percent), elementary school supervision and curriculum (10 percent), elementary school instruction (7 percent), and academic major (5 percent). Thirty-three percent of the female supervising principals had graduate majors in elementary supervision, curriculum, and instruction as opposed to only 13 percent of the men.

These descriptions strongly imply that since 1928 the principalship has moved from a role open to all who could qualify to one dominated by men. There are few indications that we might see a reversal of this trend in the next decade. Indeed, with only 2 percent of female principals under 35 and 77 percent over 50, male domination seems relatively stable. Aside from the fundamental moral and ethical issues involved, with male domination we find fewer principals prepared primarily in the areas of supervision, curriculum, and instruction. One might also infer that, since more female principals report being coaxed out of the classroom, male domination suggests that fewer principals will be oriented to or primarily identified with classroom life.

Large numbers of men, the increased number of advanced degrees, and the popularity of majors in administration suggest that the elementary school principalship is being increasingly professionalized as an entity separate from teaching and perhaps from other administrative roles. What we do not know at this point is what effect professionalization of the principalship has had on the effectiveness of the elementary school as an educational and socializing agency, on the lives of children, and on the community whose needs are served. Our own experience and that of many of our colleagues suggest that principals seem to be becoming more aloof from teachers, children, and parents. If this observation is reasonably accurate for many principals, to what extent could it be attributed to increased professionalization?

True, many have assumed that the professionalization of anything makes it better, but there are a number of negative unanticipated consequences of emerging professionalism.[4] One such unanticipated consequence is the focus on developing a role distinctly different from that of others, particularly those with lower organizational status, working in the same area. Could this account for administrators spending less and less time in teaching, with students,

---

[4] Established professional groups are probably less guilty of unanticipated consequences such as we describe here, having experienced them at an earlier time in their history.

in the classroom, with curricula, and in the community, and more and more time running the school properly? Another unanticipated consequence of emerging professionalism is the increased attention given to the maintenance and development of a professional image, often at the expense of serving people. Rights and prerogatives of position, status, protocol, and propriety often get in the way of helping, sharing, and problem solving.

Beacons and Potholes: A Study of Problems

Suppose you are an elementary school principal. What are the problems you presently face? What are the three most significant from your vantage point? What are the primary causes of these problems? What stands in the way of their resolution? As an elementary school principal, what do you consider to be your greatest strength, greatest weakness, greatest success, greatest failure? These are the kinds of questions asked recently in a national study of the elementary school principalship conducted by the Center for the Advanced Study in Educational Administration under the direction of Keith Goldhammer.[5]

Elementary school principals expressed a considerable amount of difficulty in defining and establishing an appropriate role for the principal. A general low status or left-out feeling on the part of principals in regard to participating in school-district decision making and an uneasy feeling about the principal's relationship to his teaching staff as a consequence of more intense collective bargaining were important aspects of this role problem. Principals' most critical role concern revolved around the imbalance they reported between their managerial and educational responsibilities. "The principals recognize that they must perform the managerial or 'housekeeping' chores associated with being a school building administrator, but they are uncertain about how they might delegate these responsibilities to obtain more time for supervision, planning, and evaluation." [6]

Further, while they would like to have more time for supervision, planning, and evaluation, they report a lack of necessary skills to develop appropriate programs in these important areas. Major problems reported by principals in addition to the role question include personnel selection and placement, supervision, providing for individual differences of youngsters, public relations, and community involvement and influence.

[5] Becker et al., *Elementary School Principals and Their Schools*. In earlier CASEA studies of the elementary school principal's role, it was concluded that at best only moderate agreement existed regarding perception of the principalship among principals and between them and teachers, parents, school board members, or superintendents. See, for example, John Foskett, *The Normative World of the Elementary School Principal* (Eugene: University of Oregon, Center for the Advanced Study of Educational Administration, 1967), pp. 88–95.

[6] Becker et al., *Elementary School Principals and Their Schools,* p. 6.

EFFECTIVE PRINCIPALS

As part of the "problems" study, the investigators were able to identify some outstanding elementary schools ("beacons of brilliance") and some extremely poor schools ("potholes of pestilence"). The "potholes" were characterized by weak leadership, poor teacher and student morale, control by fear, traditional and ritualistic instructional programs, a general climate of unenthusiasm, and principals just serving out their time. This was in sharp contrast to the high-morale, enthusiastic, and adaptable "beacon" schools. Principals of the "beacon" schools had several characteristics in common:

1. Most did not intend to become principals. Most indicated that they had intended to teach, but were encouraged to become principals by their superiors.
2. Most expressed a sincere faith in children. Children were not criticized for failing to learn or for having behavioral difficulties. The principals felt that these were problems that the school was established to correct; thus the administrators emphasized their responsibilities toward the solution of children's problems.
3. They had an ability to work effectively with people and to secure their cooperation. They were proud of their teachers and accepted them as professionally dedicated and competent people. They inspired confidence and developed enthusiasm. The principals used group processes effectively; listened well to parents, teachers, and pupils; and appeared to have intuitive skill and empathy for their associates.
4. They were aggressive in securing recognition of the needs of their schools. They frequently were critical of the restraints imposed by the central office and of the inadequate resources. They found it difficult to live within the constraints of the bureaucracy; they frequently violated the chain of command, seeking relief for their problems from whatever sources that were potentially useful.
5. They were enthusiastic as principals and accepted their responsibilities as a mission rather than as a job. They recognized their role in current social problems. The ambiguities that surrounded them and their work were of less significance than the goals they felt were important to achieve. As a result, they found it possible to live with the ambiguities of their position.
6. They were committed to education and could distinguish between long-term and short-term educational goals. Consequently, they fairly well had established philosophies of the role of education and their relationship within it.
7. They were adaptable. If they discovered something was not working, they could make the necessary shifts and embark with some security on new paths.
8. They were able strategists. They could identify their objectives and plan means to achieve them. They expressed concern for the identification of the most appropriate procedures through which change could be secured.[7]

[7] Becker et al., *Elementary School Principals and Their Schools*, pp. 2–3.

The more effective elementary school principals were able not only to recognize problems, but to face up to them with inspiring leadership and hard work. This leadership was supported by a belief system which resulted in an overriding commitment to children, teaching, and teachers. The ambiguities and problems presently facing the principalship do not go away, but are managed, adjusted to, and overcome by giving top priority to one's overriding commitment to children, teaching, and teachers. There is much to be said for the advice that Peter Drucker gives to executives. "Effective executives concentrate on the few major areas where superior performance will produce outstanding results. They force themselves to set priorities and stay with their priority decisions. They know that they have no choice but to do first things first." [8] The "beacons" in this study seem to have clear images of what they consider to be the most important priorities for the elementary school.

Plan of the Book

We are interested in a new kind of leadership for those who work in elementary schools—one based on intellectual foundations, to be sure, but a grass-roots kind of leadership which requires action, which is immersed in the human values of love and freedom, and which indeed does give top priority to children, teaching, and teachers. It is not enough that one think about elementary schools; one must also feel about them, for they are human institutions. Moreover, thinking and feeling need to be channeled into action. Leadership requires that one make a difference. As Starratt suggests,

> A critical quality of any leader is that he is profoundly convinced that his vision of what ought to be or could be has a dramatic significance for the lives of those for and with whom he works. He is caught up with drama and excitement of what he and his subordinates are doing, and he communicates and shares them with subordinates.
>
> When speaking of educational leaders, we must add to the above quality, a continuous, lived experience of learning, in which the educational leader shares with his subordinates his own zest for expanding his own understanding and appreciation of the human epic. [9]

Our working goal is to evoke in the reader a dynamic state of awareness of and commitment to the potentials of elementary education which leads to the action states of planning, implementing, and evaluating. This is accomplished with reference to and in interaction with a knowledge base for leader-

[8] Peter Drucker, *The Effective Executive* (New York: Harper & Row, 1967), p. 24. See also pp. 100–112.

[9] Robert J. Starratt, "Contemporary Talk on Leadership: Too Many Kings in the Parade?" *The Notre Dame Journal of Education,* Vol. 4, No. 1 (1973), 13.

ship. Each of the five parts of this book examines an aspect of this knowledge base, with Part I examining the elementary school as a unique institution, and Parts II, III, and IV examining the principal's leadership role as he works with children, teachers, and parents. Part V is designed to provide the elementary school principal with a theoretical and intellectual foundation regarding the elementary school educational program, so that he may more effectively implement his statesman's role as an educational leader.

II

First Things First: Being an Educational Leader

3

Goals and Objectives for the Elementary School

PERHAPS THE MOST IMPORTANT reason for administrators and supervisors in elementary schools to give attention to goals and purposes is that they comprise the cornerstone of an applied science of administration and supervision unique to education. What differentiates the knowledge base, role, and behavior of the educational administrator from those of administrators in general is a value system unique to education and particularly unique to elementary education.

Broudy states the importance of values to education and administration as follows:

> The educator, however, deals with nothing but values—human beings who are clusters and constellations of value potentials. Nothing human is really alien to the educational enterprise and there is, therefore, something incongruous about educational administrators evading fundamental value conflicts. . . . The public will never quite permit the educational administrator the moral latitude that it affords some of its servants. For to statesmen and

19

soldiers, men entrust their lives and future but to the schools they entrust their precarious hold on humanity itself.[1]

Educational administration is an ethical science. It is very much concerned with scientific knowledge about administration and with the social and behavioral sciences upon which much of this knowledge rests. Educational administration has its artistic features, too—experience, seasoned practice, and good judgment have much to offer. Not all scientific knowledge about administration, or for that matter artistic knowledge about what works and what gets results, is appropriate to elementary school administration and supervision. Knowledge from both of these domains, the science and the art of administration, needs to be measured against and filtered through a value system unique to the elementary school. Only what survives such scrutiny is appropriate for use. This value system is often manifested in the goals and objectives which elementary schools pursue and the way in which administrators, teachers, and children behave.

Manifest and Latent Goals

Attention needs to be given to at least two general kinds of goals with which the elementary school is concerned. One kind is explicit, usually stated in written form, and in many cases is even broken down to objectives organized by grades or levels. Such goals at the local level are often backed up by very prestigious statements from important groups such as the White House Conference on Education, The Educational Policies Commission, and the American Association of School Administrators. One finds such goals in fancy public relations documents, in textbook manuals, in the preface to unit outlines and courses of study, and too often under desk blotters and in file drawers. Another kind of goal is much more subtly a part of the educational enterprise. Goals of this sort are latent or implicit, rarely stated, and often pursued unconsciously by the school and its staff.

These implicit or latent goals may be inferred from the behavior of teachers and administrators, the assumptions they hold for each other and for children, the ways in which adults and children are treated, the degree of emphasis on control, the extent to which extrinsic reward and coercive power are used, the extent to which rules and regulations are used, the group atmosphere, the amount of trust and love people show for each other, and the ways in which decisions are made.

How the school is organized and operated tells much about what princi-

---

[1] Harry S. Broudy, "Conflicts in Values," in Robert Ohm and William Monohan (eds.), *Educational Administration—Philosophy in Action* (Norman: University of Oklahoma, College of Education, 1965), p. 52.

pals and teachers value. The rigid schedule, the no-argument approach to children, and especially the teacher-centered classroom reveal a great deal about what assumptions the teacher holds for children. Youngsters often learn more from these latent aspects of schooling than from the curriculum. It is in this context that one comes to learn much about self-respect, authority, trust, self-discipline, sharing, freedom, and the decision-making process.

Principals and teachers often do not recognize the contradiction in expecting youngsters to achieve our manifest goals of intellectual enrichment, interpersonal competence, and personal self-actualization in rigidily scheduled, high-control elementary schools which feature excessive concern for ease of adult work and smooth, orderly, and efficient operation. We need to be constantly alert to inconsistencies that exist between the goals which we are manifestly pursuing and the means (from which latent goals are inferred) which we use to pursue these goals.[2]

EXAMPLES OF GENERAL GOALS

The most significant statements of goals are those which are prepared locally by those concerned with a particular educational enterprise. Nevertheless, some examples of general goal statements might be of use to readers. In 1966 the American Association of School Administrators listed the following goals as imperatives for America's schools:

To make urban life rewarding and satisfying.

To prepare people for the world of work.

To discover and nurture creative talent.

To strengthen the moral fabric of society.

To deal constructively with psychological tensions.

To keep democracy working.

To make intelligent use of natural resources.

To make the best use of leisure time.

To work with other peoples of the world for human betterment.[3]

These are indeed global statements which are often difficult to put into operation. Yet they lend a needed perspective to schooling over and above the immediate day-by-day activities of teachers and youngsters.

---

[2] For a more complete discussion of the relationship between manifest and latent, implicit and explicit, and means-and-ends goals, see: Thomas J. Sergiovanni and Fred D. Carver, *The New School Executive: A Theory of Administration* (New York: Dodd, Mead, 1973), Ch. 2.

[3] AASA Commission on Imperatives of Education, *Imperatives in Education* (Washington, D.C.: American Association of School Administrators, 1966), p. 9.

Although we believe that what a person is is more important than what he knows, we do not view these two dimensions as opposites, but as interdependent school concerns.[4] Regardless of the desirable idiosyncrasies of locally constructed goals, we share with Starratt the belief that they should be built upon the principle of freedom for youngsters.[5] This is not to imply that we advocate an irresponsible, free-wheeling, self-indulgent kind of freedom. We are not for anarchy, but for responsible freedom. Our hope is that elementary schools will help each student to be free from fear of himself, the unknown, authority, insecurity, commitment, and risk; and free from ignorance about himself, the functioning of society, history, national phenomena, the demands of interpersonal tension, and the ability to communicate. Further, elementary schools should help each student to be free to serve and to love his family, friends, community, country, and world. Freedom to explore his environment, to respond to it appropriately, and to participate in its struggle and joys, as well as freedom to organize his values and to commit himself to a hierarchy of values, are also important. Moreover, "the student is free to accept the *limitation* of his freedom by both social and natural causes." [6]

The choice of the word "freedom" to describe these goals implies that they are arrived at or best pursued jointly by committed teachers and students, rather than imposed on students by adult authority or an impersonal curriculum. Most of these goals are not likely to be achieved merely by adult imposition.

There is no question that modern education must produce more than persons with cognitive skills, as important as such skills are. Self-actualizing persons, for example, are indeed well informed in accordance with their capabilities, but they are also possessed of positive self-concepts, open to their experiences, possessed of deep feelings, and sympathetic to other people.[7]

---

[4] A fair amount of empirical evidence exists which suggests that what a person is (his value system, self-concept, and motivational set, for example) has a direct effect on what he does know and is able to know. See, for example: Robert White, "Motivation Reconsidered: The Concept of Competency," *Psychological Review*, Vol. 66, No. 5 (1959), 297–333; Frederick Mosteller and Daniel P. Moynihan (eds.), *On Equality of Educational Opportunity: Papers Deriving from the Harvard University Faculty Seminar on the Coleman Report* (New York: Random House, 1972); Richard DeCharms, *Personal Causation* (New York: Academic Press, 1968), particularly pp. 257–357; and "Intervention Is Possible: A Model for Change from Within." Paper given at the University of Maryland Conference on Intervention, March 1971.

[5] See, for example, Robert J. Starratt's discussion of general goals for schools in Thomas J. Sergiovanni and Robert J. Starratt, *Emerging Patterns of Supervision: Human Perspectives* (New York: McGraw-Hill, 1971), pp. 270–271.

[6] Sergiovanni and Starratt, *Emerging Patterns of Supervision*, p. 271.

[7] Arthur W. Combs, *Educational Accountability Beyond Behavioral Objectives* (Washington, D.C.: Association for Supervision and Curriculum Development, National Education Association, 1972), p. 23.

The Educational Objectives Controversy

There seems to be unanimous agreement on the need for goal focus, on the establishment of aims, and on the setting of objectives for elementary school curricula and instruction. But the way in which objectives are to be formulated and stated has been and continues to be a source of controversy and professional debate. Of particular significance in recent years is the popularity of behavioral objectives. This movement has its origins in the early work of Ralph Tyler and is presently articulated by such scholars as Robert Gagné and James Popham.[8] We see much merit in the behavioral-objectives approach, but are concerned at its excesses. In this section a balanced approach to the development of educational objectives is presented, one which recognizes merit in three kinds of objectives—instructional, expressive, and informal. Curriculum development and program implementation in elementary schools need to give attention to each kind of objective, if we are to meet our commitment to both child and society.

INSTRUCTIONAL OBJECTIVES

Instructional objectives are those stated in behavioral terms. Such objectives describe student behavior rather than teaching activity. The focus is on how the student will perform as a result of an instructional treatment or exposure. The more enthusiastic advocates of behavioral objectives further specify that the instructional objective must be stated in such a way that it is measurable.

Examples of instructional objectives in the case of mathematics are: the child should be able to recognize and label squares, rectangles, circles, and triangles; use the symbols $+$ and $=$ to form sentences such as $2 + 4 = 6$; tell time to the nearest half-hour; add rational numbers expressed in numerical form such as $2\frac{2}{3} + 5\frac{5}{7}$; and use proportions to solve problems involving similar triangles.

To be sure, objectives clearly stated and sensibly defined in behavioral terms can have important value in teaching and learning. Such clear statements of objectives can help teachers select learning experiences, materials, and educational settings which will lead the student to the desired behavior. Further, organizing, sequencing, and evaluating instruction are all greatly facilitated by the statement of clear instructional objectives.

[8] Ralph Tyler, *Basic Principles of Curriculum and Instruction* (Chicago: University of Chicago Press, 1950); Robert Gagné, *The Condition of Learning* (New York: Holt, Rinehart and Winston, 1965); and W. James Popham and Eva L. Baker, *Establishing Instructional Goals* (Englewood Cliffs, N.J.: Prentice-Hall, 1970).

It is important that objectives which are stated in behavioral terms be seen as placed on a behavioral continuum with some being simple ends in themselves, others leading to more complex behavioral patterns, and still others representing major milestones in a student's growth and development. One familiar with Guilford's structure of the intellect can appreciate the difficulty in mapping the intellectual domain along an infinite behavioral continuum.[9] Nevertheless, the development of learning hierarchies, performance classification systems, and objectives taxonomies has been helpful in making decisions about objective setting and seeking.[10] Even the most enthusiastic advocates of behaviorally defined instructional objectives recognize that the kinds of pupil behavior that are the easiest to elicit are often the most trivial. Classification systems, hierarchies, and taxonomies can help guard against focusing on pedestrian and picayune objectives.

The fact is that most instructional objectives pursued by teachers require identifying, naming, and at best describing cognitive skills at the knowledge-recall-comprehension level and that not enough attention is given to objectives which emphasize the application, analysis, synthesis, and evaluation of knowledge. Further, affective objectives seem ignored for the most part. One wonders whether this lopsided attention to instructional objectives with limited potency is necessarily a function of elementary school education, and whether more advanced kinds of learning lend themselves less well to the rigor of being behaviorally organized.

We see much merit in using instructional objectives where they make sense in elementary schools. Their use becomes even more important where inferior teaching exists, for improvements can be expected in such cases as a result of instructional objectives. At the same time, too rigid an application of instructional objectives can stifle superior teaching. Robert Starratt raises some additional issues which need also to be considered.

(1) Does the specification of behavioral objectives and the learning experiences leading to their acquisition imply that every student can and must behave in exactly the *same* way in order to validate the objectives? And further, does it imply that the *only* way to achieve the objectives is by progressing through such and such a series of preordained learning experiences? If the

[9] J. P. Guilford, "The Structure of Intellect," *Psychological Bulletin*, Vol. 53, 4, (1956), 267–293.

[10] See, for example: Howard Sullivan, "Objectives, Evaluation and Improved Learning Achievement," *AERA Monograph Series on Curriculum Evaluation*, Robert E. Stake, ed. (Chicago: Rand McNally, 1967), 75–78. Also, "Individualizing Mathematical Learning in the Elementary School: A Hierarchy of Student Behavioral Objectives K–8" (Madison: Wisconsin Department of Public Instruction). Perhaps the most well-known classification system is the Taxonomy of Educational Objectives; actually, two separate taxonomies have been developed. For the cognitive domain, Benjamin S. Bloom et al., *Taxonomy of Educational Objectives, Handbook I: Cognitive Domain* (New York: McKay, 1956); and for the affective domain, David R. Krathwohl et al., *Taxonomy of Educational Objectives, Handbook II: Affective Domain* (New York: McKay, 1964).

answer to both questions is affirmative, without any qualification, then we have simply substituted one kind of dogmatism for another. Any talk about respecting individual differences becomes ridiculous, for even if students are allowed to progress at their own individual rate of learning, they must move toward the same fixed goal. (2) Do educators have the absolute, unchallengeable *right*, based on an assumption of competence, to require that their students will achieve certain objectives rather than other objectives? [11]

These issues can be resolved if instructional objectives are used with common sense. We think it makes sense to consider them as only one kind of objective with which the elementary school needs to be concerned.

EXPRESSIVE OBJECTIVES

If one were to rely only on instructional objectives, this exclusive use would imply that all knowledge is certain and can be laid out and sequenced; that all knowledge is absolute, with only one answer being appropriate; and that all knowledge is impersonal and, therefore, the same for all.[12] Such is not the case, however, for knowledge is filtered through and mediated by the personal meanings which the learner brings to the setting and, therefore, is often unpredictable in terms of outcome. Objectives which are achieved as a result of an individual's encounter with knowledge or a knowledge setting are referred to as expressive objectives.

> Expressive objectives differ considerably from instructional objectives. An expressive objective does not specify the behavior the student is to acquire after having engaged in one or more learning activities. An expressive objective describes an educational encounter: it identifies a situation in which children are at work, a problem with which they are to cope, a task they are to engage in—but it does not specify the form of that encounter, situation, problem, or task they are to learn. An expressive objective provides both the teacher and the student with an invitation to explore, defer or focus on issues that are of peculiar interest or import to the inquirer.[13]

The use of expressive objectives requires that we focus less on the specific desired outcome for each child and more on arranging an educational encounter which will permit the emergence of a number of worthy outcomes. Permitting youngsters in the first grade to spend time in the science corner playing (they make little distinction between work and play) with magnets and materials might be an example of an educational encounter. Who can say

[11] Sergiovanni and Starratt, *Emerging Patterns of Supervision,* p. 230.

[12] James MacDonald and Bernice Wolfson, "A Case Against Behavioral Objectives," *The Elementary School Journal,* Vol. 71, No. 3, 1970, p. 126.

[13] Elliot Eisner, "Instructional and Expressive Educational Objectives: Their Formulation and Use in Curriculum," *AERA Monogram Series on Curriculum Evaluation: Instructional Objectives,* Robert E. Stake, ed. (Chicago: Rand McNally, 1967), 15–16.

what the youngsters will learn or should learn as they engage in this experience and share it with others? It is after the encounter that educational outcomes are identified and appraised. How restrictive it would be to decide beforehand what educational outcomes a group of sixth graders, white children with black masks and black children with white masks, should achieve as they debate the merits and consequences of busing children to school to achieve integration. Think of all the learnings which would be missed by focusing on only those items previously specified by the teacher as a group of second graders visits the zoo in a neighboring city. How unfortunate if the subway ride, the hustle and bustle of downtown, the slum, the corner grocery store, and the urban schoolyard were all ignored because we were committed to objectives which did not include them!

Expressive objectives permit the youngster to enter the learning encounter on an equal footing. True, the teacher assumes a major role in deciding and arranging the learning setting, but the learner has the option of responding to this setting in a number of ways. Objectives in this setting, then, emerge as a result of the educational encounter.

INFORMAL OBJECTIVES

Informal objectives differ from instructional and expressive objectives in that they focus less deliberately on content and concept *per se* and more on processes. Informal objectives are derived from a class of purposes and activities which have value whenever they occur. The development of personal meanings in learning, intrinsic satisfaction in motivation, interpersonal enjoyment in interaction, and love of self and others in life are desirable whenever they occur in school settings. Add to these more cognitively oriented process goals such as exploring, feeling, sensing, sorting, clarifying, creating, and the like, and we begin to sense the flavor of informal goals. Informal and unpredictable, when they do occur, they should be nurtured and valued.

Informal objectives, when combined with instructional and expressive objectives, add the necessary balance of how something is learned to what is learned. To be sure, what is learned is not unimportant, but the procedures used by youngsters in learning are often of more lasting value.

For instance, the kindergarten teacher has an instructional objective which is that the youngster be able to differentiate among objects which are rough, smooth, and squishy. However, she recognizes, as any sensible teacher would, that providing youngsters with several encounters with a variety of materials can lead to a number of alternate (but just as worthy) objectives relating to touch senses and differentiating powers. One child, for example, might discover that the feel of an object can change as the physical state of that object changes. He might observe that gelatin cubes, which are squishy at first, melt and become smooth when placed in a sunny window. If he places a bowl of gelatin cubes outside, he notes that the gelatin freezes and turns rough. This is an example of only one of several expressive objectives which could emerge as a result of such an educational encounter.

An educational encounter can lead to informal objectives when the focus of activity or content widely departs from that previously planned. A second child engaged in the same feeling and differentiating activity might note with some puzzlement while juggling two objects that the larger one is heavier and the smaller one is lighter. To turn aside this observation in order to bring the learning experience back to its "proper" course does not make sense. A number of informal objectives are beginning to emerge. Curiosity and discovery are in themselves of sufficient value to be nurtured and rewarded when experienced by youngsters, particularly the very young. This is to say nothing of the content possibilities relating to weights, measurement, volume, and density which seem begging for exploitation by the alert teacher.

Identifying School Needs

The 1970s will be remembered for many developments in education, but none will rival the interest in and movement toward the development of goals for schools and the use of objectives in teaching. The behavioral-objectives movement began to receive widespread attention in the 1960s and is presently in the prime of adolescence. Management by Objectives (MBO), Evaluation by Objectives (EBO), and Planning Programming Budgeting Systems (PPBS) are further blossomings of the objectives movement.[14] The interest in educational objectives is a manifestation of pressure from a number of sources for educators to plan more deliberately, to allocate resources more carefully, to upgrade teachers and educational programs—in short, to be more accountable.[15]

Needs assessment plays an important role in many state-mandated evaluation programs and is becoming accepted as a necessary prerequisite to the establishment of goals and objectives for schools. In most needs assessment programs, needs are determined by the ranking of goals by community representatives. Once community perceptions of school district priorities are de-

[14] See, for example, Peter Drucker, *The Effective Executive* (New York: Harper & Row, 1967); John D. McNeil, *Toward Accountable Teachers* (New York: Holt, Rinehart and Winston, 1971); and Harry Hartley, *Educational Planning-Programming-Budgeting: A Systems Approach* (Englewood Cliffs, N.J.: Prentice-Hall, 1968).

[15] California's Stull Act (1972), for example, requires that all certified personnel including the superintendent be evaluated according to objective guidelines including pupil gain. As part of its "Fair Dismissal Law" enacted in 1971, the Oregon school code requires "The district superintendent . . . shall cause to have made at least annually an evaluation of performance for each teacher employed by the district to measure teachers' development and growth in the teaching profession. A form shall be prescribed by the State Board of Education." The school code defines administrators as teachers. State-mandated evaluation also exists in Florida, South Dakota, Hawaii, Connecticut, Washington, Virginia, and Illinois.

termined, the school is evaluated by estimating the extent to which each of the goals is being emphasized and achieved. Discrepancies between the importance of goals and the extent to which the school is emphasizing or achieving these goals constitute in a general sense the needs of the district.[16]

The following is an example of one set of goal statements used by many school districts in assessing needs, distributed by the Commission on Educational Planning of Phi Delta Kappa.

1. Learn how to be a good citizen.
2. Learn how to respect and get along with people who think, dress, and act differently.
3. Learn about and try to understand the changes that take place in the world.
4. Develop skills in reading, writing, speaking, and listening.
5. Understand and practice democratic ideas and ideals.
6. Learn how to examine and use information.
7. Understand and practice the skills of family living.
8. Learn to respect and get along with people with whom we work and live.
9. Develop skills to enter a specific field of work.
10. Learn how to be a good manager of money, property, and resources.
11. Develop a desire for learning now and in the future.
12. Learn how to use leisure time.
13. Practice and understand the ideas of health and safety.
14. Appreciate culture and beauty in the world.
15. Gain information needed to make job selections.
16. Develop pride in work and a feeling of self-worth.
17. Develop good character and self-respect.
18. Gain a general education.[17]

Individuals in classes or workshops will find it useful to rank each of the goal statements and then to compare individual rankings with others in a

[16] In ranking goals to identify perceived priorities of the community and of community subgroups, it is often useful to provide rankers with a list of generally accepted goals. If items on the list are clearly not acceptable, they can be deleted, and glaring omissions from the list can be added. For examples of goal statements and suggestions for use, see: *Educational Goals and Objectives: A Model Program for Community and Professional Involvement* (Administrator's Manual) (Bloomington, Ind.: Phi Delta Kappa Commission on Educational Planning); and Lawrence Downey, *The Tasks of Public Education: The Perceptions of People* (Chicago: Midwest Administration Center of University of Chicago, 1960). See also Robert Stake and Dennis Gooker, "Measuring Educational Priorities," *Educational Technology*, Vol. 11, No. 9 (1971), 44–48.

[17] *Educational Goals and Objectives*, Appendix, p. 9.

small group setting. The object is to reach a consensus in the general ranking of goals and to identify major irreconcilable differences. Areas of general agreement represent the value core of the group or school. Major differences in ranking of goal statements may suggest the importance of providing options or alternatives for those holding strong minority opinions.

Another idea is to write each of the goal statements on a separate card or slip of paper. Divide the goal statements into three categories—those perceived to be very important, moderate, and less important. The goal statements should be broken into seven piles as follows:

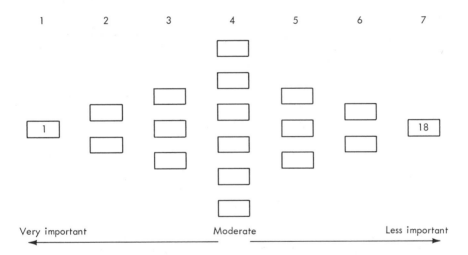

Goal statements may now be sorted within each of the seven piles to reflect actual rankings from 1 (most important) to 18 (least important). These rankings or priorities can be translated into needs by rating the school against each of the goal statements; that is, how well are the school's current programs and efforts meeting each of the goals? Raters may consist of students, teachers, and community members. The Phi Delta Kappa program suggests that the school be evaluated against each goal on a 1-to-15 scale as follows:

Extremely poor	Poor	Fair but more needs to be done	Leave as is	Too much is being done
1 2 3	4 5 6	7 8 9	10 ⑪ 12	13 14 15

As the scale suggests, need discrepancies can take the form of deficiencies or sufficiencies. For example, it may be possible that not enough is being done with respect to one goal, but too much is being done with respect to another. Discrepancies, of course, have more serious implications for highly ranked goals.

DEVELOPING OBJECTIVES

Working with statements of general goals as described above can be a useful activity for the school, but the real value is determined by the extent to which such general statements are translated into educational goals and imperatives that can be used to guide educational program decisions. Further, educational goals need to be translated into instructional, expressive, and informal objectives, which in turn can be used to guide teacher decision making in the classroom. This process is illustrated in the model for building consensus and variation which appears in Figure 3-1.

As the pattern of moving from perceptions of general district goals to district and school needs, to educational goals and imperatives, to teacher-established instructional, expressive, and informal objectives develops, the pattern of agreement and disagreement changes. The process moves from little known agreement at the community level to building a general consensus with regard to goals, imperatives, and working philosophy, to less agreement on proxy objectives,[18] to wide variation in educational program formats and methods of teaching which are designed to meet the general goals and imperatives.

Deciding what goals the schools should pursue, what knowledge is worth knowing, what educational policies should be developed, and what methods should be used are value questions of prime order. These are not questions to be neatly answered by formula or questions on which one is likely to readily obtain narrow agreement. If one insists on or forces agreement with respect to these questions, the task of evaluation, for example, is admittedly easier, but becomes arbitrary, oppressive, and lacking in credibility. But, although evaluation is certainly tougher and more complex without complete agreement, it is not impossible.

Certainly a program such as we describe is not possible without some common agreement on what the school should do and on the prevailing assumptions under which it works. Further, the relative priorities given to these common goals and assumptions also need reasonable agreement. But, as these

---

[18] Proxy objectives are those objectives which are generated from general goals. Because they tend to be more specific or descriptive, they are better able to guide teachers and administrators as they make decisions about educational programs, instruction, and activities.

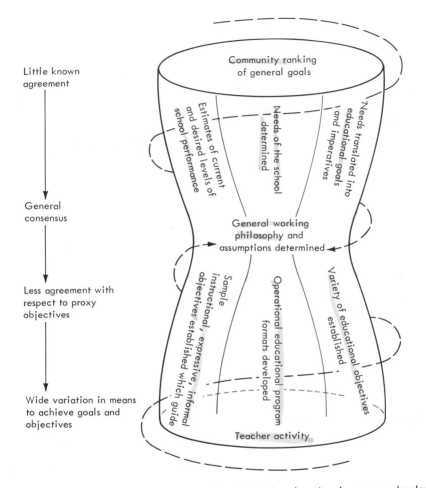

Little known
agreement

General
consensus

Less agreement with
respect to proxy
objectives

Wide variation in means
to achieve goals and
objectives

Community ranking
of general goals

Needs translated into
educational goals
and imperatives

Needs of the school
determined

Estimates of current
and desired levels of
school performance

General working
philosophy and
assumptions determined

Variety of educational objectives
established

Operational educational program
formats developed

Sample
instructional, expressive, informal
objectives established which guide

Teacher activity

FIGURE 3-1.   Consensus and variation in educational program development.

From Thomas Sergiovanni, "Synergistic Evaluation," *Teachers College Record,*
75, *4,* May 1974.

goals and assumptions are articulated in the form of educational programs
and proxy objectives, disagreement can be expected to increase. This is the
way it should be. If we accept the notion that students are different, parents
are different, and teachers are different—all individuals with unique personalities, needs, beliefs, competencies, and aspirations—we should not be surprised if youngsters differ in their responses to the same educational program,

or surprised if some teachers feel more comfortable with one approach to teaching than another, or surprised when parents differ with regard to what they want from schools.

PROVIDING OPTIONS AND ALTERNATIVES

Rather than work to hide one's differences, schools need to sharpen differences and legitimize them in the form of optional educational programs. Options are not necessarily in conflict with seeking common purpose. They can maintain separate identities by developing different proxy objectives for these common purposes and by developing different approaches to achieving them.

An elementary school faculty, for example, might agree that attention should be given to the basic skills, that educational programs and instructional activities need to be tailored individually for youngsters, that self-concept development and feelings of self-worth need to be manifested in the educational program, and that schooling should be an intrinsically satisfying experience in which learning is an enjoyable activity. Add to this list two other common agreements—that a quality education can be obtained through a number of alternate methods or programs with no one method or program being objectively better than another, and that teachers should be allowed to use the approach they prefer—and we may have enough common agreement. That is, we have a faculty which agrees on common purpose and pursues this purpose in a variety of ways in a mutually supportive atmosphere of respect and commitment. Evaluation in this setting places less emphasis on estimating the worth of programs and activities with respect to one standard and more emphasis on evaluating for integrity within options. Reasonably clear description and definition of objectives, beliefs, and assumptions within options and descriptions of how options, objectives, and activities support common purposes greatly facilitate the evaluation process.

One school's attempt to define options and to make them available to parents is illustrated in Figure 3-2. This document is a letter to parents describing three general but distinct ways of working with children. The descriptions are general and brief, given the letter form, and need backing by "in house" documents which more richly and clearly describe the working assumptions of teachers about how children learn and the nature of knowledge. Further, more complete descriptions of classroom life, instructional organization, and curriculum content, as well as samples of instructional, expressive, and informal objectives, would also be part of the working documents of the school.

A key question is how much ambiguity can an organization such as the school tolerate? The answer is probably much less ambiguity with regard to general goals, beliefs, and assumptions than most schools now have, but much

URBANA SCHOOL DISTRICT 116
BOARD OF EDUCATION
ADMINISTRATIVE OFFICES

Dear Parent:

The teaching staff has been examining the instructional program at Leal during the last few months. One of the characteristics that seemed evident as a result of this consideration is the great diversity of teaching styles that are utilized at Leal. The staff recognized that some children seem to profit from one type of teaching style and program while other children work better in another setting. In the past we have not given a great deal of attention to these kinds of individual differences and needs in our placement of children; however, after due consideration, it seems logical that we do this. Therefore, we are interested in providing options to parents with regard to their child's placement for the 1973-74 School Year. A meeting will be held at the school on the evening of Monday, May 21st, at 7:30 P.M., in the Gym to provide you with additional information concerning this process. In the meantime, we are providing the following preliminary information so that you will have some background concerning the options that could be available. Please note that the options are being offered in terms of program and teaching style descriptions rather than specific teachers.

The Leal School Staff is committed to providing youngsters with a quality education. In this effort, all Leal Teachers agree that:

a. Attention should be given to the basic skills.
b. Educational programs and classroom instructional activities need to be tailored individually to fit the needs of youngsters.
c. Goals such as self-concept development and a feeling of self-worth are of critical importance.

33

d. School should be an intrinsically satisfying
   experience in which learning is an enjoyable
   activity.

e. A quality education can be obtained through a
   number of alternate methods or programs. No
   one of these alternate methods or programs may
   be objectively better than another though different students may respond better to one
   method or program than another.

f. Teachers too are individuals and some feel more
   comfortable and successful using one type of
   method or program rather than another.

The Leal School Staff is prepared to offer three
options or choices of educational program to parents
and students of each age level. The three options are
described below; each of the options share the simi-
larities described above as agreed to by the entire
staff. At the same time each option is sufficiently
different from the other two. In order to avoid
prejudicing one or another option, we have simply
labeled the options "A," "B," and "C."

GENERAL CHARACTERISTICS OF LEAL PROGRAM OPTIONS

OPTION A

Teacher guided or directed—teacher makes most
   decisions about subject matter, procedures, etc.
Formally structured—although individualized, all
   students have reading at the same time, math
   at the same time, etc. Classroom probably more
   formal in physical arrangement.
Emphasis on teacher-established goals and teacher
   directed methods.
Largely separate subjects and basal text oriented
   with project methods used when appropriate.
Self contained classroom with children of same age
   or two age levels together.

OPTION B

Teacher guided or directed—teacher makes most
decisions about subject matter, procedures, etc.

Informally structured—Students given certain requirements with flexibility as to when they are
completed and what supplementary work is done.
Physical arrangement of classroom probably based
more on interest centers.

Emphasis on teacher-established goals with some
student choice in deciding methods of achieving
these goals.

Largely activity, project, and problem oriented.

Self-contained classroom with some teaming and
some multi-age grouping.

OPTION C

Teacher and student guided or directed—teacher
and students together make decisions about some
subject matter, procedures, etc.

Informally structured—Individualized, certain requirements as determined by teacher and student
with flexibility as to when they are completed.
Physical arrangement of classroom probably more
informal.

Emphasis on goals generated by both teacher and
students with as much choice as makes sense for
students with regard to deciding methods to
achieve goals.

Activity, project, and problem oriented—textbooks
used as a resource.

Multi-aged classrooms with grouping for instructional purposes.

It should be noted that overlap exists in each of
the program options and that our descriptions refer
only to a general orientation to the programs. It is
entirely possible, for example, that on any given day,
an "A" program might look more like a "C" program, and
vice versa.
We realize that the information we have provided

does not give a complete description of each program and does not answer all of your questions; thus, we urge you to attend the meeting at 7:30 P.M. on May 21st.

It would be greatly appreciated if you would complete the attached questionnaire and return it to your child's teacher by May 16th. Your response will help the staff make decisions about the program for next year. This is only a survey and is in no way a commitment, it is not necessary to indicate your child's name, only his/her grade level.

OPTION SURVEY FORM

Based on the background information that you have been provided thus far, we are interested in knowing how you feel about the program options being considered for Leal School for 1973-74. This is only a survey and not a commitment, we need only your child's grade level, not his/her name. Please designate an option for each of your children.

Which option do you think is best for your child? (Please make a first and second choice for each child.)

CHILD'S PRESENT GRADE LEVEL	OPTION A	OPTION B	OPTION C	NO PREFERENCE
————	————	————	————	————
————	————	————	————	————
————	————	————	————	————
————	————	————	————	————
————	————	————	————	————

Please return to your child's teacher by May 16th.

Richard C. Lanaghan
Principal

FIGURE 3-2.   Educational program options.

more ambiguity with respect to proxy objectives and means to achieve these objectives than most schools now permit.

PROVIDING HELP IN WRITING OBJECTIVES

The development and writing of objectives by teachers is not an easy task by any means. Some frustration is to be expected, but extreme frustration and confusion at this early stage in defining more deliberately what we believe and how these beliefs are articulated into educational program dimensions can result in the task of objective writing becoming little more than an administrative annoyance to be dealt with rather than an aid to teaching.

Objectives differ in their focus, specificity, and observability. As has been indicated earlier, the focus of objectives should not be limited exclusively to student behavior, but should also include teacher behavior and intention. What the teacher would like to accomplish, the kinds of learning settings and experiences to be provided and carried out are a class of objectives as important as what behaviors the teacher anticipates in children.

An objective is most useful in teaching when it is specific enough to help the teacher make decisions about such characteristics as teaching methods, curriculum materials, class organization, the student role, and time, scope, and sequence. At the same time, an objective needs to be general enough so that normally a particular series of teaching acts are not defined in detail beforehand. That is, an objective should not rob the teacher of decision-making discretion, but should help him to make better decisions.

Focusing on student behavior for a moment, the objective "The student will develop an appreciation of literature" does little more than provide general (albeit, important) direction to the teacher. A proxy for that objective might be, "The student has gained an appreciation of the writings of Edgar Allan Poe." This objective is more specific and somewhat sharpens the teacher's intention. A proxy for this objective might be, "In story form, the student will compare attributes of any of Poe's characters with his own attributes." Direction and intent are clear with this objective, but considerable discretion still remains for the teacher. With "Given a list of Poe's characters, the student will be able to match them with correct book titles," we arrive at a level of specificity often recommended by behavorial-objectives enthusiasts, but which, when used in excess, unduly limits the discretion of both teacher and students.

The extent to which a particular behavior is observable further defines the objectives. More covert objectives are those which seek to elicit awareness and appreciation, for example. As imprecise as this type of objective is, its importance cannot be denied. The challenge, of course, is to develop good overt objectives which will proxy the intent of the covert objective, or to define teacher intentions, educational situations, and encounters in such a way that, after they occur, expressive objectives can be determined and the more covert general objectives can be inferred.

Three methods of generating objectives are illustrated in Table 3-1. The downward-generation method has been described in earlier sections. It assumes the capability of teachers to move from general beliefs to the logical development of teaching objectives. Easy to describe on paper and certainly not insurmountable in practice, the approach, nevertheless, represents an extremely difficult task for teachers.

The topic-display method is often easier for teachers and may well be the place to start in initially defining objectives. The topic-display method starts with concepts and ideas which are more concrete and familiar to the teacher. Care needs to be taken, however, to insure that teachers go beyond the topic display in order to avoid an imbalance in favor of objectives which are concerned with cognitive or intellectual matters. Objectives dealing with learning processes and with affective concerns can also be generated from the topic display though they may initially be less obvious to teachers.[19]

TABLE 3-1. Generating objectives.

Downward-Generation Method	Topic-Display Method	Turn-On Method
Start with broad goals, values, beliefs, assumptions. Derive educational goals and objectives. Derive instructional, expressive, and informal objectives.	1. Gather and display all topics you plan to teach. 2. Include concepts, generalizations, subject titles, units, outlines, and facts. 3. Use old lesson plans, curriculum guides, textbooks, experience, and unit outlines for ideas. 4. Place them in some order or sequence (subject, logic, difficulty, or unit). 5. Formulate objectives for topics identified.	1. Identify an important goal or objective. 2. Brainstorm without regard to evaluation. Generate as many proxy objectives as you can. 3. Sort and categorize. OR 1. Identify an important topic, idea, activity, or concept. 2. Brainstorm to generate as many "things that can be learned" as you can.

[19] Teachers might find Clark's book a helpful and practical guide to writing and using objectives. The book tends to honor instructional over expressive and informal objectives and favors student-focused objectives almost exclusively, but if one keeps these biases in mind, one will find the book to be well written and useful. See D. Cecil Clark, *Using Instructional Objectives in Teaching* (Glenview, Ill.: Scott, Foresman, 1972).

The turn-on method is described more fully in Chapter 11 as we discuss staff development. This technique is an excellent vehicle for in-service education, not only in generating objectives, but in developing curricula and in sharing ideas.

In addition to goals and objectives, the principal as an educational leader must be concerned with other important dimensions of educational programs. In the next chapter, we discuss the learning environment, or the context for learning. That chapter is followed by a consideration of patterns for classroom organization and their influence and effect on the quality of educational programs which the elementary school provides for children.

4

An Environmental
Design for Learning

In Chapter 3, we talked of goals and objectives which could be stated or identified either before, during, or after a learning encounter and those which are latent, inferred, or hidden in the cultural web of the school. We proposed that the way in which the school is organized, the extent and nature of student-control ideology and procedure, the emphasis or deemphasis on teacher self-actualization, the status system, the use of rules and regulations, and the extent to which parents feel a sense of partnership in the school are examples of goal-laden conditions. One can learn more of what the school values and what it indirectly communicates to children by studying such factors than by giving attention to what the school lists as its goals and purposes. A school which speaks of helping young people to become more responsible and to develop a self-concept, but at the same time implements a series of rigid checks and controls on student behavior, may in fact be pursuing goals opposite of those which it intends. One wonders what a youngster learns about trust, authority, responsibility, and self-discipline in a school where every time he leaves the classroom without teacher escort he is required to carry (or if quite young, have pinned on him) a hall pass which states the time he left, his destination, and the time he returned. Indeed, the climate of living in any elementary school has a critical effect on the climate of learning and growing. We will discuss what principals can do to improve school climate in Part III, as we focus on organizational leadership for principals.

In this chapter, we concern ourselves with the context of learning and the goals and objectives implicit in this context. Much of the previous discussion applies here. The environmental context of learning shares, and perhaps exceeds, the importance of the substance or content of learning. One manages only a small glimpse of purpose and goals if he pays attention only to stated objectives and to substantive content. These can only be appreciated, understood, and evaluated within the context of the learning environment— a point too often ignored by those for whom "performance only" counts.

The Three Dimensions in the Learning Context

The context of learning is defined in terms of three dimensions, each of which partly determines the extent to which human growth is realized.[1] One dimension is the extent to which the learning context emphasizes intrinsic (being) or extrinsic (becoming) motivation for learning. Another dimension is the extent to which the learning context emphasizes personal meanings brought to the educational encounter by the learner, or culturally defined meanings built into the educational encounter by the teacher, curriculum writer, textbook or lesson plan, or by some societal demand or necessity. All of these are elements of the growth process for healthy individuals. The third dimension of learning context refers to interpersonal setting which moves from individual thought and action, to conversation with another, to action and discussion in a group. Each of these dimensions is examined and related to each other in nine possible contexts for learning. The nine contexts must be actively sought, planned for, and nurtured if the elementary school is to function effectively not only as a transmitter of knowledge and culture, but also as a developer of human potential. We should remember that no guaranteed positive relationship exists between the two. History is replete with evidence showing that knowledge in and of itself is not virtuous.

INTRINSIC AND EXTRINSIC MOTIVATION

Why someone does something is an important reflection of his personal maturity. One whose life focuses on *becoming* something or someone, on striving for success, on reaching the next milestone, to the virtual exclusion of

---

[1] Thomas J. Sergiovanni and Robert J. Starratt, *Emerging Patterns of Supervision: Human Perspectives* (New York: McGraw-Hill, 1971). This discussion is adapted from Starratt's design for a human curriculum presented in Chapter 13.

being able to enjoy who he is, where he is, or others for who they are, may have lived, but has missed the whole point of life. True, an emphasis on being is not enough in our complex society, for many others are dependent upon what we become. Nevertheless, becoming in and of itself represents for any man a rather shallow and empty view of life.[2] What differentiates being from becoming is the end intended. Being seeks no other end outside of itself, other than the sheer satisfaction intrinsic to the knowledge or activity, while becoming is instrumental, that is, used to solve problems or answer questions or gain a specific objective.

School words which come close to describing being and becoming are "intrinsic" and "extrinsic." Are we motivating children to learn only because they will get something from us in return such as a passing grade, being able to move to the next step in a learning sequence or hierarchy, winning our approval, getting more free time, or avoiding homework? Do we encourage students to engage only in learnings and activities which youngsters find intrinsically meaningful and satisfying? Or, do we attempt a balance between the two motivations for learning? So far, we have described one dimension in defining and mapping a learning environment: the extent to which being or intrinsic motivation and becoming or extrinsic motivation or combinations of the two are being emphasized and nurtured.

PERSONAL MEANING AND CULTURALLY DEFINED MEANING

Personal meanings are those which the youngster brings to any learning encounter. Indeed, personal meanings act as filters through which all learnings are processed. The outcome for any learning encounter is, therefore, different for each learner. Culturally defined meanings, on the other hand, are heavily laden with expectations which reflect the values which others hold for the learner.[3] What the teacher expects youngsters to learn in a given lesson or through a given learning experience, or what a text discussion or workbook exercise is supposed to do are examples of specific culturally defined learnings. Generally, schools, communities, nations, and societies make rather manifest a set of expectations in regard to what knowledge is worth knowing. This knowledge comprises the core of culturally defined meanings to which the school is obligated to give some attention. It is doubtful, however, if culturally defined meanings can ever be fully understood and appreciated by focusing on them at the expense of personal meanings.

[2] See, for example, Abraham H. Maslow, "Some Basic Propositions of a Growth and Self-Actualization Psychology," in Arthur W. Combs (ed.), *Perceiving, Behaving, Becoming* (Washington, D.C.: Association for Supervision and Curriculum Development, National Education Association, 1962), p. 41.

[3] See, for example, James MacDonald, "An Image of Man: The Learner Himself," in Ronald D. Doll (ed.), *Individualizing Instruction* (Washington, D.C.: Association for Supervision and Curriculum Development, National Education Association, 1964), p. 39.

For example, a group of youngsters is asked to write an essay or report describing the homes, people, and traffic patterns they observed from the bus window returning home to the suburbs from a field trip to a pier in a nearby city. The teacher expects them to compare these observations with their own community as part of a social studies unit on neighborhoods. Jimmy, who lived for many years in a brownstone much like hundreds of others passed in the crowded neighborhoods of the nearby city, might write an essay quite different from those of his new suburban classmates. Indeed, his rich and warm version of the urban neighborhood, the alley, the corner candy store, the hot nights spent sleeping on the roof under the stars, stickball, Italian ices, and the feeling of comradeship in sitting on the stoop with his family and friends could help him wind up with a poor paper if it were judged according to the objective and fact-oriented comparative criteria set forth by the teacher. The word "neighborhood" has a culturally defined meaning, but for Jimmy this meaning would be colored and enriched by his own personal experiences.

Combs criticizes the neglect of personal meanings in schools when he states:

> In our zeal to be scientific and objective, we have sometimes taught children that personal meanings are things you leave at the schoolhouse door. Sometimes, I fear, in our desire to help people learn, we have said to the child, "Alice, I am not interested in what you think or what you believe. What are the facts?" As a consequence, we may have taught children that personal meanings have no place in the classroom, which is another way of saying that school is concerned only with things that do not matter! If learning, however, is a discovery of personal meaning, then the facts with which we must be concerned are the beliefs, feelings, understandings, convictions, doubts, fears, likes, and dislikes of the pupil—these personal ways of perceiving himself and the world he lives in.[4]

It is the interaction of gaining new information and discovering personal meanings which results in learning beyond the recall level. As Nyberg argues, learning is a "product of two functions: acquiring information and, more importantly, discovering and developing *personal meaning*. It's the interaction of the two for the learner which results in a behavioral change. Learning = Information + Personal Meaning ———→ Behavioral Change."[5]

A second dimension in defining or mapping the learning environment at

---

[4] Arthur W. Combs, "Personality Theory and Its Implications for Curriculum Development," in Alexander Frazier (ed.), *Learning More About Learning* (Washington, D.C.: Association for Supervision and Curriculum Development, National Education Association, 1959), p. 11.

[5] David Nyberg, *Tough and Tender Learning* (New York: National Press Books, 1971), p. 127. See also Arthur W. Combs, *Educational Accountability Beyond Behavioral Objectives* (Washington, D.C.: Association for Supervision and Curriculum Development, National Education Association, 1972), p. 39.

any given time is the extent to which personal meaning and culturally defined meanings or combinations of the two are being emphasized. This dimension can be combined with the first dimension so that one learning environment might emphasize personal meanings with intrinsic motivation, another personal meanings with extrinsic motivation, a third culturally defined meanings with intrinsic motivation, and still another culturally defined meanings with extrinsic motivation.

THE INTERPERSONAL SETTING

Conversation, two people working together, the helping relationship, and expressions of friendship are among the most natural modes of interpersonal relationships for adults. They are at the center of marriage, of the family, of our social activities, and have become an important part of our work culture. Bridges and cities will be built, the air will be cleaned, and cancer will be conquered as a result of teamwork—people working and sharing together in pursuit of these problems. The day of individuals working alone and in competition with others to solve man's problems seems past.[6] Yet the schools seem to continue their emphasis on learning contexts comprised of interpersonal settings which pit one person against another. Conversation, working together, the helping relationship, and expressions of friendship seem at best tolerated and more often frowned upon or punished. Two children enjoying conversation, or helping each other with their schoolwork are admonished for "talking" or for "copying."

> Group activities and discussions contribute to the person's ability to relate to others, to share in group goals, and to surrender selfish attitudes and values for the benefit of the group. Sometimes, however, group participation in school activities can be made a fetish. Conversation with another person can usually be carried on at a deeper level than discussion in a group and can lead to the formation of the stronger ties of friendship. And there are times when it is good for the person to be alone, to work alone, to simply get away from all the talk and think things over on his own. This third dimension of human growth can be represented as a continuum moving from individual activity to conversation and activity with a friend to discussion and activity in a group.[7]

Schools need to provide students with learning experiences in each of the three interpersonal settings. To be alone, to work closely with another, and to function as a member of a group in pursuit of personal and culturally defined meanings expand the options we have in facilitating learning as well as providing youngsters with experience in a variety of interpersonal settings.

---

[6] See, for example, John Kenneth Galbraith, *The New Industrial State* (Boston: Houghton Mifflin, 1967), particularly Ch. 6.

[7] Sergiovanni and Starratt, *Emerging Patterns of Supervision,* p. 249.

The Nine Contexts for Learning

As the relationship setting is added to motivation and meaning, we now have three dimensions which comprise the raw material necessary for building and classifying any learning encounter by context. True, the content of a learning encounter also needs to be considered, but will be assumed for the purposes of this discussion. The three dimensions are illustrated in the diagram below.

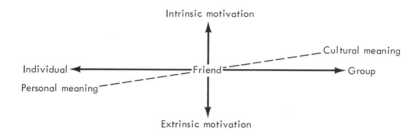

Various combinations of the three dimensions provide us with nine contexts for learning as illustrated in Figure 4-1. It would be useful to classify learning activities you observe or experience in elementary schools by locating them on Figure 4-1.

With a learning activity clearly in mind, how would you classify the motivational set of the learners? Were they engaged in the activity because they were responding to adult authority, because they needed to complete this step to get to the next, or because they found it intrinsically satisfying? Did the activity emphasize predetermined expectations or objectives, or were youngsters interacting with knowledge on their own terms? Did the learning activity emphasize youngsters working alone, in conversation or friendship settings, or in group settings? Our observations are that of the nine contexts, contexts 7 and 8 (contexts ICE and GCE in Figure 4-1, or those which emphasize extrinsic motivation and culturally defined meanings in either individual or group settings) account for the major focus in most elementary schools.

Most learning encounters which emphasize skill mastery followed by testing and grading of some kind, or by contest or competition reward, would be found in contexts 7 and 8. These would include memorizing multiplication tables, vocabulary lists, state capitals, and the parts of a grasshopper. Drawing and painting sessions in which the best works on pollution (a topic proposed by the art teacher) are selected for display in the corridor on parents' night, or music classes geared only to preparing youngsters for the Christmas

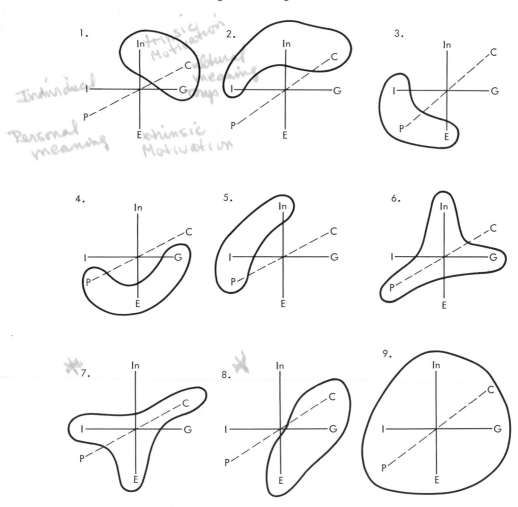

FIGURE 4-1.   Contexts for learning. Today's schools focus primarily on contexts 7 and 8 (ICE and GCE) which emphasize extrinsic motivation and culturally defined meanings in individual and group settings.

Adapted from: Thomas J. Sergiovanni and Robert J. Starratt, *Emerging Patterns of Supervision: Human Perspectives* (New York: McGraw-Hill, 1971), p. 256.

song fest are further examples. The day-by-day progression, page by page, paragraph by paragraph, through textbook after textbook, followed by group discussion of questions at chapter endings and by tests, is also likely to be classified in contexts 7 and 8. Committee work in social studies units prepared and assigned by the teacher, which is followed by graded written and oral reports, as well as science fair competition projects, more often than not find themselves in the same contexts. The key to classifying learning activities in these settings is that the activity or outcome is largely determined by the teacher and curriculum, and the student is expected to come up with something in order to win a prize, get a grade, successfully compete with other children, move on to the next unit, or to obtain adult approval.

Building a series of tunnels in the sand corner, reading a book on the life of Andrew Jackson, figuring out the number of square feet of floor space in the classroom, or reading up on the mechanics of how to use a slide rule out of sheer curiosity might be examples of contexts 1 and 2 (BCG and IBC in Figure 4-1). Four youngsters who because of interest become involved in constructing a bar graph showing the height relationship of boys and girls by age in the third and fourth grades would be a further example of context 2. Any of the learning activities mentioned so far could shift to contexts emphasizing personal meanings, if student interpretation and valuing are encouraged and if student self-awareness and concept development are nurtured. Examples might include drama in which youngsters act out important incidents in history or current events, discuss and debate major social issues, and are encouraged to take positions and to describe "what something means to me" or "how I feel about it." However, if their themes become handy topics for a teacher-initiated "creative writing" session, as so often happens, we may find ourselves back in contexts 7 and 8.

All of us can recall learning activities where we had everything going for us. As rare as they may be, when they do occur, they are long remembered and treasured. Context 9 would probably be used to classify these peak learning experiences.

The learning context discussion presented in this chapter provides an alternate way of examining, evaluating, and planning educational experiences for youngsters in schools. As in our discussion of goals and objectives, we advocate a balance among learning contexts which emphasizes cognitive as well as humanistic settings for youngsters and which provides a sufficient array of options and approaches to better accommodate the idiosyncracies of school learnings and individual personalities.

> While an appeal to these basic human qualities of life is considered unscientific and sentimental by some, a curriculum which effectively programs these qualities of human life out of existence is self-defeating. To be fair, a curriculum focusing solely on interpersonal relations and esthetic contemplation can produce a flaccid and ineffective personality. It is not a question, however, of either-or. The schools can provide an atmosphere and a curriculum for both intellectual and personal growth. And, consonant with the theme developed earlier, one can enter upon personal growth most humanly through knowledge of the world and can grow intellectually precisely by an internalization and integration of knowledge in one's personal life.[8]

8 Sergiovanni and Starratt, *Emerging Patterns of Supervision,* pp. 258–259.

We have maintained that the one-dimensional view of educational objectives, particularly when limited to only instructional objectives, lacks the necessary potency and understanding to help the elementary school function effectively as a human organization. As we give attention to expressive and informal as well as instructional objectives, and to context as well as content of learning, our chances for making a human difference in elementary education are greatly increased.

5

Teacher-Student Influence and Instructional Organization

"THE OBJECTIVES MUST determine the organization or else the organization will determine the objectives," reads the 1918 Cardinal Principles of Secondary Education. This statement is true for any organization, although its consequences seem particularly critical for the elementary school. Most readers would agree that the form of an elementary school educational program should follow its function but, in spite of stated goals and objectives (or in the absence of these, what the teachers say they are doing), we can readily observe large numbers of schools where function follows form.

This chapter is concerned with the organization and operation of the school's educational program. Our discussions of goals and objectives and of learning contexts in Chapters 3 and 4 should provide the reader with the necessary background to critically analyze the educational programs we describe in terms of stated and implied goals. This analysis should then be appraised in reference to the values in elementary education and the goals and objectives with which the school should be most concerned. Consider, for example, the extent to which a specific program provides for a balanced approach to instructional, expressive, and informal objectives. Are personal meanings as well as culturally defined meanings encouraged and nurtured? Does the instructional approach rely on intrinsic learning and being behavior, or primarily on extrinsic reasons for learning, which results in becoming behavior? Does an instructional approach limit student activity to group settings, or are individual work settings provided for students? Is the program based on principles of student cooperation, sharing, and teamwork, or on student competition? Is freedom to learn as important as learning itself?

In order to facilitate the analysis and evaluation of various program options, a model for classifying and understanding patterns of instructional organization and teaching strategies is developed and presented. The utility of this model is increased when it is used in conjunction with the educational-objectives categories and the learning-context concepts previously discussed.

The Teacher-Student Influence Model

One way in which a classroom can be described is on the basis of student influence and teacher influence; that is, to what extent do students and teachers influence and contribute to classroom goals and objectives, curriculum decision making, and instructional activities? Great variability exists in the amount of influence which teachers and students exercise as one views elementary school classrooms. In some schools, the teacher is very influential in deciding goals and objectives—what will be studied, how, and when. Such teachers may very well have the students' interests at heart and, indeed, may demonstrate this by flexible and creative teaching, but it is understood that students will have little to say about such decisions. In other classrooms, teachers function in a mindless way as they implement a curriculum which they have little identity with and often do not understand. Here, neither teacher nor student assumes responsibility for goal selection and curriculum decision making. In a few classrooms, teachers and students exercise major influence as they participate together in goal and objective development and in curriculum decision making. In an occasional classroom, one may find that the teacher exercises virtually no influence, having abdicated the responsibility for goal selection and curriculum decision making entirely to the students.

The teacher-student influence model is presented in grid form in Figure 5-1. The line forming the base of the grid (the horizontal marginal axis) represents the influence of the teacher in developing and selecting goals and in deciding the nature, scope, sequence, and pace of learning activity in the classroom. The lower the influence exhibited by teachers, the further to the left on this line they would rate, with 1 representing virtually no influence

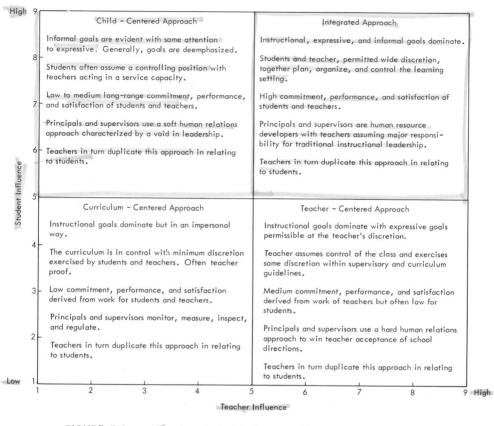

FIGURE 5-1.   Teacher-student influence grid.

and 9, maximum influence. The line forming the left side of the grid (the vertical marginal axis) represents the students' influence in developing and selecting goals and in deciding the nature of learning activity in the classroom, with 1 on this line representing virtually no influence and 9, maximum influence. The ratings (1 to 9) on each of the two lines should be considered equivalent. Therefore, a classroom with a teacher-contribution rating of 3 and a student-contribution rating of 3 would suggest that teacher and students would have approximately the same (albeit, small), amount of influence and control over what they do.

It is important at this time for the reader to make a first estimate of his location on the grid.[1] Further, we should realize that we are dealing con-

[1] If it is not possible to make an estimated rating of your own classroom, rate a classroom with which you are familiar, perhaps your child's classroom.

ceptually with these ideas, and, while it may not be possible to speak of exact location of a classroom on the grid, we believe that it is useful to speak of approximate location. After studying the grid, based on our previous discussion, rate your classroom from 1 to 9 on both marginal axes. For example, if you rate yourself as 7 and the students in your class as 4, your location in the grid would be in the teacher-centered quadrant as follows:

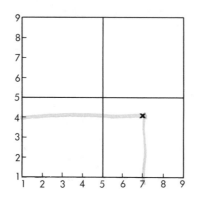

Perhaps in the classroom you are rating, the teacher and students are not permitted or do not assume much influence over goals, directions, and activities; that is, these decisions are made elsewhere, and the teacher is largely expected to implement a heavily prescribed curriculum or to follow the textbooks systematically and faithfully. If this classroom is rated as 4 in teacher influence and as 2 in student influence, it would be located in the curriculum-centered quadrant on the grid as follows:

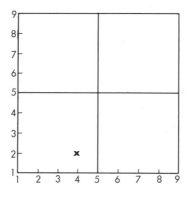

Estimates of classroom location on the grid would need to be made based on patterns of influence which are exhibited over a long period of time. This is important, for at any given instant a class whose modal pattern places it primarily in one location could find itself in any other location.

The nine possible ratings for each of the axes permit 81 different estimates of location for a particular classroom. The grid is divided into four quadrants. Realizing that the nine-point rating scheme permits 20 different locations within a quadrant, it still is useful from a conceptual standpoint to speak of each quadrant representing a classroom climate for learning that is comprised of a set of modal characteristics. The deeper one finds oneself in any quadrant (that is, the further one gets from the center of the grid) the more applicable are the characteristics we describe as we examine each of the quadrants more specifically.

TEACHER-CENTERED APPROACH

Large numbers of elementary school classrooms are characterized by teachers who assume leadership functions which include planning objectives, goals, strategies, programs, activities, and policies; organizing methods, materials, equipment, and children; teaching through instructing, mediating, communicating, and developing; and controlling by measuring, evaluating, correcting, rewarding, and punishing. These leadership functions are often assumed by dedicated teachers who have the best interests of students at heart, but who feel that they know best what youngsters need. Students are treated with kindness and consideration, but their classroom roles are limited primarily to responding to teacher planning, organization, and leadership, by doing or implementing the instructional programs and then by submitting to controls which measure effectiveness.

This approach to teaching is suggested in the lower right-hand quadrant of Figure 5-1 and is referred to as the teacher-centered approach. Here, teacher contributions to class activity are reasonably strong but limited. For example, all students may be required to study long division before Christmas of the fourth grade, or to learn how to write a business letter during the sixth grade, or to study two "hot" countries and two "cold" countries in the third grade, but the choice of materials, methods, and approaches, within approved limitations, is largely up to the teacher not the textbook writer, the curriculum developer, or the supervisor. The teacher is free to adjust materials and methods according to his perception of student needs providing that certain specified content areas are covered.

Classrooms patterned after this quadrant are likely to employ learning contexts which primarily emphasize culturally defined meanings, although, with some imagination, personal meanings can be occasionally included. Individual and group settings rather than conversation, friendship, or team settings are likely to be observed. In this quadrant, intrinsic motivation and being behaviors are likely to be neglected because of the heavy emphasis placed on following the teacher's lead. The emphasis is likely to be on the achievement of instructional objectives with expressive objectives only possible from time to time.

Teachers typically find some enjoyment in their work, though many are still hampered from reaching full satisfaction by constraints imposed in terms of prescribed curriculum guidelines. It is frustrating to have to stop at the border of fourth- and fifth-grade content when one is in hot pursuit of learning with a group of well-motivated children because of curriculum fragmentation, particularly when children in this quadrant may only rarely be well motivated.

Teachers need to engage in selling, persuading, convincing, appealing, and other human-relations skills in order to get serious commitment from youngsters. Sometimes this is too difficult or time consuming, and the teacher falls back on horse trading: "When you are finished with the assignment, you may take a game from the shelf and play quietly at your desk," or "Tomorrow we will have a test and this assignment will help you pass."

CHILD-CENTERED APPROACH

The upper left-hand quadrant would describe classrooms where the teacher rarely, if at all, exercises leadership. Responsibility for learning is abdicated completely to students. Classrooms such as these are usually part of educational experiments such as Summerhill-type schools and are found only rarely in the public schools. Some consider that schools and classrooms associated with this quadrant offer an attractive approach to elementary education, but we believe the approach to be limited because of the passive role assigned to the teacher.

THE INTEGRATED APPROACH

Each of the two approaches previously discussed assumes that student initiative, freedom, and personal self-actualization and academic goals, cultural expectations, and societal demands to which the school must respond are in conflict with each other. The upper right-hand quadrant, characterized by autonomy and involvement for the teacher and the student, represents an integrated approach to elementary school teaching and learning. In this approach, no conflict is assumed between student needs and academic goals. Indeed, the two are seen to be interdependent under the premise that youngsters find rich personal meanings only through engaging in worthwhile educational experiences. Further, the difference between intellectual enrichment and merely going through the motions of schooling in order to accumulate information is the initiative, excitement, commitment, and meaning which the youngster brings to any learning encounter.

In the integrated approach, teachers and students assume major responsibility for planning, organizing, and controlling the learning environment with the supervisor's leadership (instructing, mediating, communicating, developing, delegating, and motivating) supporting this effort. Since teacher and student involvement in setting goals and in planning work are high, commitment and intrinsic motivations are assured. These in turn are likely to result in high performance by teachers and students as they pursue instructional, expressive, and informal goals. Culturally defined meanings and extrinsic motivation are not sacrificed, but they are not pursued at the expense of personal meanings and the nurturing of intrinsic interest in learning and in life for its own sake.

THE CURRICULUM-CENTERED APPROACH

The least satisfactory and most dehumanizing approach to schooling is represented in the lower left-hand quadrant. This quadrant contains a non-leadership approach which many observers feel characterizes a large percentage of American schools. Here, the controlling force is the textbook, the highly structured and sequenced curriculum, and other materials which for the most part determine class and school goals and objectives, decide pacing, sequencing, and scope of instruction, and so on. Teachers and students only need to follow directions, and supervisors see to it that directions are followed. In classrooms of this type, teacher and students have abdicated all rights and responsibilities to an impersonal expert manifested in the text, the overly structured curriculum, or whatever it is which commands how teachers and students are to behave and defines the nature of activities with which they will be engaged.

The fallacy in this approach becomes readily apparent when youngsters are taught and tested on subject matter which two weeks previously was totally unfamiliar to the teacher and which too often becomes unfamiliar to both shortly after the test. Teachers rated deep in this quadrant have deserted the class in terms of providing leadership and have become mere followers and givers of directions.

The question is not simply one of texts, materials, and curricula, but one of control. Do teachers use texts, materials, and curriculum guides as means to achieve individual and school goals, or are these things ends in themselves? This is not merely a rhetorical question, but one relevant to the survival of teaching as a profession as opposed to an occupation. We will always have teachers, but professionals in teaching may become extinct as more and more classrooms drift into this quadrant. In some respects, this quadrant simplifies the "job of teaching," but makes the job of keeping control of students more difficult, for the typical student response is largely indifference, protest, and slowdown. Soon teachers respond similarly.

Educational Program Alternatives

We have no intention of presenting a historical summary of educational program development in elementary schools and promise no annotated list of alternate methods of curriculum design. These make interesting reading for one who has a need for such information, but are readily available from a number of other sources. In the remainder of this chapter, some general approaches to the development and implementation of various educational programs are considered. Among these are the familiar or habitual approach (sometimes referred to as the traditional or subject-centered approach) and the continuous progress approach. We conclude the chapter with a consideration of the Multiunit School and Individually Guided Instruction as more concrete examples of educational program and school organization. In Chapter 6, we consider informal or open approaches to elementary education. These have tremendous potential if properly conceived, understood, and implemented by committed teachers.

For this discussion to be a useful one, the reader will need to interact with what is written from the perspective of his reservoir of personal meanings. Which of the approaches we discuss here and in Chapter 6 make you feel most uncomfortable? Why? What values and goals are implicit in each by virtue of the way the educational program is organized and operated? Are these implicit values and goals different from those which are claimed by advocates? How do they measure up to your values and goals for elementary education?

HABITUAL (TRADITIONAL) SCHOOLING

We like to cherish traditions, for, in addition to sentimental value, they provide us with strength, stability, and continuity. We like what is familiar to us, for the familiar helps us feel comfortable. It is for these reasons that traditions are venerated and respected. In spite of this, the graded subject-centered school which has for so long dominated elementary education has too many shortcomings for it to enjoy such veneration and respect. Its perseverance, therefore, seems more appropriately attributed to habit than to tradition. One follows tradition with purpose in order to enjoy its meaning. Few people could find purpose in habitual schools. Indeed, goals and objectives are systematically avoided in most habitual classrooms, and in their place one finds an emphasis on covering subjects, materials, units, and pages.

Although some attempts are made to individualize instruction, most teachers in habitual classrooms teach to the group. Usually the classroom group is homogeneous in the sense that attempts have been made to group children by ability. Grouping decisions are made on the basis of standardized tests in reading and math in addition to teacher evaluation. Often, the motivation behind such grouping is *to make children easier to teach* rather than to individualize instruction.

Once class assignments of students are made, teachers work on the assumption that no wide range of interests and needs exists. To be sure, subgroupings in reading and math are used within the classroom group, but what is often not recognized is that individuals within any group may require special consideration with respect to learning style, rate, mode, materials, and activities. Typically, children are assigned to the same basal texts with subgroupings which allow for faster or slower coverage. The various subgroups receive the same basic assignments, cover the same workbook pages, and complete the same worksheets. Not only is the material basically the same, but little adjustment is found in learning styles, activities, and methods for each of the groups.

The use of basal texts in each of the subject-matter areas does not prevent a teacher from individualizing instruction, but it does discourage such practices. Teachers can, and many do, use multiple texts and other instructional materials to fit their estimates of a youngster's needs, interests, performance levels, and learning style, but such practices threaten to upset the integrity of the habitual system. For the most part, teachers in habitual schools feel that if they try to diverge from the text in an attempt to individualize instruction beyond simple pacing, a child will miss an important skill, or material which is supposed to be covered at a particular level will be neglected. In many respects the decisions of curriculum administrators who decide what materials will be studied are assumed infallible. Thelen describes very nicely the three main features of habitual classrooms—a *teacher-centered* culture which emphasizes *extrinsic motivation* and *culturally defined meanings*.

> In present classrooms we note that it is generally assumed that children would be easier to teach if they were grouped for *similarity* of readiness, sophistication, or ability, and that, obviously, they will achieve best and most meaningfully if they are set in *competition* with each other. . . .
>
> The competition is directed by the teacher, and to make it "fair" he must pick tasks that are equally "distant" or distasteful to all the children. (If he let them dictate their interests, the person whose interest won would be believed to have an unfair advantage.) Even goals that are "fair" are too easy for some, too hard for others, and just right for a small minority. Since this must always be the case in a competitive situation, there is no point in finding out whether the goals are meaningful to the students, for changing the goal does not eliminate the unmeaningfulness; it only redistributes it.
>
> Since the goals are not necessarily congruent with the needs of more than

a few students, the rest may not be able to tell when the goals have been satisfied. But the teacher knows and will tell the student; therefore, *satisfying the goal* and *pleasing the teacher* are identical processes. Since the child can, through teacher study, learn to please the teacher even though the goals remain senseless and arbitrary, for him the teacher becomes the only significant target; and a goal is whatever the teacher, in the name of his official and certified office, demands.

Since the children cannot make deductions from goals to procedures, or from ends to means, the teacher must specify the procedures. These are concrete and require activity on the part of the student. To him, carrying out the teacher-required procedures is the heart of learning and the goal of activity; and the teacher-stated goals are only rationalizations or trust-building assurances that the teacher, at least, knows what he is up to.[2]

Imaginative teachers, principals, supervisors, and curriculum workers have always found ways to work creatively within any system. Thus, in many schools which are locked into habitual education, one finds teachers using subjects as means to achieve goals of intellectual enrichment, individualization, and self-actualization. For such gifted teachers the focus is on problems with subjects treated experientially through activity-oriented teaching techniques. Teacher-pupil planning is used extensively to determine what aspects of the prescribed curriculum are worth studying, as opposed to covering, and how these problems might best be studied. Classroom schedules are listed as blocks of time rather than as subject-matter modules. Not all of the "subjects" need be covered for a specified number of minutes, or for that matter at all, each day. Subjects are integrated around problems, and blocks of "free time" when youngsters are permitted to study or work in areas or subjects of their choice are built into the schedule.

CONTINUOUS PROGRESS APPROACHES

A popular alternative to the habitual approach to schooling in elementary education is the nongraded plan. Recently, advocates of nongraded education have used the term "continuous progress" to describe their approaches. Continuous progress plans are designed to individualize the *rate* of instruction by breaking the lock-step feature found in graded schools.[3] Youngsters are not customarily taught in groups or classes, but are engaged in individual

[2] Herbert Thelen, "Secularizing the Classroom's Sacred Culture," *School Review*, Vol. 79, No. 1 (November 1970), 12–14.

[3] Examples of continuous progress approaches are Individually Prescribed Instruction (IPI) and Project PLAN. IPI is a project of the Learning Research and Development Center at the University of Pittsburgh, and Project PLAN of the American Institute for Research in Behavioral Sciences and the Westinghouse Learning Corporation. See, for example: John Bolvia, "Individually Prescribed Instruction," *Educational Screen and Audiovisual Guide*, Vol. 47, No. 4 (April 1968), 17–22; and Thomas Quirk, "The Student in Project PLAN: A Functioning Program of Individualized Instruction," *The Elementary School Journal*, Vol. 71, No. 1 (October 1970), 42–54. Perhaps one of the best examples

activities more or less specifically designed for them. The acceptance of individual differences in learning rates (and sometimes styles) is considered fundamental to such programs. The student, thus, becomes the baseline from which to measure growth, and the curriculum is organized into a series of levels through which youngsters are programmed. Hillson and Hyman propose the following as a nonexhaustive list of advantages to continuous progress education.

Learning skill sequences that are operationally defined and developed to meet the needs of the learner population involved generally reflect better teaching opportunities as well as learning opportunities.

Children are taught skills from learning sequences ranging from readiness to competency or mastery, and the development of skills is more carefully attended to.

The elimination of promotion or nonpromotion eliminates much of the threat that brings about unhappiness in school.

Children who are deliberate learners, but no less intelligent than their faster counterparts, can move at their own pace without the penalty of being nonpromoted simply because necessary coverage over a given year is defined as a grade. When multiaging is used in skill development programs, older children frequently become leaders when working with slower or younger children and teach them how to use manipulative and mechanical materials.

When multiaging is used, children who would not make a contribution because of their peer critics now tend to do so in a group where they are at a relevant, problem-solving level.

There are no gaps in instruction because there is no grade to skip.

There is no repetition of material that the child already knows since he begins each year where he left off.

There is a greater opportunity for flexibility in grouping procedures and this allows for appropriate and pertinent placement of youngsters.

Because of the problem-solving nature of the program attendant to the need of the child, the reduction in behavior problems is great.

There is much more teamwork on the part of faculty members when they are involved in a collaborative planning program that allows them to evaluate and to deal with the needs of the individual youngsters.

There is increased awareness of pupil individuality since individual differences are the very core of continuous progress.

Where multiadult exposure (through team teaching) takes place, a

---

of continuous progress can be found in the film *Charlie and the Golden Hamster* distributed by IDEA. This film is a portrayal of the ungraded UCLA laboratory school.

greater opportunity for real evaluation of the quality of the learner is made.

There is no fear of encroachment on materials supposedly reserved for a particular grade.

There is no ceiling on learning in a continuous progress program.

The pressures normally found in graded education to achieve end-of-term goals and to maintain standards that may be clearly outside the attained abilities of pupils are eliminated since the norm in continuous progress is the child. His placement and work are always appropriate to his capacity, readiness, or competence.[4]

It should be noted that in those curriculum areas where continuous progress is used, usually reading and math, individualization usually takes place not in what is learned but in the pacing of learning. Youngsters and often teachers still have little say about the substance of the delivery system of education to which they are exposed. The autonomy of teachers increases in some areas and decreases in others. They assume much more responsibility for placing students on learning tracks and adjusting placement decisions through diagnosing learning difficulties and measuring individual progress. On the other hand, many continuous progress plans are so rigidly structured and sequenced that little or no discretion is permitted by the teacher in determining objectives and curriculum. In such cases, the teacher's job becomes one of monitoring the learning process. Other plans permit teachers to select goals and objectives according to their assessment of student needs. Each of these objectives is accompanied by a curriculum package of some sort which the teacher then utilizes. Still others permit the teacher wide discretion in opting not only for goals and objectives, but for developing learning experiences as well. Needless to say, plans that permit only modest teacher discretion do guarantee some protection against weak or incompetent teaching, but will also stifle creative teaching.

In summary, continuous progress plans as they presently operate are basically pacing plans in which rates of learning are adjusted in accordance with individual needs of students. As such plans move from their adolescence to maturity, perhaps we can hope to see more than a token accommodation to what is learned based on individual needs. This will require that more attention be given to expressive and informal objectives and to expanding contexts of learning. In their present state, most continuous progress plans are marvels of efficiency in delivering what so-called infallible experts feel youngsters should learn, but are still primitive in involving the student as an equal partner in learning encounters.

[4] Maurie Hillson and Ronald Hyman (eds.), *Change and Innovation in Elementary and Secondary Organization* (New York: Holt, Rinehart and Winston, 1971), pp. 35–36.

A Specific Example: The Multiunit
School and Individually Guided Education

The Wisconsin Research and Development Center for Cognitive Learning has developed a comprehensive plan for school organization and curriculum implementation which is gaining wide acceptance. Our treatment of this approach to individualize elementary education is admittedly too brief and perhaps oversimplified, but our intent is only to introduce the reader to the possibilities which this model and others like it represent.[5]

An unanticipated consequence of adopting any model is the danger of focusing on the model *per se* rather than on what it represents. The Multiunit School (MUS-E) and Individually Guided Education (IGE) are no exceptions to this danger. The IGE model has potential to provide the guidelines for developing a responsive educational program which gives attention to multiple learning contexts and to expressive and informal as well as instructional objectives. It can also become a sterile marvel of engineering efficiency designed to do little else but pack more information at faster rates into the minds and hearts of students. The MUS-E model has potential for bringing together teams of teachers dedicated to their own growth and development as well as those of their youthful charges, or it can become a monster of management science designed to simplify the job of teaching through task specialization and other assembly-line techniques.

THE MULTIUNIT ELEMENTARY SCHOOL

MUS-E is a plan of school organization which incorporates family or multiage grouping, differentiated staffing, and shared group decision making to accompany a philosophy of individualized instruction. The school faculty is divided into teams or units, each charged with planning and implementing an educational program for about 150 students. Students are grouped into families according to ages. Each team or unit is comprised of a unit leader or lead teacher and several teachers, assistants, and interns. The unit leader or lead teacher is a new role specifically responsible for educational programs, curriculum development, and teaching leadership as opposed to administrative leadership functions. Each of the units assumes responsibility for planning, carrying out, and evaluating *as a team* the instructional program for the children of the unit. Staff development through cooperative teaching and mutual sharing and planning are important features of the MUS-E model.

---

[5] See, for example: Herbert J. Klausmeier et al., *Individually Guided Education in the Multiunit Elementary School: Guidelines for Implementation* (Madison: University of Wisconsin, Wisconsin Research and Development Center for Cognitive Learning, 1971); and "The Multiunit Elementary School and Individually Guided Education," *Phi Delta Kappan,* Vol. 53, No. 3 (November 1971), 181–184.

INDIVIDUALLY GUIDED EDUCATION

IGE is described by Klausmeier as:

> . . . a comprehensive system of education and instruction designed to produce higher educational achievements through providing for differences among students in rate of learning, learning style, and other characteristics. IGE is more comprehensive than individualized instruction if the latter is viewed as instruction in which a student learns through interacting directly with instructional materials or equipment with little or no assistance from a teacher. In IGE self-instructional materials or systems are simply one important kind of material or medium to be used in instructional programming for the individual student.[6]

An instructional program model for IGE is presented in Figure 5-2. The model is a useful one, rationally conceived, well planned, and designed for orderly implementation of an educational program. Yet its strengths are its shortcomings, for intellectual enrichment, growth, and development, as well as personal self-actualization, are not exclusively (and perhaps not primarily) the by-products of such orderly learning.

As a plan of organization, MUS-E has enormous potential for more deliberately developing learning encounters in each of the nine contexts for learning we referred to in Chapter 4. Further, family grouping offers the advantage of young people's working cooperatively rather than competitively in schools. The faculty unit team makes management and motivational sense as well as educational sense by permitting people to opt for varying levels of commitment and responsibility at work. IGE as presently conceived should be of enormous assistance in increasing our capacity to achieve instructional objectives. However, the model would be vastly improved if it were more manifestly designed to include expressive and informal objectives.

MUS-E and IGE concepts are considered further in the next chapter as we explore American approaches to informal education.

Evaluating Instructional Approaches

At their very best, habitual approaches and continuous progress approaches to schooling permit students to express individual needs within prescribed limits. These are basically curriculum-oriented and teacher-centered models which, when expressed ideally, have the interests of students in mind. Students, however, are expected to be relatively passive recipients of these good intentions. Their involvement ranges from having little or no say to one of being consulted by the teacher. In any case, either the curriculum or the

[6] Herbert J. Klausmeier et al., *Individually Guided Education and the Multiunit Elementary School Elementary Education for the 1970s* (Madison: University of Wisconsin, Wisconsin Research and Development Center for Cognitive Learning), p. 12.

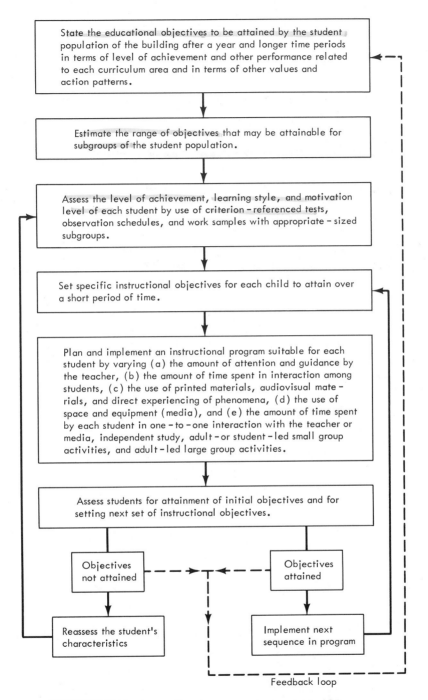

FIGURE 5-2. Instructional programming model in IGE.

From Herbert J. Klausmeier et al., *Individually Guided Education and the Multiunit Elementary School Elementary Education for the 1970s* (Madison: University of Wisconsin, Wisconsin Research and Development Center for Cognitive Learning), p. 13.

teacher knows what is best. The absurdity in this presumed infallibility of curriculum and teacher is evidenced in the wide disagreement which exists among teachers and curriculum workers in regard to what knowledge is worth knowing. Knowledge in and of itself seems to be less important than the learnings gained and enjoyed in confronting knowledge. Further, concepts and processes experienced in this confrontation with knowledge generally are not dependent upon any given body of knowledge. Youngsters in Brazil, Japan, or Sierra Leone manage to learn, understand, and appreciate the relationships between cultural norms and environmental determiners and how these affect one's life style without ever studying American Indians, and acquire simple principles of geography and economics without studying the products of the states or regions of the United States.

As the emphasis in learning shifts from mere accumulation of knowledge to higher-order cognitive processes, such as comprehension through interpretation and extrapolation, application, analysis, synthesis, and evaluation,[7] student involvement in the learning encounter must increase. The higher the cognitive process, the more student initiative, commitment, and involvement are necessary. This principle applies as well to affective goals such as awareness, responding, and valuing.

At their very best, habitual approaches and continuous progress approaches as they are presently conceived would probably be rated as 9 on teacher involvement and as 5 on student involvement on the Teacher-Student Influence Grid presented earlier (Figure 5-1). At their worst, such approaches would rate a 1 on each of the dimensions as follows:

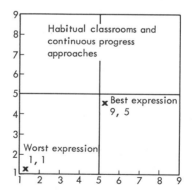

---

[7] Benjamin S. Bloom et al., *Taxonomy of Educational Objectives, Handbook I: Cognitive Domain* (New York: McKay, 1956).

In the 9,5 setting, habitual and continuous progress teachers have generous autonomy within loosely prescribed limits to do as they wish in developing and implementing the educational program, and youngsters are involved not as equal partners in learning but as respected consultants. In the 1,1 setting, teachers and students blindly follow the directions necessary to cover a curriculum which is placed before them—in the case of habitual classrooms page after page in textbook and workbook, and in continuous progress classrooms sheet after sheet in sequential learning modules. Most habitual and continuous progress classrooms could probably be located at a variety of points somewhere between the influence settings we describe.

6

Informal
Approaches to
Elementary Education

AMERICA'S RENEWED INTEREST in informal education is largely a result of glowing reports from a number of distinguished educators and private citizens of exciting developments occurring in many of the infant schools (ages 5, 6, and 7) and junior schools (ages 8 and 9) in Britain. In this chapter, both British-style and American-style informal approaches to education are considered. These approaches are then related to our previous discussions of goals and objectives and learning contexts. Further, the teacher's role in informal education is compared to that in habitual and continuous progress approaches.

The term "open education" is commonly used to refer to informal approaches to elementary education in the United States. "Open classroom," "open corridor," "open space," and "open door" are additional terms sometimes used to refer to such approaches. In many respects open education represents an attitude, an approach to elementary education, rather than a model of program development and implementation.

If properly conceived and implemented, informal approaches offer enormous potential for improving the quality of intellectual and personal growth for children, for upgrading the profession of teaching, and for bringing school and community closer together. On the other hand, instant adoption of informal approaches on a wide scale can be disastrous. To begin with, an informal classroom run without complete knowledge of and appreciation for its philosophy and inner workings promises a miserable experience for children and teacher. Second, principals' commanding changes to informal teaching results at best in teachers' going along with new room arrangements, scheduling, gimmicks, and methods with little change in actual behavior.

Informal Education, British-Style

The following description represents an "eye witness" report of informal classrooms and how they operate in Britain. The "reporter" is Lillian Weber, an early advocate of open education in the United States who has wide experience in British primary schools.[1]

An old stone building, a wall, a bare playground, but with large tubs for planting. Inside, suddenly all is light, movement, color. The first impression is of lovely things on the eye level of five-year-olds, in corners that invite use and lingering—flowers and potted plants, easy chairs, books, paintings, shelves filled with china, a length of soft patterned fabric, a lovely bit of sea glass in the midst of an arrangement of blue pottery. The blue pottery is just one part of a total pattern of beauty—all for seeing and touching and arranging into new compositions. There are precious things, lovely things, colorful things where children can see them and handle them or, seated around a small table, enjoy quiet reading near them. Some of the corners display musical instruments, all laid out for children to see, to handle, to use. In fact, in all the corners all the objects seem to be set out with confidence that the children will handle beautiful things carefully and with respect. And also on view are things the children themselves have made with clay and wood, with paint and paper, with shells and stones.

An environment bursting with invitation, bursting with all the things children are producing right then and there. In the entry way is a paint table

[1] A number of excellent descriptions and reports of informal education in Britain and the United States are available. See, for example: Vincent R. Rogers (ed.), *Teaching in the British Primary School* (New York: Macmillan, 1970); Casey Murrow and Liza Murrow, *Children Come First, the Inspired Work of the English Primary Schools* (New York: American Heritage Press, 1971); Charity James, *Young Lives at Stake* (London: Collins Press, 1968); Joseph Featherstone, "Schools for Children," *The New Republic* (August 1967), 17–21; "Report Analysis: Children and Their Primary Schools," *Harvard Educational Review*, Vol. 38, No. 2 (Spring 1968), 317–328; and *Schools Where Children Learn* (New York: Liveright, 1971); *Children and Their Primary Schools, A Report of the Central Advisory Council for Education, Lady Plowden, Chairman, Volume 1: Research and Surveys* (London: Her Majesty's Stationery Office, 1967. In the United States: British Information Services, 845 Third Avenue, New York, New York 10022); and Charles Silberman, *Crisis in the Classroom* (New York: Random House, 1970). This book reports on a study of American education supported by the prestigious Carnegie Foundation, sponsors of the famous Conant studies of a decade or so ago.

and three children at work painting. The hall itself is large, with five doors opening out on it. Six children are there, painting a large sheet, barefoot so they can get in on the painting. The teacher is right in there with them, offering them material. Three children are at a workbench. A couple are selling cakes they had made, making sales and change with real money. Another couple sit at a table writing; still another, quietly reading. Through an open door one catches a glimpse of three girls using weights, weighing flour, making some cakes; of others in a housekeeping corner; of two children building blocks on the floor; of a boy arranging number trays of nails, buttons and conkers (our American horse chestnuts); of another measuring with knotted string on the floor.

All over the classroom wall—under paintings, on shelves, in front of clay figures, attached to woodwork—are words. "I used three pieces wood." "My boat is 11 and ¾ inches long." "This girl has a red dress." "It is a man." A little boy dictates to the teacher and watches while the teacher writes. Another writes his own sentence and asks for a word. A couple of children are absorbed at a water trolley with tubing, and with all shapes and sizes of plastic bottles, funnels, strainers, and a really fine collection of measuring cups. In the library are eight children, each one at his own task, which seems to be phonetics. The teacher helps each one separately in whatever way he needs. All during the day, groups or individuals, after asking permission, use the library, but book corners are in every room as well as in the corridor and in the big hall, often with easy chairs grouped around them and flowers on the table.

The classroom does not contain the class. The children spill all over in little groups going to use things in various areas of the room and hall. The teacher is not behind a desk but moving to all these children. The headmistress is in the midst of it all, too, knowing everyone, helping wherever needed. Talk is going on all the time. Words for activities are being sought all the time. The children seem to know just what they want to do, where to get material, how to go about it. The children move with self-assurance, *using* their school. . . .

In another infant school, also an old building, drab and gray, in one step I am in a gymnasium-sized room—the central hall—with five rooms leading off from it. I stop a child to ask for the headmistress. He takes me up to a lady in the center of a group around a workbench. They are cutting lino-prints. Another group nearby is printing for a book they are designing. Another is printing fabric. Two little girls are drawing thick wool threads through a standing pegboard, following a design they have drawn on the pegboard with colored chalk.

The room is full of activity. In one corner, two girls are marking what, on inquiry, I discover to be the register! Children collect milk money and sell snacks, using real money. Children are going in and out of a supply room that contains pieces of wood, different kinds of paper, thread and fabrics, buttons, boxes, animal supplies, wheels, paint—all sorted and labeled. A sign advertises: "Animal Grooming in Room C," and the cost; "Animal Food," and the cost. One little girl is weighing an amount of animal food. While a boy is giving out a circular describing the offerings of this animal clinic, another is making a sign needed for this. At a table six children and a teacher are cooking. An older child is helping a sewing group, and another is helping a child to read. Over in one corner two children are writing. Three little girls are walking about, holding and fondling guinea pigs, "loving them," they tell me. There seem to be no groups of more than six.

Even the old building poses no limits to possibilities of use. I begin to see that the use of the big hall and the corridor permits the breakthrough from classroom to use of *all* the school areas, thus creating a new unity of school life. Classroom doors are open to corridors or hall where children can go to acting boxes, to workbench, to musical instruments, to library corner. No child moves as part of a class; he moves as an individual to things he chooses to do and the teacher and the headmistress move to help him do these things. The classroom, the class, the teacher behind the desk—all are metamorphosed, all are changed.

Each classroom contains the standard equipment of blackboard, chairs, and tables. Though there are enough chairs to construct a large circle if desired, it is usually a few chairs around a number area, around a book corner, around an interest table, around a table covered with junk material or with clay, or around a table for children sitting writing. A good deal of empty space is left for block building, for floor projects, for all sorts of use. Children sit on the floor for storytelling, for group teaching, for a group reading. Children can always be seen writing, sprawled comfortably on the floor.[2]

CONCRETE EXPERIENCES

Advocates of informal education believe that children learn best through repeated encounters with concrete experiences. Such experiences are provided through an experiential or activity approach to teaching which relies heavily on a rich environment capable of stimulating or motivating children and freedom of choice which enables youngsters to discover learning. Further, informal educators believe that it is a waste of time to teach young children anything that they cannot learn through their senses. Feeling about things is as important as thinking about them. Abstract thinking and concept development, say informal education advocates, must be built upon layers of direct experience which include seeing, hearing, touching, smelling, and feeling.

Things make the best teachers. The emphasis is on the interface between the student and the concrete settings which comprise his educational environment. Learning takes place as children proceed through or interact with a series of educational encounters—some planned, to be sure, but many accidental in the sense that they represent spin-offs or new learnings and discoveries not anticipated by the teachers. In some respects "the medium is the message," and activities are often worthwhile in and of themselves.

INDIVIDUALIZATION IN CONTENT AND PACE

Individualized instruction to the informal educator means adjusting learning rates for children and learning styles. Not only do children develop and learn at different rates of speed, but the way they learn varies so that one method or approach may work for Jimmy but not for Johnny. Johnny does not fail for not learning; rather the teacher searches for an alternate

[2] Lillian Weber, *The English Infant School and Informal Education* (Englewood Cliffs, N.J.: Prentice-Hall, 1971), pp. 62–64.

approach to his learning style. Further, individualized education requires flexibility in student choice of what is learned.

> What children learn is never unimportant; but if we take the view that the attitudes, beliefs, and values that are learned during the years in school count for more than the facts acquired and memorized, if we think that the ability and the desire to go on learning beyond these years are valuable criteria of the work of the educative process, then how children learn is extricably bound up with what they learn.[3]

The separation of work and play is only rarely made in informal classrooms. Play is seen as a natural expression especially for the five-, six-, and seven-year-olds in the primary school. Often British schools are "family grouped" with youngsters of different ages assigned to the same teacher. A teacher typically finds himself with a group of 35 to 40 students. Sometimes 100 students and three or so teachers live and work together in a large classroom or in several adjacent classrooms or bays which open to a commons area. As in many real families, school family grouping permits youngsters to help each other. Further, it helps children to set their own pace rather than having to worry about competing with others. The emphasis is on sharing, helping, and cooperating as compared with working alone but in competition with other class members.

CONVERSATION AND COOPERATION

The importance for learning of conversation which results from the friendship setting in informal classrooms cannot be underestimated. Mutual appreciation, cooperation, understanding, and love are nurtured and enjoyed through conversation. The paired relationship is a natural one for human beings at any age, but seems particularly important in helping young people to grow in intellect and humanity. It is through conversation that deep involvement in one's work is enhanced. Conversation leads to the testing of ideas, to concept development, and to feedback. Conversation builds feelings of security, of belonging, and of self-esteem in young children. Further, conversation is natural. It is for these reasons that children in informal classrooms are encouraged to talk with each other and to work together—a far cry from many habitual classrooms which so often emphasize silence, order, and control.

THE IMPORTANCE OF STRUCTURE

Contrary to popular belief, well-conceived informal classrooms are structured, but deceptively. Their success depends on careful planning and goal setting by the teacher or teacher group. Children typically enter the school

[3] Marie Muir, "How Children Take Responsibility for Their Learning," in Rogers, *Teaching in the British Primary School*, p. 17.

and classroom when they arrive and become immediately involved in work and play. Sometimes the teacher is present, but often he is visiting with other teachers in the halls or lounge. The formal day usually begins with a meeting of the whole class. This meeting provides the teacher with an opportunity to visit with children as a group, to point out any new features or changes in the educational environment, and to plan the activities for the day with the children. Typically, youngsters discuss with teachers activities they wish to engage in; teachers clarify, encourage, urge, approve, and when necessary tactfully disapprove by "guiding" children in developing balanced learning-activity plans. Time is set aside for group activities such as physical education, a walk in the park, a school assembly, or a play that one group wishes to perform before the class.

Much planning goes into arranging the educational environment, in selecting and displaying materials, and in establishing educational settings that will be attractive to youngsters. Lack of money for schools, while in general no asset, does encourage teachers to be creative in selecting materials and to be ingenious in using them. Discarded wire, paper, bottles, milk cartons, cans, old motors, TV tubes, and broken radios; old paint, foil, ribbons, wallpaper and carpet samples; floor tile, ceramic tile, wood chips, buttons, skulls, and bones from the meat market; string, rubber bands, bricks, mason jars, bottle tops, plastics, nuts and bolts, bits and pieces of wood, old clothes, material samples, piping, corks, reels, acorns, tubing, books, magazines, tools, furniture, and similar items, all normally considered junk, often possess greater potential for stimulating creative work than most educational devices and equipment available in school supply catalogues. The arrangement and availability of these materials are important components in developing exciting and challenging educational encounters for youngsters.

The rooms resemble the layout of workshops rather than classrooms as we typically know them. These arrangements are flexible and designed for frequent adaptation to the needs of children. Indeed, good informal classrooms are well structured in the sense that careful decisions are made in arranging the environment so that certain predictable ends can be met.

THE HEAD TEACHER

The administration of the informal school is focused primarily on the instructional program. The principal or head teacher is an instructional leader who is actively involved in working alongside teachers and helping them grow in professional skill and stature. The faculty of the school operates as a team, helping each other develop the curriculum and developing themselves as professionals.

The head teacher is very much in charge of the school, and it is his manner, personality, perception of life, and educational philosophy which largely determine the climate and flavor of the school and the functioning of teachers, to the point that schools in Britain are often referred to by the head's name—Turk's School or Johnson's School. Indeed, in some schools he is so omnipresent that for all practical purposes the head is the teacher and teachers are his assistants.

The strength of the British head brings about a unity of purpose and a consistency of program not readily found in the United States. Further, since it is expected that the head exert strong leadership, he is in a position to command changes of his liking. This relatively autocratic leadership style is not a condition possible or desirable for American principals to imitate. In the United States, teacher autonomy is too important, and images of professionalism among teachers are too strongly established. Unlike their British counterparts, American teachers do not expect principals to behave in such a manner. Nevertheless, one characteristic of the head which seems amiable to imitation is his interest in and emphasis on educational program. Leadership approaches more suited to American schools are described in Part III of this book.

Informal Education, American-Style

The ideas and descriptions which appear in the previous section are not unfamiliar to most Americans who are interested in elementary education. Although these are not new ideas, their use in the United States is not widespread. Much value exists in adopting informal methods more deliberately and on a wider basis in this country. But one should not regard informal education as one does a magic elixir—as a major cure-all guaranteed to produce instant success. Successful informal methods require deep understanding, commitment, hard work, and a supportive environment. What is really unique about informal education in England is that they are doing on a broad scale what we have for so long talked about and until recently have only been able to accomplish on a modest scale.

If conceived, understood, and implemented properly, these approaches seem to provide a better than average chance for developing balanced educational experiences which give attention to instructional, expressive, and informal objectives for children. Further, enormous opportunity exists for generating learning contexts which give alternate or simultaneous attention to personal meanings and culturally defined meanings, to being behavior and becoming behavior, and to learning settings which emphasize the individual, conversation with another, and the group. At their very best, informal approaches to elementary education would rate 9 on teacher involvement and 9 on student involvement on the Teacher-Student Influence Grid presented and developed in Chapter 5. At their worst, such approaches would rate 9 on student involvement and 1 on teacher involvement as shown below.

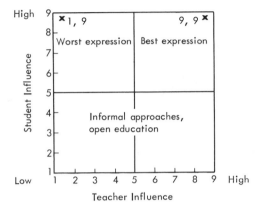

In the 9,9 setting, teachers and students have generous autonomy within broadly described limits to do as they wish in developing and implementing educational programs. Teachers and youngsters are involved as equal partners in learning. This partnership is based on the teacher's respect for the rights of children in expressing personal meanings and in enjoying being behavior and the respect of children for the teacher's prerogative to balance this emphasis with generous doses of culturally defined meanings and becoming behavior. No conflict is assumed between being and becoming, between personal and culturally defined meanings, between student rights and teacher prerogatives. In each case they are seen as being interdependent with the successful expression of one possible, but not maximized, without the other.

The 1,9 setting characterized by high student involvement and influence but low teacher involvement and interest may be caused by those who would too hastily and perhaps too enthusiastically adopt informal methods, resulting in exclusive attention on being behavior and on personal meanings in learning. The child can contribute much in deciding what is important to him, but we cannot assume that only the child knows what knowledge, information, and understanding he will need any more than we can assume that only adults have this insight. True, in many habitual and continuous progress classrooms the emphasis has been exclusively on the other extreme with the child's assuming no role in selecting his learning experiences. Informal approaches have reversed this trend by accepting the integrity of children and giving them an important say in such decisions. Ignoring adult input, a characteristic of a weak informal classroom, is as dangerous as ignoring input of children in habitual and continuous progress classrooms. Rogers speaks of the problem of balance as follows.

> This does not negate the argument that there *are* some things worth knowing; that some ideas help to order and explain our lives and the lives of others, while other ideas do not. It seems to me that the great weakness one observes in both British and American schools is the lack of knowledge about and understandings of such ideas among teachers.
>
> It would be foolish indeed to suggest that a discipline like anthropology has developed no ideas that are really worth teaching to children; no concepts that help to order, classify, and explain the social world in which we find ourselves. The real value, the ultimate utility of such ideas, however, lies not in the creation of prepackaged "teacher-proof" curricula; rather, it is the classroom teacher who must grasp them and utilize them at the appropriate moment. In other words "structure" belongs in the minds of teachers.[4]

Assumptions about Learning and Knowledge

Before one begins to seriously consider adopting informal approaches to education, it is important that one understand the assumptions that are basic to these approaches. To do otherwise often results in adopting all of the manifestations of open education—interest areas, free choice, family grouping, corridor usage, open spaces—without altering basic philosophy, attitude, and ways of behaving. The result of this kind of change is usually to be no different from, and probably worse off, than before.

Roland Barth has developed a very simple survey instrument which will help you assess your attitudes about children, learning, and knowledge (see Table 6-1). Take a moment to respond to it.

TABLE 6-1. Assumptions about learning and knowledge.

Instructions: Make a mark somewhere along each line which best represents your own feelings about each statement.

Example: School serves the wishes and needs of adults better than it does the wishes and needs of children.

strongly agree	agree	no strong feeling	disagree	strongly disagree

[4] Vincent R. Rogers, "An American Reaction," in Rogers, *Teaching in the British Primary School*, p. 300.

TABLE 6-1. Assumptions about learning and knowledge. **(cont.)**

I. Assumptions about Children's Learning

MOTIVATION

Assumption 1: Children are innately curious and will explore their environment without adult intervention.

strongly agree	agree	no strong feeling	disagree	strongly disagree

Assumption 2: Exploratory behavior is self-perpetuating.

strongly agree	agree	no strong feeling	disagree	strongly disagree

CONDITIONS FOR LEARNING

Assumption 3: The child will display natural exploratory behavior if he is not threatened.

strongly agree	agree	no strong feeling	disagree	strongly disagree

Assumption 4: Confidence in self is highly related to capacity for learning and for making important choices affecting one's learning.

strongly agree	agree	no strong feeling	disagree	strongly disagree

Assumption 5: Active exploration in a rich environment, offering a wide array of manipulative materials, will facilitate children's learning.

strongly agree	agree	no strong feeling	disagree	strongly disagree

Assumption 6: Play is not distinguished from work as the predominant mode of learning in early childhood.

strongly agree	agree	no strong feeling	disagree	strongly disagree

TABLE 6-1. Assumptions about learning and knowledge. (**cont.**)

Assumption 7: Children have both the competence and the right to make significant decisions concerning their own learning.

strongly agree	agree	no strong feeling	disagree	strongly disagree

Assumption 8: Children will be likely to learn if they are given considerable choice in the selection of the materials they wish to work with and in the choice of questions they wish to pursue with respect to those materials.

strongly agree	agree	no strong feeling	disagree	strongly disagree

Assumption 9: Given the opportunity, children will choose to engage in activities which will be of high interest to them.

strongly agree	agree	no strong feeling	disagree	strongly disagree

Assumption 10: If a child is fully involved in and is having fun with an activity, learning is taking place.

strongly agree	agree	no strong feeling	disagree	strongly disagree

SOCIAL LEARNING

Assumption 11: When two or more children are interested in exploring the same problem or the same materials, they will often choose to collaborate in some way.

strongly agree	agree	no strong feeling	disagree	strongly disagree

Assumption 12: When a child learns something which is important to him, he will wish to share it with others.

strongly agree	agree	no strong feeling	disagree	strongly disagree

TABLE 6-1. Assumptions about learning and knowledge. **(cont.)**

INTELLECTUAL DEVELOPMENT

Assumption 13: Concept formation proceeds very slowly.

strongly agree	agree	no strong feeling	disagree	strongly disagree

Assumption 14: Children learn and develop intellectually not only at their own rate but in their own style.

strongly agree	agree	no strong feeling	disagree	strongly disagree

Assumption 15: Children pass through similar stages of intellectual development, each in his own way and at his own rate and in his own time.

strongly agree	agree	no strong feeling	disagree	strongly disagree

Assumption 16: Intellectual growth and development take place through a sequence of concrete experiences followed by abstractions.

strongly agree	agree	no strong feeling	disagree	strongly disagree

Assumption 17: Verbal abstractions should follow direct experience with objects and ideas, not precede them or substitute for them.

strongly agree	agree	no strong feeling	disagree	strongly disagree

EVALUATION

Assumption 18: The preferred source of verification for a child's solution to a problem comes through the materials he is working with.

strongly agree	agree	no strong feeling	disagree	strongly disagree

TABLE 6-1. Assumptions about learning and knowledge. (**cont.**)

Assumption 19: Errors are necessarily a part of the learning process; they are to be expected and even desired, for they contain information essential for further learning.

strongly agree	agree	no strong feeling	disagree	strongly disagree

Assumption 20: Those qualities of a person's learning which can be carefully measured are not necessarily the most important.

strongly agree	agree	no strong feeling	disagree	strongly disagree

Assumption 21: Objective measures of performance may have a negative effect upon learning.

strongly agree	agree	no strong feeling	disagree	strongly disagree

Assumption 22: Learning is best assessed intuitively, by direct observation.

strongly agree	agree	no strong feeling	disagree	strongly disagree

Assumption 23: The best way of evaluating the effect of the school experience on the child is to observe him over a long period of time.

strongly agree	agree	no strong feeling	disagree	strongly disagree

Assumption 24: The best measure of a child's work is his work.

strongly agree	agree	no strong feeling	disagree	strongly disagree

TABLE 6-1. Assumptions about learning and knowledge. **(cont.)**

II. Assumptions about Knowledge

Assumption 25: The quality of being is more important than the quality of knowing; knowledge is a means of education, not its end. The final test of an education is what a man *is,* not what he *knows.*

strongly agree	agree	no strong feeling	disagree	strongly disagree

Assumption 26: Knowledge is a function of one's personal integration of experience and therefore does not fall into neatly separate categories or "disciplines."

strongly agree	agree	no strong feeling	disagree	strongly disagree

Assumption 27: The structure of knowledge is personal and idiosyncratic; it is a function of the synthesis of each individual's experience with the world.

strongly agree	agree	no strong feeling	disagree	strongly disagree

Assumption 28: Little or no knowledge exists which it is essential for everyone to acquire.

strongly agree	agree	no strong feeling	disagree	strongly disagree

Assumption 29: It is possible, even likely, that an individual may learn and possess knowledge of a phenomenon and yet be unable to display it publicly. Knowledge resides with the knower, not in its public expression.

strongly agree	agree	no strong feeling	disagree	strongly disagree

From Roland S. Barth, "So You Want to Change to an Open Classroom," *Phi Delta Kappan,* Vol. 53, No. 2, October 1971, 98–99.

Barth has found that most British and American advocates of open or informal education "strongly agree" with most of these statements. He does not argue that strong agreement with these statements assures success in developing informal classrooms, but does feel that disagreement will assure failure. Assumptions are an important starting place in bringing about change in the direction of open or informal education, for in the final analysis these approaches are less a model of curriculum implementation or teaching strategy and more a way of thinking and feeling about and educating and living with children.

THE NEW PROGRESSIVISM

It would be a mistake to assume that all children learn all things best through informal methods. Indeed, some respectable evidence exists that suggests that for many children, structured approaches to teaching are far more effective in raising achievement levels than informal methods.[5]

Further, many parents and school board members express doubts about the apparent lack of discipline or academic seriousness of informal methods. They are unaccustomed to such approaches and seem to mistrust the unfamiliar. For many, logically sequenced learning experiences linked to behaviorially defined instructional objectives provide predictability and security. Further, the use of hardware in the form of computer consoles, teaching machines, cassettes, and the like, adds that technical and scientific touch which is reassuring to Americans who have had a long and amorous relationship with machines and electronic gadgets. It would be reckless for elementary school principals to ignore these tendencies.

Is it possible that structured approaches such as continuous progress, individually prescribed instruction, and individually guided education are able to do some things better and that informal methods and approaches are able to do other things better? We think so and believe that both should be incorporated into the elementary school's educational program. For many students, the structured, highly predictable, and well-managed educational environment seems to be the most efficient means to accomplish highly specific instructional objectives, such as those relating to reading and math skills, which are reasonably dependent upon logically sequenced learning hierarchies.[6]

[5] See for example, Miriam Stearns, "Report on Pre-school Programs: The Effect of Pre-school Programs on Disadvantaged Children and Their Families," report submitted to the Office of Child Development, United States Office of Education, Washington, D.C., 1971; and Standard Research Institute, *Longitudinal Evaluation of Selected Features of the National Follow-Through Program* (Menlo Park, Calif.: Standard Research Institute, 1971).

[6] Highly sequenced and structured instructional approaches are not without their fallacies. Roe, for example, finds that children seem to learn just as well when the frames of programmed instruction are presented in random order as they do when the frames are presented in an order considered logical by experts: K. V. Roe, H. W. Case, and A.

Informal methods, on the other hand, seem more suitable for adding context, relevance, and personal meaning to these skills. For example, the joy or intrinsic satisfaction in reading, as manifested by reading without being asked or reading outside of school, is a goal seemingly best achieved through informal methods, while the acquisition of fundamental reading skills seems for many children more favored by structured methods. Ideally, joy and skill need to be developed simultaneously, for one reinforces the other.

The advocates of informal methods and those of continuous progress approaches represent the two major educational thrusts in elementary education today. Unfortunately, each often sees the views of the other as being in conflict with and incompatible with his own. Each insists that elementary school principals and faculties accept one or another of these approaches rather than the best of both.

We advocate a new progressivism in elementary education—one which capitalizes on the technical and rational approach of continuous progress in pursuit of instructional objectives without losing sight of the importance of informal methods in facilitating expressive and informal objectives. Skill mastery, scholarship, and intellectualism are important goals for elementary schools. These goals are best pursued in an educational environment which encourages children to accept responsibility for their own decisions and actions, to be autonomous, to have the ability and desire to set their own goals, to possess self-discipline, to learn self-direction, to develop the capacity for long-term involvement in activities of their own choosing, to have self-confidence, to trust themselves and others, and to be free to learn and grow as thinking and caring human beings. A new progressivism which is firmly grounded in the beliefs and practices of informal approaches to education and which has the ability to incorporate the best features of the more structured, continuous progress approaches seems to be our best hope for achieving these goals.

ONE MIDDLE-RANGE APPROACH

Approaches to working with children within the context of the elementary school need not stand alone. Indeed, any number of them can be valuably combined if such combinations are thoughtfully conceived, developed, and implemented. Informal methods, for example, might be tried within the context of the self-contained classroom. Social studies and science might be experienced in an informal way for the first or last two hours of the day with the rest of the day conducted in the habitual teacher-centered fashion. Continuous

Roe, "Scrambled v. Ordered Sequence in Autoinstructional Programs," *Journal of Educational Psychology,* Vol. 53, 2 (April 1962), 101–104. One of Piaget's findings often quoted by informal educators is that children below the age of 12 are not very good at logical thinking. They maintain that logical sequencing is not always necessary and that youngsters are quite capable of making "conceptual leaps."

progress and habitual approaches are already being combined in many different ways.

For those interested in trying informal methods, moving slowly makes sense. Much can be said for starting with habitual or continuous progress and moving toward informality in one or two areas and only gradually increasing informal time as teachers and students feel more comfortable in these settings.

One combination which we feel has particular promise is that of continuous progress and informal education. The Multiunit School (MUS-E) and Individually Guided Education (IGE), for example, can be used along with informal methods quite successfully. In this arrangement one could work within the context of family grouping to provide each youngster with a continuous progress experience in reading and math skills for about one and one-half hours on the average each day. The rest of the day would be operated in an experiential or activity-oriented informal way. The math and reading continuous progress "modules" could be scheduled for a specific time—first thing in the morning or last thing in the day for everybody—or could be opted for by the student at any time during the day.

An MUS-E school which combines IGE reading and math modules [7] with informal education might be located on the Teacher-Student Influence Grid as follows:

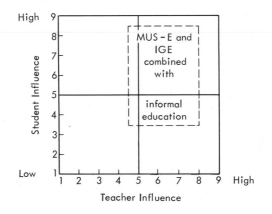

[7] We use MUS-E and IGE here as examples and recognize that a number of other approaches to family grouping and continuous progress could be combined with informal methods quite successfully. "Freedom" and "Structure" are being successfully combined in over 350 classrooms in Hartford, Connecticut, as that school district blends together informal concepts of open education with the traditional teacher-centered approach. For a description of this program, see Joseph D. Randazzo and Joanne M. Arnold, "Does Open Education Really Work in an Urban Setting?" *Phi Delta Kappan*, Vol. 54, No. 2 (October 1972), 107–110.

Such a pattern has a number of advantages. It provides teachers, parents, and community groups with some assurance that reading and math skills will be considered systematically. At the same time, this combined approach permits youngsters to be involved in informal settings which seem more suitable for achieving important expressive and informal objectives. Perhaps in time, as we acquire more confidence and skill, the total educational program could consist of informal experiences.

Summary

This chapter concludes Part II of the book. Readers should now have had sufficient opportunities to explore their own beliefs and assumptions regarding elementary education and school program. They should be able to differentiate one approach to teaching and program from another by using such indicators as (1) the implied assumptions regarding learning and knowledge manifested in the approach; (2) the amount of teacher and student influence permitted; (3) the nature and degree of balance among instructional, expressive, and informal objectives; and (4) the learning contexts which are emphasized. We have made no attempt to hide our own value system in regard to those issues, though we offer it more for analysis, discussion, and consideration than for mindless adoption.

In Part V, we present a more systematic basis for our view as we examine educational program development, the nature of human knowledge and knowing, principles of human development, and strategies for curriculum development and implementation. Our aim is not to provide the elementary school principal with technical skills in these areas, but to give him a foundational base which will permit him to operate more effectively as an educational leader as he works with teachers and community in program development.

In Part I we spoke of the importance of matching means with ends in education. How teachers function and behave in the classroom seem directly related to the goals they actually pursue regardless of their intentions. The same relationship holds as well for how the school is operated, its organizational or management climate, the behavior of the principal, his relationship to teachers, and their relationship with each other. We can learn much about what a school values and what its actual goals are, though they may be latent and quite contrary to the stated goals, from the way it is organized and operated. These are the primary concerns of Parts III and IV.

III

Organizational Leadership: A Behavioral Science View

7

The Principal's
Assumptions and
Leadership Behavior

IN EARLIER CHAPTERS we discussed the relationship that exists between the school's organizational climate and life style and the development and implementation of its educational program. We concluded, for example, that it would be most unlikely for a school to maximize its efforts to provide youngsters with an intellectually rich and self-actualizing educational experience in a school whose operation was characterized by a rigid and tightly controlled, bureaucratically oriented structure.

One important ingredient in defining a school's organizational climate and life style is its leadership system. This leadership system includes such components as general styles or ways in which principals express leadership and administrative behavior, the ways in which power and authority are used and expressed, the decision-making processes and procedures, the character of communication processes, the quality and pattern of interpersonal relationships, processes for developing goals and directions, and methods of control, supervision, and evaluation.

The ways in which the principal expresses leadership, uses power and authority, arrives at decisions, and in general interacts with teachers and others are all influenced by preexisting psychological factors, including his past experiences, his personality, and his system of values and beliefs, which in turn are expressed in the form of a set of assumptions the principal develops, believes in, and holds for people with whom he works. In this chapter, we are interested in examining the assumptions of principals and the affects of these assumptions on leadership style.

The Principal's Assumptions

Examining one's assumptions about people is a valuable aid to the analysis of leadership. Responding to the inventory which follows will help. Each of the statements, arranged in pairs, represents an assumption about people. Assign a weight from 0 to 10 to each statement to show the relative strength of your belief in the statements which comprise each pair. If, for example, you believe the first sentence of a paired statement to be mostly true and the second to be only occasionally true, you may wish to allocate 7 of your 10 points to the first of the paired sentences and 3 to the second. Any combination of point distribution is possible (10-0, 0-10, 5-5, 2-8, 6-4, and so on) depending upon the relative strength of your beliefs. The points assigned to each pair, however, must equal 10. Place your point distribution to the right of each statement in the spaces provided.

Assumptions Inventory

1. a. It's only natural for students to do as little work as they can get away with.
   b. When students avoid work, it's usually because their work has been deprived of its meaning.

1. ___2___ .
2. ___8___
   10

2. a. Because a principal or supervisor is entitled to more respect than those below him in the school hierarchy (a teacher or custodian, for example), it weakens his prestige to admit that a subordinate was right and he was wrong.
   b. Because people at all levels are entitled to equal respect, a principal or supervisor's prestige is increased by admitting that a subordinate was right and he was wrong.

3. ___0___

4. ___10___
   10

3. a. If teachers have access to any information they want, they tend to have better attitudes and behave more responsibly.

5. ___9___

     b. If teachers have access to more information than they need to do their immediate job, they will most likely misuse it.

6. ___1___
10

4. a. One problem in asking for the ideas of teachers is that their perspective is too limited for their suggestions to be of much practical value.

7. ___0___

     b. Asking teachers for their ideas broadens their perspective and results in the development of many useful suggestions.

8. ___10___
10

5. a. If students are allowed to set their own goals and standards of performance, they tend to set them lower than the teacher would.

9. ___1___

     b. If students are allowed to set their own goals and standards of performance, they tend to set them higher than the teacher would.

10. ___9___
10

6. a. Because people at all levels are entitled to equal respect, a teacher's prestige is increased when he admits that a student was right and he was wrong.

11. ___10___

     b. Because a teacher is entitled to more respect than those below him in the school hierarchy, it weakens his prestige to admit that a student was right and he was wrong.

12. ___0___
10

7. a. If teachers don't use much imagination and ingenuity in their work, it's probably because relatively few teachers have much of either.

13. ___3___

     b. Most teachers are imaginative and creative, but may not show it because of limitations imposed by supervision and the job.

14. ___7___
10

8. a. People tend to work harder if they are accountable for their own behavior and for correcting their own mistakes.

15. ___8___

     b. People tend to lower their standards if they are not watched over and corrected for their misbehavior and mistakes.

16. ___2___
10

9. a. If you give people enough money, they are less likely to be concerned with such intangibles as responsibility and recognition.

17. ___2___

     b. If you give people interesting and challenging work, they are less likely to complain about such things as pay and supplemental benefits.

18. ___8___
10

10. a. If teachers are allowed to set their own goals and

standards of performance, they tend to set them
higher than the principal or supervisor would.   19. __8__

b. If teachers are allowed to set their own goals and
standards of performance, they tend to set them   20. __2__
lower than the principal or supervisor would.[1]   10

Your "score" on the assumptions inventory is the sum of the amounts
which appear in blanks numbered 2, 4, 5, 8, 10, 11, 14, 15, 17, 19. We will
consider the assumption-inventory score later in this chapter. At this point, we
take a general look at the nature and importance of assumptions.

THEORY X ASSUMPTIONS AND PATTERN A BEHAVIOR

Assumptions are important, for they provide the data base for our
thoughts and actions about people. If, for example, we assume that youngsters
cannot be trusted in the halls and corridors of the school, then we develop
and implement a set of procedures and controls to regulate corridor behavior.
Or, if we assume that teachers will work harder toward objectives to which
they are committed, then we will spend more time with teachers dealing with
general means and ends, and less time closely supervising their day-by-day
work.

Assumptions are deceptive in many respects, particularly because they
may develop through irrational processes, such as superstition or stereotyping.
Most of us have only foggy notions about the assumptions we hold about
others and usually attribute our behavior to more rational sources. In spite
of this, these assumptions seem so readily communicated to others—particularly those to whom our behavior is directed. Indeed, although we are so
vague about our own assumptions, we are quick to perceive the assumptions
that others hold about us. The net effect of this phenomenon is that one tends
less to respond to what others say and more to the assumptions which they
hold. This phenomenon is often referred to as "the self-fulfilling prophecy."

An interesting study by Rosenthal and Jacobson illustrates the power
of the self-fulfilling prophecy in elementary classrooms. In this study, elementary school teachers believed that they were assigned children who on the
basis of an aptitude test were identified as those most likely to show an
academic spurt. Indeed they did, when compared with a control group, though
in both cases students were randomly assigned to the "academic spurt" or
control group. This study strongly suggests that the mental development of

---

[1] The Assumptions Inventory is patterned after Douglas McGregor, *The Human
Side of Enterprise* (New York: McGraw-Hill, 1960), Chaps. 3 and 4 and after Scott
Myers, *Every Employee a Manager* (New York: McGraw-Hill, 1970), p. 19.

youngsters was influenced by the expectations that teachers held for them.[2] Rensis Likert's study of supervisors of highly effective work groups in industry strongly suggests that a subordinate generally responds well to the supervisor's high evaluation and genuine confidence in him and works hard to justify the supervisor's expectations.[3]

Theory X is the title given by Douglas McGregor to a set of assumptions administrators have about people.[4] This theory is comprised of several systematic and interrelated generalizations which significantly influence one's behavior. The assumptions basic to Theory X are:

1. The average human being has a natural dislike of work and will avoid it if he can.

2. Because of this inherent dislike of work, most people must be persuaded, rewarded, punished, controlled, coerced, and directed in order to get them to put forth satisfactory effort toward achieving work goals.

3. The average person prefers to be directed, lacks ambition, wishes to avoid responsibility, and wants security above all.[5]

4. In sum, the average person is inherently self-centered, indifferent to organizational needs, and resistant to change by nature.

The behavior typically manifested in Theory X assumptions is labeled by Argyris as Pattern A.[6] Pattern A takes two forms: hard and soft. In the school, the hard version is a no-nonsense approach characterized by strong leadership, tight controls, and close supervision by the teacher in a classroom setting and by the principal in a total school setting. The soft approach relies heavily on buying, persuading, or winning people through good (albeit, superficial) human relations and benevolent paternalism to obtain compliance and acceptance of direction from superiors. The emphasis in both soft and hard versions of Pattern A is on manipulating, controlling, and managing people.

[2] Robert Rosenthal and Lenore Jacobson, *Pygmalion in the Classroom* (New York: Holt, Rinehart and Winston, 1968). For a critical examination of the Rosenthal study as well as an extensive review of other studies relating expectations of teachers to educational achievements, see: Jeremy D. Finn, "Expectations and the Educational Environment," *Review of Educational Research,* American Educational Research Association, Vol. 42, No. 3 (1972), 387–410.

[3] Rensis Likert, *New Patterns of Management* (New York: McGraw-Hill, 1961), see, for example, Ch. 1.

[4] Douglas McGregor, *The Human Side of Enterprise* (New York: McGraw-Hill, 1960).

[5] McGregor, *The Human Side of Enterprise,* pp. 3–31.

[6] Chris Argyris, *Management and Organizational Development* (New York: McGraw-Hill, 1971), pp. 1–26.

The assumptions that the principal holds remain the same regardless of whether the hard or soft approach is used.

There are many problems with Theory X and Pattern A as management systems in organizations in general, though the problems seem more acute in the school. As basic philosophies, Theory X and Pattern A seem inconsistent with the hopes of teachers and principals who are interested in raising the quality of life for young people in schools.

THEORY Y AND PATTERN B

This book is rooted in Theory Y tradition in its approach to educational philosophy, goals and purposes, and educational program development and implementation. Theory Y is the label given by McGregor to a second set of assumptions which differ quite dramatically from those which comprise Theory X. Theory Y assumes that people have integrity, will work hard toward objectives to which they are committed, and will respond to self-control and self-direction as they pursue their objectives. Further, the capacity to exercise a high degree of imagination, ingenuity, and creativity in the solution of organizational problems is widely distributed among people, and the average person under proper conditions is not only capable of accepting responsibility, but will seek it out. In sum, work is as natural to an adult as play is to a child, and *under proper conditions* he will respond to work with similar joy, vigor, and enthusiasm.

Pattern B is the label which Argyris attaches to manifestation of behavior associated with Theory Y assumptions. Basic to Pattern B is the dependence upon building identification and commitment to worthwhile objectives in the work context and upon building mutual trust and respect in the interpersonal context. Success in the work and interpersonal contexts is assumed to be dependent on meaningful satisfaction for individuals being achieved within the context of accomplishing important work as well as upon authentic relationships and the exchange of valid information. "More trust, concern for feelings, and internal commitment; more openness to, and experimenting with, new ideas and feelings *in such a way that others could do the same,* were recommended if valid information was to be produced and internal commitment to decisions generated." [7]

The differences between Theory X assumptions and behavior of the hard or tough variety and Theory Y assumptions and behavior are readily ob-

---

[7] Argyris, *Management and Organizational Development,* p. 18. Argyris does not recommend that a person be completely open and trusting, but that he be open to an extent that permits others to be open. He argues that trust and openness exist only in interpersonal relationships and, therefore, the question is: How open is the relationship between person A and person B? In Argyris's words, "To say what you believe is to be honest; to say what you believe in such a way that the other can do the same is to be authentic."

servable and understood. Theory X *soft* and Theory Y, however, are often deceptively similar. One should not be fooled by this similarity, for soft X is readily exposed as one probes just slightly below the surface. Theory X soft is often referred to as the human-relations model and Theory Y as the human-resources model. These approaches are contrasted in Table 7-1.

TABLE 7-1. Distinguishing between human relations and human resources.

Theory X Soft	*Theory Y*
Human-relations model	Human-resources model

Attitudes Toward People

1. People in our culture, teachers and students among them, share a common set of needs—to belong, to be liked, to be respected.	1. In addition to sharing common needs for belonging and respect, most people in our culture, teachers and students among them, desire to contribute effectively and creatively to the accomplishment of worthwhile objectives.
2. While teachers and students desire individual recognition, they more importantly want to *feel* useful to the school and to their own work group.	2. The majority of teachers and students are capable of exercising far more initiative, responsibility, and creativity than their present jobs or work circumstances require or allow.
3. They tend to cooperate willingly and comply with school goals if these important needs are fulfilled.	3. These capabilities represent untapped resources which are presently being wasted.

Kind and Amount of Participation

1. The principal's basic task (or in reference to students, the teacher's basic task) is to make each worker believe that he is a useful and important part of the team.	1. The principal's basic task (or in reference to students, the teacher's basic task) is to create an environment in which subordinates can contribute their full range of talents to the accomplishment of school goals. He works to uncover the creative resources of his subordinates.
2. The principal is willing to explain his decisions and to discuss his subordinates' objections to his plans. On routine matters, he encourages his subordinates in planning and in decision making. In reference to students, the teacher behaves similarly.	2. The principal allows and encourages subordinates to participate in important as well as routine decisions. In fact, the more important a decision is to the school, the greater the principal's efforts to tap faculty resources. In reference to students, the teacher behaves similarly.

TABLE 7-1. Distinguishing between human relations and human resources. **(cont.)**

3. Within narrow limits, the faculty or individual teachers who comprise the faculty should be allowed to exercise self-direction and self-control in carrying out plans. A similar relationship exists for teachers and students.

3. Principals work continually to expand the areas over which subordinates exercise self-direction and self-control as they develop and demonstrate greater insight and ability. A similar relationship exists for teachers and students.

Expectations

1. Sharing information with subordinates and involving them in school decision making will help satisfy their basic needs for belonging and for individual recognition.

1. The overall quality of decision making and performance will improve as principals and teachers make use of the full range of experience, insight, and creative ability which exists in their schools.

2. Satisfying these needs will improve faculty and student morale and will reduce resistance to formal authority.

2. Subordinates will exercise responsible self-direction and self-control in the accomplishment of worthwhile objectives that they understand and have helped establish.

3. High faculty and students morale and reduced resistance to formal authority may lead to improved school performance. It will at least reduce friction and make the school principal's job easier.

3. Faculty satisfaction and student satisfaction will increase as a by-product of improved performance and the opportunity to contribute creatively to this improvement.

Adapted from Thomas J. Sergiovanni and Fred D. Carver, *The New School Executive: A Theory of Administration* (New York: Dodd, Mead, 1972), Ch. 3. Raymond E. Miles contrasts these approaches in more detail in his article, "Human Relations or Human Resources?" *Harvard Business Review,* Vol. 43, No. 4 (1965), pp. 148–63.

MOVING FROM XA TO YB

Pattern A behavior is usually associated with Theory X and Pattern B with Theory Y, though these relationships need not and indeed do not always hold. The following table shows four combinations of assumptions and behavior.

Notice that one who believes in X assumptions about leadership and people often uses Pattern A, but might also use Pattern B. The consequence of adopting a B pattern when not committed to or believing in Y assumptions is that behavior usually takes the form of deception, manipulation, or a "snow job." We speak here of involving people just enough to keep them contented without really valuing their input, "setting up" someone by being especially nice and attentive before you hit him with a request, order, or direction. In short, becoming more open, concerned, and trusting with others in order to *use* them somehow.

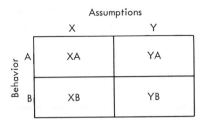

One who subscribes to Theory Y may find himself using the A pattern on occasion. To do otherwise would suggest that he is a perfect human being and few are. Being honest with our feelings, on occasions, without regard to how others feel—"bawling someone out"—may be an example. Adopting a style of close supervision for a particular person who seems not to respond to the B pattern may be another example. As we discuss in a later chapter, many teachers are not interested in and a few are not capable of developing high commitment to work regardless of our efforts. These will require YA approaches to administration and supervision. The exceptions to Theory Y are real but few. Principals and teachers who complain that large numbers of subordinates are unresponsive to Theory Y may indeed still be working under X assumptions without realizing it.

In the following illustration we predict the long-term consequences of using one or another leadership system in educational administration and supervision.

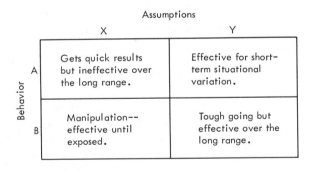

Theory X approaches have often been found to be effective for a short period of time, but soon result in ineffectiveness.[8] XA combinations so seriously neglect the welfare of the human side of organizational life that in time they have a wearing effect on performance. XB, as is the fate of manipulation in general, is soon discovered for what it is and within a short time backfires

[8] Rensis Likert, *The Human Organization* (New York: McGraw-Hill, 1967).

with negative organizational consequences. The most effective leadership system for schools is YB with occasional situational and short-term expressions of YA.[9]

Moving from XA to YB in classrooms and in the school is not an easy task. Argyris discusses the difficulty in making this transition in the industrial setting.

> The trip from XA toward YB is not an easy one. And why should it be? As we shall see, most leaders in any type of organization tend to be programmed by their society to value theory X and to behave according to pattern A. They are taught that strong leaders are those who control and manage others. They are cautioned not to become too self-conscious or get too close to people. In business you've got to be fair and you've got to be firm. But, by jessuz, you've got to be firm. They are admonished not to accept a new idea about management until it has been proven by someone else. They are cautioned not to trust the average worker's motivation. As one executive put it, "five percent of the people work; ten percent think they work; and 85 percent would rather die than work."[10]

The task seems even more awesome in educational settings for tradition has it that youngsters are not to be trusted and schoolwork is not to be enjoyed. Teachers, it is claimed, are not capable of individual initiative and substantial responsibility. Because of this tradition, principals and teachers alike seem to lack confidence in themselves and in young children. Many believe that giving students a choice is an invitation to anarchy and that taking away the teachers' manual, mimeograph machine, and rigidly prescribed schedule are the first steps to the collapse of our educational system. These traditions are true only because we believe them to be so.

A Beginning for the Principal

If we are serious about beginning the journey of converting our classrooms and school leadership systems from XA to YB, the way to begin is to examine our own assumptions and those of teachers and colleagues. This is

---

[9] Readers interested in samples of theoretical and research support for these views might examine, for example: Likert, *New Patterns of Management;* and *The Human Organization;* Chris Argyris, *Interpersonal Competence and Organizational Effectiveness* (Homewood, Ill.: Dorsey Press and Richard D. Irwin, 1962); and *Integrating the Individual and Organization* (New York: John Wiley and Sons, 1954); Tom Burns and G. M. Stalker, *The Management of Innovations* (London: Tavistock, 1961); Robert Blake and Jane Mouton, *Building a Dynamic Corporation Through Grid Organization Development* (Reading, Mass.: Addison-Wesley, 1969); Warren Bennis, *Organizational Development: Its Value, Origin and Prospects* (Reading, Mass.: Addison-Wesley, 1969); and *Changing Organization* (New York: McGraw-Hill, 1968); McGregor, *The Human Side of Enterprise;* and *The Professional Manager* (New York: McGraw-Hill, 1967).

[10] Argyris, *Management and Organizational Development,* p. xii.

ideally a group process—one best pursued and understood by teacher, supervisor, and principal together. Earlier in this chapter you responded to the Assumptions Inventory. You were asked to sum the numbers which appeared in blanks 2, 4, 5, 8, 10, 11, 14, 15, 17, and 19. Each of these blanks represented responses to Theory Y assumptions. The blanks not summed represent responses to Theory X assumptions. Scores range from 0 to 100, but yours most likely falls somewhere between 50 and 100 since educators tend to overrate Y assumptions in inventories of this type. That is, we have found that a tendency exists for educators to respond in terms of how they feel educators should respond rather than how they actually feel. Scores ranging from about 65 to 100 suggest that one would at least like to try to accept Theory Y assumptions and give Pattern B a chance. Scores from 90 to 100 may suggest an overly optimistic perspective which could result in unrealistic expectations for success. It is important to remember that within Theory Y one should expect occasional Pattern A behavior.

After principals and teachers have had an opportunity to explore the assumptions they hold (on an inventory such as we describe here, perhaps the Assumptions about Learning and Knowledge inventory reprinted in Chapter 6, or through other means), the next step might be to examine the ways in which they are presently behaving toward each other, toward the children they serve and toward the parents with whom they must work. The discrepancies which they identify between ideal assumptions and their present behavior patterns as expressed in classrooms and school operations are the raw material for meaningful change in the school beginning the journey from XA to YB.

As we shall see in a later chapter, the process of change is a slow one indeed, especially when success of a change depends upon acceptance, identification, and commitment of people. YB is not a result of introducing continuous progress, open classroom, multiunit, team teaching, in-service workshops, unit leaders, advisors, or what have you, though these may be acceptable options within the transition; it is a basic alteration of the way teachers, parents, children, and principals think about and see each other as they work and live together in school.

8

Expressions
of Leadership

THIS BOOK ADVOCATES a revitalization of the principal's role to give
first priority to educational leadership responsibilities. The effective principal
knows and understands elementary school programs and children and pos-
sesses high standards and a sense of mission with respect to the elementary
school. But this is not all, for he also must know how to implement the
standards he holds and how to build the quality of life in the school as an
organization.

In recent years, the emphasis seems to have shifted from educational
leadership to organizational leadership for principals. That is, principals are
prepared knowing less about educational program matters and more about
organizational matters relating to leadership behavior, communication, decision making, and morale. Some feel as we do that perhaps we have gone
overboard in emphasizing the principal's organizational skills. Others would
have a shift in emphasis entirely away from organizational leadership, proposing that the American principal adopt more of the characteristics of the

British head—emphasizing strong educational leadership and insisting on conformity from subordinates to his image of how the school operates. This is really a silly argument which proposes a fallacious dichotomy. We advocate knowledgeable and visionary principals with respect to educational program and competent principals with respect to organizational matters such as staff growth and development and building commitment to the school. It is educational and organizational leadership together which characterize the effective principal in today's schools.

Leadership Behavior and School Effectiveness

Many have suspected that, at best, traditional inputs have limited impact on effectiveness of educational organizations. Facilities, materials, money, certification credentials, length of the school day, academic degrees and duration of training of teachers, teacher-pupil ratio, and the number of feet of library shelf space, and similar variables which can be readily counted and sorted are examples of traditional inputs. To be sure, a certain minimum amount of educational effectiveness can be attributed to such factors and the absence of many contributes heartily to ineffectiveness. But if Coleman, Mosteller, Moynihan, and Jencks are right, variables of this sort have only limited influence and insure only a minimum or foundation level of effectiveness in schools.[1]

There is convincing evidence, however, that certain school variables—for example, those more social or psychological in nature—are more potent and elastic influences on organizational effectiveness than the traditional inputs. Rensis Likert's theoretical and research work is one such example of this evidence. External forces notwithstanding, Likert finds that organizational effectiveness is largely determined by the condition or health of the organization's human fabric.[2]

---

[1] James S. Coleman et al., *Equality of Educational Opportunity.* 2 vols. (Washington, D.C.: Office of Education, U.S. Government Printing Office, 1966), OE-3800 1; Frederick Mosteller and Daniel P. Moynihan (eds.), *On Equality of Educational Opportunity* (New York: Random House, 1972); and Christopher S. Jencks et al., *Inequality. A Reassessment of the Effects of Family and Schooling in America* (New York: Basic Books, 1972).

[2] Rensis Likert, *New Patterns of Management* (New York: McGraw-Hill, 1961); and *The Human Organization, Its Management and Value* (New York: McGraw-Hill, 1967). This is a position held by a number of theorists in educational administration. See, for example: Matthew Miles, "Planned Change and Organizational Health," in *Change Processes in the Public Schools* (Eugene: University of Oregon, Center for the Advanced Study of Educational Administration, 1965); and Andrew Halpin, *Theory and Research in Administration* (New York: Macmillan, 1967), pp. 131–249. See also T. J. Sergiovanni and R. J. Starratt, *Emerging Patterns of Supervision: Human Perspectives* (New York: McGraw-Hill, 1971).

With specific reference to the school, effectiveness—as measured by student performance, teacher performance, lower absence and turnover rates of teachers, lower absence and dropout rates of students, improved teacher-board relations, and improved school community relationships—is more likely to be attained in schools where faculties display greater group and school loyalty, higher performance goals for themselves, greater identification with and commitment to school goals, more interest in the work itself, and other intrinsic factors, less feeling of unreasonable pressure, more favorable attitudes toward supervisors and administrators, and higher levels of motivation to work.[3]

The condition of a school's human fabric or organization cannot be exclusively accounted for by school factors. True, if you want motivated teachers, hire motivated people. Nevertheless, the extent to which a teacher's potential as a person and as a professional is being fully realized and his identification with and commitment to the school and its students are strong are largely dependent upon such school factors as the nature of administrative and supervisory assumptions; manifestations of organizational structure; style and philosophy; the character of interaction and influence; the ways in which goals are identified, set, and ordered; and the general climate of openness and trust in the school. These factors in turn are largely determined, developed, and articulated by the nature and quality of leadership which the elementary school principal provides to the school.

By definition, leadership is different than administration in that the former involves introducing something new or helping to improve present conditions, while administration, on the other hand, refers to the maintenance, support, and service of the status quo. Separating leadership from administration in this manner has a number of technical advantages, but for our purposes both behavioral types will be considered as variations in leadership style.

For some people leadership comes easily and naturally. But most people who are in positions of leadership are not born leaders. The skills and insights which are necessary for one to be an effective leader can be learned through training and experience. At one time it was thought that a single best leadership style could be identified. This would have certainly made things easier, for the principal would need only to find out what the best style is, learn it, and use it.[4] Unfortunately, leadership effectiveness is much more complex

---

[3] See, for example, Lonnie Wagstaff, "The Relationship Between Administrative Systems and Interpersonal Needs of Teachers." Doctoral Dissertation (Norman: University of Oklahoma, University Microfilms 702343); and Allan Ferris, "Organizational Relationship in Two Selected Secondary Schools." Doctoral Dissertation (New York: Columbia University, University Microfilms 658839).

[4] Approaches associated with the Leadership Behavior Description Questionnaire and with the Managerial Grid seem to hold the view that one best style exists. See, for example, Andrew Halpin, "How Leaders Behave," in his *Theory and Research in Administration* (New York: Macmillan, 1966), pp. 81–130; and Robert Blake and Jane Mouton, *The Managerial Grid* (Houston: Gulf, 1964).

than this, and any number of styles or approaches could be effective given the proper circumstances. In this chapter, we are concerned with the major expressions of leadership styles and with the situations which determine their effectiveness.

LEADERSHIP DIMENSIONS

The research tradition dealing with leadership style in educational and noneducational settings has identified two key dimensions of leadership. These dimensions have been given a variety of labels. Subtle differences may exist within and among the labels, but, by and large, experts agree that leadership style is defined by the extent to which the leader seems to show concern for, focuses on, or seems oriented toward getting work done or accomplishing tasks; and the extent to which he seems to show concern for, focuses on, or seems oriented toward the needs or feelings of people and his relationships with them.

In this discussion we will use the phrase "task oriented (TO)" to refer to tendencies for the leader to show concern for work and "relations oriented (RO)" for his tendency to show concern for people as he displays leadership behavior. Each of these dimensions of leadership style is illustrated conceptually in Figure 8-1.

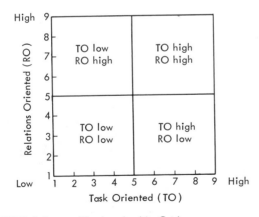

FIGURE 8-1.   The Leadership Grid.

This diagram or grid is arranged very much like the Student-Teacher Influence Grid presented in Chapter 5 and could be read similarly. That is, the horizontal marginal axis which forms the base of the grid represents the extent to which the leader's behavior shows a concern for task accomplishment (TO) with a high concern to the right and a low concern to the left.[5] You might estimate the extent to which your leadership style shows concern for task by checking one of the numbers (1 to 9) on this line. The vertical marginal axis which forms the left side of the grid represents the extent to which the leader's behavior shows a concern for people and relationships (RO) with the top representing high concern and the bottom low concern. Again, estimate the extent to which you show concern for people and relationships in expressing leadership by checking one of the numbers on this line. To find your location in the grid based on the estimates you have made, simply find the point where lines drawn from each of your checks on the numbers would intersect. For example, if you checked a six on the TO line and 7 on the RO line your position on the grid would be indicated by the X which appears on the grid below.

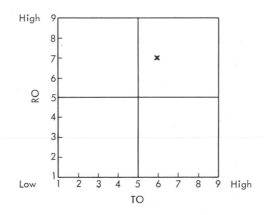

You can check your self-perception of leadership style by responding to the leadership questionnaire which follows. Your style estimate as well as your score on the questionnaire should provide you with a fairly accurate indication of your tendency to emphasize each of the dimensions, task and relationship, as you express leadership.

The following items describe aspects of leadership behavior. Respond to each item according to the way you would be most likely to act if you were the leader of a work group. Circle whether you would be likely to behave in

---

[5] Samples of the leadership literature upon which this discussion is based include Fred E. Fiedler, *A Theory of Leadership Effectiveness* (New York: McGraw-Hill, 1967); Robert Blake and Jane Mouton, *The Managerial Grid* (Houston: Gulf, 1964); and W. J. Reddin, *Managerial Effectiveness* (New York: McGraw-Hill, 1970). The first book is research oriented; the second, concept oriented; and the third, practice oriented.

the described way always (A), frequently (F), occasionally (O), seldom (S), or never (N).

If I were the leader of a work group . . .

A F O S N   1. I would most likely act as the spokesman of the group.

A F O S N   2. I would allow members complete freedom in their work.

A F O S N   3. I would encourage the use of uniform procedures.

A F O S N   4. I would permit the members to use their own judgment in solving problems.

A F O S N   5. I would needle members for greater effort.

A F O S N   6. I would let the members do their work the way they think best.

A F O S N   7. I would keep the work moving at a rapid pace.

A F O S N   8. I would turn the members loose on a job, and let them go to it.

A F O S N   9. I would settle conflicts when they occur in the group.

A F O S N   10. I would be reluctant to allow the members any freedom of action.

A F O S N   11. I would decide what shall be done and how it shall be done.

A F O S N   12. I would push for increased production.

A F O S N   13. I would assign group members to particular tasks.

A F O S N   14. I would be willing to make changes.

A F O S N   15. I would schedule the work to be done.

A F O S N   16. I would refuse to explain my actions.

A F O S N   17. I would persuade others that my ideas are to their advantage.

A F O S N   18. I would permit the group to set its own pace.

To score the questionnaire,

1. Circle the item number for items 1, 3, 9, 10, 11, 15, 16, and 17.

2. Write a "1" in front of the *circled items* to which you responded S (seldom) or N (never).

3. Write a "1" in front of *items not circled* to which you responded A (always) or F (frequently).

4. Circle the "1's" which you have written in front of the following items: 2, 4, 5, 6, 8, 10, 14, 16, and 18.

5. Count the circled "1's." This is your score for concern for people, your RO score.

6. Count the uncircled "1's." This is your score for concern for task, your TO score.[6]

Return to the leadership grid and, using your TO and RO scores as revealed by the questionnaire, plot yourself into the grid. To what extent does your previous estimate agree with your score on the questionnaire?

School people are fully aware of the importance of the human dimension in schools and are likely to react to the social acceptability of expressing people concerns by estimating that they exhibit a relatively high concern for people as they express leadership in classrooms and schools. This tendency remains as one responds to the questionnaire.[7] You might find it helpful to have others who know of your work or who are the targets of your leadership describe you on the same questionnaire. Do not be surprised if others see you differently than you see yourself.

THE BASIC LEADERSHIP STYLES

In this section we are concerned with what each of the four quadrants of the leadership grid represents. The lower right-hand quadrant (TO high and RO low) represents a style of leadership characterized by a good deal of drive and *dedication* to work with little overt concern for the relationship dimension. The upper left-hand quadrant (TO low and RO high) represents a style of leadership which emphasizes *relationships* with little overt concern for the task dimension. The upper right-hand quadrant (TO high and RO high) represents an *integrated* style that expresses people concerns through emphasizing meaningful work and work concerns by bringing together and stimulating committed groups of individuals. The lower left-hand quadrant (TO low and RO low) represents a style of leadership which expresses very little concern for both dimensions. In a sense the leader *separates* himself from both task and people. We refer to each of these styles as homogeneous and discrete patterns only conceptually, for in reality most of us would probably fall on grid locations which require less clear descriptions. It is possible for one to occupy any of 81 different locations on the leadership grid.

Many disagreements exist over which of the leadership styles is best.

---

[6] The items which comprise this questionnaire are adapted from the "Leadership Behavior Description Questionnaire" (Columbus: Ohio State University, The Bureau of Business Research, College of Commerce and Administration, 1962). The format for this questionnaire is adapted from J. William Pfeiffer and John E. Jones, *Structured Experiences for Human Relations Training, Volume I* (Iowa City: University Associates Press, 1969), pp. 7–10.

[7] A number of more sophisticated approaches to measuring leadership style exist. Examples previously cited are Fiedler's LPC Scale, Blake and Mouton's Managerial Grid Inventory, and Reddin's Management Style Diagnosis Test.

Early research in education seemed to suggest that the integrated style characterized by high TO and high RO was best. Recent thought, however, assumes that effective leadership style can only be understood within the context of the leadership situation.[8] That is, any of the four basic styles of leadership we discuss could be effective or not effective depending upon the situation. W. J. Reddin's 3-D theory of leadership does an excellent job of illustrating the importance of situation in determining effectiveness. He assumes that related, integrated, separated, and dedicated are only four basic styles, each with an effective and an ineffective equivalent depending upon the situation in which it is used. These effective and ineffective equivalents result in eight leadership styles as shown in Figure 8-2.

Using Reddin's terminology, the basic *integrated* style when displayed in an inappropriate setting might lead to compromise, but when displayed in an appropriate setting leads to executive effectiveness. The basic *related*

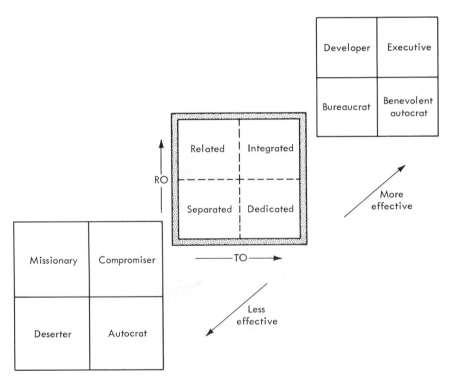

FIGURE 8-2.   Reddin's 3-D Theory of Leadership.

From W. J. Reddin, *Managerial Effectiveness* (New York: McGraw-Hill, 1970), p. 13.

[8] Fiedler, *A Theory of Leadership Effectiveness;* and Reddin, *Managerial Effectiveness.*

style expressed inappropriately may be perceived as missionary behavior, but when the situation is ripe for this style, development of people takes place. If one behaves in a *separated* way given appropriate conditions, one is displaying an appropriate bureaucratic response; but if involvement in task or people or both is needed, but not forthcoming, one is a deserter. The *dedicated* person who is an inspirational and driving force given appropriate circumstances is seen as a benevolent autocrat; but when this style is displayed in inappropriate situations, he is viewed as an interfering, dominant, and repressive autocrat. The key to this theory is the notion that the same style expressed in different situations may be effective or ineffective. For example, a principal who uses the integrated style with a teacher who is in need of personal support may be seen as compromising the person dimension by not giving exclusive attention to the needs of the individual. This same principal who relies exclusively on support and understanding when a teacher is groping for a task solution to his problem may be seen as a "sobbing," "sticky" missionary lacking in forceful leadership. This style, if used in the first instance, would have been perceived as being most effective.

Understanding Situational Leadership Variables

The situational determinants of leadership style effectiveness are difficult to identify entirely and even more difficult for the principal to completely read and formally catalogue as he approaches a given situation. Nevertheless, some useful generalizations can be made about situational variables and their relationships to leadership style. With a little practice one's ability to match appropriate style to situation can be improved considerably. Perhaps the three most important aspects of any situation to consider are: (1) the kinds of demands on leadership made by the job, (2) the nature and distribution of power and authority, and (3) the expectations held by significant others (teachers, parents, superintendents) for the leader's behavior.

One persistent theme throughout this book is that compatibility between means and ends (that is, how we do something and what it is we hope to accomplish) is an important determinant of effectiveness in all human organizations, including schools. In many respects, this compatibility is an insurance policy since product and process in elementary schools are diffused and defy separation. When one works with people in order to achieve human ends such as intellectual and personal self-actualization, excessively formal models which clearly separate these dimensions are dangerous to say the least and unworkable in the long run except for the most routine and pedestrian school tasks.

Generally speaking, therefore, we can assume that educational settings and particularly leadership situations in elementary schools will only occasionally call for separated and dedicated styles, for in each of these cases the human dimension is neglected. We are not suggesting that occasions will not exist when low-concern-for-people styles are appropriate, only that the focus of leadership in general will be in the related and integrated quadrants in those schools who wish to make a human difference.

A number of exceptions to this generalization come to mind. In each case the job demands are such that the dedicated style which emphasizes task but not people will probably be most effective. One exception deals with routine situations with simple, clear, and uncontroversial goals and objectives, where the paths to reach the goal are few in number and clearly marked. Another exception relates to situations where very favorable leader-member relationships exist. Here, members trust the leader and are willing to follow him. A third exception relates to situations characterized by excessive interpersonal tension, confusion, and stress. Short-term success in these situations can be accomplished through use of the dedicated style. This style, however, will only be the aspirin which controls the pain so that people can function adequately—the problem does not go away, nor will it stay controlled indefinitely under this leadership style. The leader's formal position in the school hierarchy is another important condition. When too much positional or hierarchial distance exists between leader and members, it is often less stressful for everyone if the leader uses a more directive or task-oriented style.

CONTINGENCY LEADERSHIP THEORY

Fiedler summarizes many of these conditions in his contingency theory of leadership.[9] His extensive research strongly indicates that task-oriented leaders perform best in group situations that are either very favorable or very unfavorable to the leader. Relationship-oriented leaders, on the other hand, perform best in group situations that are intermediate in favorableness. Favorableness is defined by the degree to which the situations enable the leader to exert his influence over the group. Three major situational variables seem to determine whether a given situation is favorable or unfavorable to the leader: (1) leader-member relations; (2) task structure; and (3) position power to the leader. The contingency theory provides for eight leadership contexts, each defined by the situational variables (see Figure 8-3).

Leadership contexts 1, 2, and 3 provide the leader with the most favorable opportunities for influence, and Fiedler finds that task-oriented leadership is the most effective style. Leadership context 8 provides the leader with the least amount of influence, and again the task or directive style is found to be effective. The remaining four contexts, according to the contingency leadership theory, seem best suited to the relationship-oriented style.

[9] Fiedler, *A Theory of Leadership Effectiveness.*

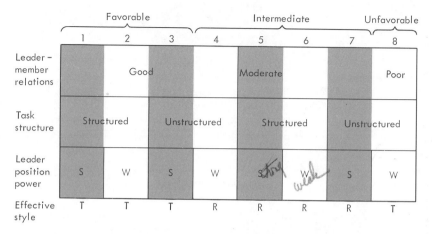

| | Favorable | | | Intermediate | | | Unfavorable |
	1	2	3	4	5	6	7	8
Leader–member relations		Good			Moderate			Poor
Task structure	Structured		Unstructured		Structured		Unstructured	
Leader position power	S	W	S	W	S	W	S	W
Effective style	T	T	T	R	R	R	R	T

FIGURE 8-3.   Fiedler's Contingency Theory of Leadership.

In his study of leadership effectiveness in elementary schools Lanaghan found that, overall, relationship-oriented principals were more effective than their task-oriented counterparts, and he raises the question that perhaps the elementary school is generally a situation of intermediate favorableness.[10] Lanaghan was referring to the principals' overall style, noting that at any specific time the effective principal will use task or relationship style depending upon the situation.

THE ZONE OF INDIFFERENCE

We cannot assume that all teachers have a uniform desire to participate in the decision-making processes of the school or, for that matter, wish to be involved in the same things. When the content of decision making is of little or no concern to an individual (that is, when it is in his zone of indifference), a more task-oriented approach from the principal would be appropriate. Teachers, for example, are not likely to be terribly interested in many of the purely management aspects of running the school and would probably look with pleasure at a principal who can regulate them in a dedicated but unobtrusive way. Teachers often resent being involved in trivial matters, serving on committees of dubious value, and sitting through long meetings on topics and affairs which are of little interest to them. As the zone of indifference on a particular matter decreases, however, teachers will need to be more involved

[10] Richard Lanaghan, "Leadership Effectiveness in Selected Elementary Schools." Unpublished Doctoral Dissertation (Urbana: University of Illinois, 1972), pp. 137–144.

and the relationship-oriented style becomes more appropriate. These relationships are shown in Figure 8-4.

It is important to note that a broad range of styles exists between the two extremes of task and relationship. Further, it is difficult to conceptualize leadership on the task and relationship continuum only. For example, as one moves to the extreme right on Figure 8-4, to where the principal defines limits and asks teachers to make decisions and permits teachers to function within limits defined by agreed-upon goals and objectives, concern for task and concern for people are both present. These are the essential characteristics of the integrated style illustrated in Figure 8-2. Nevertheless, it seems appropriate to generalize that, as the content of decision making moves closer to the day-by-day work of teachers and as potential changes in operations and procedures require attitudinal and behavioral changes from teachers, the zone of indifference is likely to decrease. In such cases, leadership styles which include a generous component of relationship orientation are most likely to be effective. A relationship similar to that appropriate for the zone-of-indifference concept holds for the competency, maturity, and commitment levels of teachers. We discuss these factors in Chapter 10, which deals with motivating teachers to work.

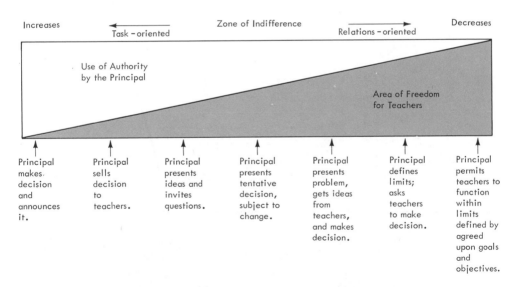

FIGURE 8-4.   Leadership Continuum and Zone of Indifference.

Adapted from: Robert Tannenbaum and Warren Schmidt, "How to Choose a Leadership Pattern," *Harvard Business Review,* Vol. 36, No. 2 (March–April 1957), 95–101. This article is reprinted along with fresh insights by the authors in *Harvard Business Review,* Vol. 51, No. 3 (1973), 162.

Authority Relationships
and Leadership Effectiveness

One important source of tension, frustration, and confusion in elementary schools is the conflict that exists between formal authority and functional authority.[11] Formal authority is that authority associated with the role or position one occupies in any organization and is sometimes referred to as hierarchical, legal, position, or office authority. This authority is defined by the schools, the bureaucratic structure, and the legal system rather than by the person who occupies a given role. Principals rely on formal authority by using school rules, regulations, and policies or by "pulling rank." Formal authority is exemplified by teachers in habitual classrooms who obtain compliance from children because "the teacher says so." Youngsters here are engaged in educational activities, not in pursuit of instructional, expressive, and informal objectives, but in obedience to the teacher's wishes. Functional authority refers to the authority which an individual who occupies a given role or position brings to the position. His competence, ability, or expertise in functioning on the job and his interpersonal skills in working with others within the job context (expert and referent authority) are examples of functional authority.

The dedicated style (TO high and RO low) is one which relies heavily on the formal authority which exists within the position one occupies. The principal has the right to decide on a change, announce it to his faculty, and implement it because he is the "boss" or the head of the school. The separated style (TO low and RO low) is also heavily dependent upon formal authority. The emphasis is not on position or "boss" power but on legal authority. A principal who strictly enforces the sign-in–sign-out system might do so because he perceives himself as obligated to enforce school district rules and not because he really wants to. Legal authority is very objective, and the separated style permits principal and teacher to blame the impersonal system for any inconvenience they incur as rules are enforced. Teachers like to use legal authority in disciplining children because it permits them to act "objectively" and "impersonally." An example of legal authority in relating to parents is teachers' blaming impersonal examination test scores for a youngster's failures. Use of legal authority often results in the person being subjected to it feeling quite helpless.

Expression of functional authority by principals usually results in their reliance on related and integrated (TO low–RO high and TO high–RO high) leadership styles. Successful related styles rely heavily on the interpersonal skills which the individual brings to his position; successful integrated styles require substantial competence and expertise in educational matters as well as in interpersonal skills. These relationships are shown in Figure 8-5.

[11] See, for example, Robert L. Peabody, "Perceptions of Organizational Authority: A Comparative Analysis," *Administrative Science Quarterly,* Vol. 6, No. 4, (1962), 463–482; and Victor Thompson, *Modern Organization* (New York: Knopf, 1961).

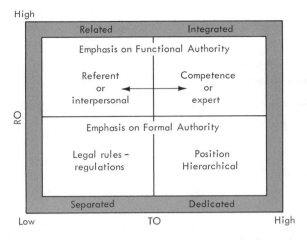

High

FIGURE 8-5.   Authority bases for the basic leadership styles.

One important difference between formal authority and functional authority is that the superordinate always has the former, while often the subordinate has the latter. Formally, the principal is responsible for introducing an individualized reading program into the primary grades, but functionally the teachers have the understanding and ability for accomplishing this task. Principals who are anxious about authority relationships, protocol, and status systems might be inclined to override the functional authority of teachers in order to preserve formal authority relationships and assume the major leadership role.

When the principal finds himself in a situation where he has both formal and functional authority, he is fortunate indeed. This seems to be an ideal setting for effective use of the integrative style. When he has only formal authority, he should be prepared to let the locus of leadership shift to where functional authority exists. He might even use his formal authority to legitimize the functional authority which others have by giving them *ad hoc* formal responsibility.

Substantial evidence exists to show that workers in educational and noneducational settings are more satisfied and seem to work harder and more willingly when exposed to functional authority. Response to legal uses of formal authority by workers is often one of indifference. Position or hierarchical forms of authority, particularly when expressed in terms of sanctions, paternalism, rewards, and punishments evoke negative responses and seem to result in poorer performance in the long run.[12] It seems reasonable to expect

[12] See, for example, Peabody, "Perceptions of Organizational Authority"; J. R. P. French, Jr., and B. Raven, "The Bases of Social Power," in D. Cartwright and A. F. Zander (eds.), *Group Dynamics: Research and Theory,* 2nd ed. (Evanston, Ill.: Row

that similar relationships hold for children as they are exposed to the teacher's authority in elementary school classrooms.

Role Expectations
and Leadership Effectiveness

Another important determinant of the principal's leadership effectiveness is the expectations which important others, such as his superintendent and his teachers, have for his performance as a leader. Of further importance is the extent to which these role expectations agree with each other and agree with how he feels he needs to behave.[13] One need not have mirror agreement with superiors and subordinates in regard to role expectations, but, generally speaking, reasonable agreement and mutual understanding of areas of disagreement seem to be prerequisite for leadership effectiveness. This section deals with expectations and their relationship to leadership effectiveness for the elementary school principal. We focus on the principalship throughout our discussion, but considerations are appropriate for all of the roles which comprise the school membership including those of teacher and student.

THE ROLE EXPECTATION EXERCISE

Twenty phrases are listed below which could be used to describe the role of the principal, supervisor, or adviser as he relates to and works with children in elementary school classrooms [14]:

_____ To listen	_____ To measure
_____ To motivate	_____ To control
_____ To administer	_____ To trust
_____ To complete	_____ To advise
_____ To accept	_____ To direct
_____ To interact	_____ To encourage
_____ To integrate	_____ To participate
_____ To organize	_____ To innovate
_____ To initiate	_____ To maintain
_____ To examine	_____ To evaluate

Peterson, 1960), p. 612; Jerald D. Bachman et al., "Bases of Supervisory Power: A Comparative Study in Five Organizational Settings," in Arnold S. Tannenbaum (ed.), *Control in Organizations* (New York: McGraw-Hill, 1968), p. 229; and Harvey A. Hornstein et al., "Influence and Satisfaction in Organizations: A Replication," *Sociology of Education,* Vol. 41, No. 4 (1968), 389.

[13] See, for example: Jacob Getzels and Egon Guba, "Social Behavior and the Administrative Process," *School Review,* Vol. 65 (Winter 1957), 423–441; and W. J. Reddin, *Managerial Effectiveness* (New York: McGraw-Hill, 1970), especially Ch. 8.

[14] Reddin, *Managerial Effectiveness,* p. 94.

To be sure, each of the 20 phrases may be valid descriptions of the principal's role or the teacher's role at any given time. Some of them, however, will occur with more frequency depending upon who the leader is and upon the particular leadership role. The following procedures are suggested for selecting the words which best describe the role with which you are concerned.

1. Read through the 20 phrases.
2. Select the 10 words of the 20 that best describe what you as a _____ expect of your _____. Place an X to the left of each of the 10 words.
3. Circle the X's of the five words of the 10 that are most descriptive of what you expect of the above role.

As suggested in step 2, these procedures can be followed by describing what you as a principal expect of yourself; what you as a principal expect of your teachers; what you as a teacher expect of your principal; what you as a superintendent expect of your principal, and so on. Any number of role combinations can be examined and compared by using this method.

The 20 statements which appear above are illustrated again in Figure 8-6, but this time they are grouped into quadrants of the leadership grid on the basis of identification with a particular leadership style. The five statements which seem most descriptive of the related style are listed in the upper left-hand quadrant and other statements are similarly grouped in each of the three remaining quadrants.

The five statements you have selected provide a general idea of how

Related	Integrated
To listen	To interact
To accept	To motivate
To trust	To integrate
To advise	To participate
To encourage	To innovate
To organize	To examine
To initiate	To measure
To direct	To administer
To complete	To control
To evaluate	To maintain
Separated	Dedicated

FIGURE 8-6.   Basic Style Indicators.

From W. J. Reddin, *Managerial Effectiveness* (New York: McGraw-Hill, 1970), p. 94.

you see the principal's or teacher's role. Taking the role of the principal for a moment, if teachers have role expectations for his performance which are different from his, we have a problem which will usually result in teacher dissatisfaction and ineffective leadership behavior by the principal.[15] This problem would be further confounded by the superintendent's expectations for the role behavior of the principal. The principal is likely to find himself in deep trouble if his role perceptions differ markedly from those of both superintendent and teacher. A certain amount of disagreement on role expectations for the principal probably should be expected in the elementary school. Teachers, central office staff, students, room mothers, custodians, bus drivers, PTA officials, and parents differ in their needs and demands as they relate to the school. They make the differences felt on the principal in terms of expectations for his behavior.

Particularly in his relationships with teachers and with his superiors, the principal's effectiveness will be improved as he develops reasonable agreement between their expectations for him and his own perception of his role. Further, areas of disagreement should not only be small, but should be understood and accepted by concerned parties. These principles apply as well to the teacher's role, working with youngsters in the classroom.

A number of studies dealing with the importance of role expectation in schools were conducted at The University of Chicago in the fifties and sixties.[16] By and large the researchers conclude, as Chase does, that (1) there is a close relationship between teachers' evaluation of the principal's leadership and the extent of their satisfaction; (2) teacher evaluations of leadership are largely determined by the extent to which the principal conforms to expected roles; and (3) principals need to understand the expectations of teachers in order to bring about effective group action.[17]

THEY ONLY SEE PART OF THE JOB

Can the principal afford to let others determine what his role should be? We hardly subscribe to this point of view though the perceptions of significant others are important considerations in determining the principal's role. The principal needs to view his role not only in relation to how others

---

[15] Robert Kahn et al., *Organizational Stress: Studies in Role Conflict and Ambiguity* (New York: John Wiley and Sons, 1964); and Jacob Getzels, "Administration as a Social Process," in Andrew Halpin (ed.), *Administrative Theory in Education* (New York: Macmillan, 1967), are helpful references in understanding role theory, role expectations, and role conflict and ambiguity.

[16] See, for example, those summarized in Jacob W. Getzels, James M. Lipham, and Ronald F. Campbell, *Educational Administration as a Social Process Theory, Research, Practice* (New York: Harper & Row, 1968).

[17] Francis S. Chase, "How to Meet Teacher Expectation of Leadership," *Administrator's Notebook,* Midwest Administrator's Center, University of Chicago, Vol. 1, No. 9 (1953).

see him, but also in terms of his own values, beliefs, and perceptions of the needs of the school and the children.

One reason for not simply responding to any and all expectations regardless of their form and content is that others often see only one part of the principal's job. The superintendent and other central office officials, for example, may want the principal to be prompt and thorough in developing and submitting his reports; to avoid conflict and controversy; to handle people problems efficiently and with minimum fuss; to avoid new ventures, changes, and innovation; and in general, to maintain the status quo, for to do otherwise confuses and compounds the job at the central office.

Buffinton and Medster, in studying how parents and teachers describe the effective principal, point out that one sees a different portrait of the principal's role, depending upon which group one looks at.[18] Teachers view these behaviors as being most important in a principal: he builds teacher morale and unity; evaluates teacher performance as a basis of upgrading and helping teachers; shares decisions and responsibilities with teachers; and maintains discipline in the school, particularly by working with parents on the solution of discipline problems. Parents, on the other hand, describe the effective principal as one who organizes and guides parents' groups unobtrusively and who makes school facilities available to them. He needs to be an able speaker who interprets the school and the program in language that laymen can understand. Further, he should handle parental complaints in a constructive manner, take prompt action on complaints, and provide ample opportunity for parents to state their problems. In each case, however, neither group cited as critical the principal's behavior in developing and improving curricula or in general supervision of instruction. The researchers conclude that parents and teachers judge the principal's effectiveness primarily on the basis of his personal relationships with them rather than on the quality of the instructional program in the school. Very early in this book we argued that the effective principal is one who displays educational leadership in three important areas—human resource development, community development, and educational program development. Each of these areas needs to be included as an integral part of the principal's role description and behavior.

Summary

We have described two essential components in defining a particular leadership style: the extent to which the principal shows concern for task (TO), and the extent to which he shows concern for people (RO). Four basic

---

[18] Reed L. Buffinton and Leland L. Medster, "Teachers and Parents Describe the Effective Principal's Behavior," *Administrator's Notebook,* Vol. 4, No. 1, 1955.

styles were identified from different expressions of these dimensions: dedicated, related, separated, and integrated. Any one of these styles can be effective or not depending upon the unique nature of the leadership situation. Situational variables discussed here include the nature of the work to be done, the relationship that exists between leader and members, the amount of stress and tension in the situation, the position power of the leader, the distribution of ability and authority among leader and members, the zone of indifference of members, and the expectations which others hold for the principal. In Chapter 10 we will be concerned with motivational and commitment levels of teachers—extremely important determinants of leadership style effectiveness.

IV

Working with Teachers and Parents

9

Bringing About Change: Some Theoretical and Practical Considerations

PERHAPS ONE REASON why change seems so difficult to accomplish and so slow in coming in schools is that we have been confused about who should assume responsibility as the agent of change. Teachers are usually the best agents of change inasmuch as they usually live with and implement school changes.[1] Yet the literature suggests that administrators and supervisors are the change agents, and teachers are clients of change.[2] This orientation often encourages teachers to feel that they are helpless and powerless,

---

[1] Emil Haller finds, for example, that teachers look to other teachers as the most favored and trusted model for change. Emil Haller, *Strategies for Change* (Toronto: The Ontario Institute for Studies in Education, 1968).

[2] Faber and Shearron describe the change-agent conception of the principal as follows: "The principal as a *change agent* has become an important concept, since the emphasis on innovation, so prominent during the 1960's. The principal is one of the administrative agents through which change enters the school. . . . The principal as a change agent not only senses the potential for educational improvement that exists within a new approach and convinces others to accept it, but he also translates each new idea into a program of action." Charles F. Faber and Gilbert F. Shearron, *Elementary School Administration Theory and Practice* (New York: Holt, Rinehart and Winston, 1970), p. 211.

manipulated, or treated as pawns.

A basic assumption of this book is that bringing about change is the *goal,* but not the primary *task,* of principals, supervisors, and advisers in elementary schools. Forcing changes in schools—even "good" ones—endangers the goal of improving the human potential of the school. Further, forced changes only rarely result in a lasting change in teacher behavior or in the operation of the school. Some of the most creative and ingenious behavior is expressed by teachers who manage to operate in basically the same way as always, after having been subjected to and seemingly having accepted sweeping, often radical, changes.

If teachers are to be the real agents of change, what role will administrators, supervisors, and advisers assume? They will indeed assume the change-agent role under those circumstances where successful change does not require the support and commitment of teachers. Where support and commitment of teachers are important—for example, when changes affect the student-teacher relationship and the educational program—the principal's role will approximate that of a change environmentalist and helper.

This chapter explores the change environmentalist-and-helper role. In general, this role requires that the principal give attention to the development of a school climate that encourages and supports change and to the development of an interpersonal context which frees, encourages, and helps people to experiment with change. Basic to this experimentation is the right of free choice for the teacher. As disappointing as it may be, free choice implies that the hopes and aspirations of the principal will not always be realized. But, when free choice does result in change, one can be sure that the change is genuine as opposed to a superficial drama expertly played by teachers at work.

Starting with Teachers

The most popular educational changes have been patterned after "linear" or sequential models and have emphasized structural changes in schooling. Teachers have been seen as objects to be reshaped to conform to these changes. In a sense, change is something which is researched, developed, demonstrated, and disseminated, and teachers are viewed as rational entities to be convinced, untrained entities to be taught, psychological entities to be persuaded, economic entities to be bought, and so on.[3] Indeed, if the object is the dissemination of information or materials, or temporary change in the structure of teaching or work in education, linear or sequential thinking may have merits. But, as the sole or primary method for bringing about lasting change, this approach has been disappointing.

[3] See, for example, Egon Guba, "Diffusion of Innovations," *Educational Leadership,* Vol. 25, No. 4, (January 1968), 292–295. Ronald Havelock et al., *Planning for Innovation Through Dissemination and Utilization of Knowledge* (Ann Arbor: University of Michigan, Center for Research on Utilization of Scientific Knowledge, 1969).

Sizer attributes this disappointment in part to our failure to recognize teaching as a "labor intensive" field with wide actual discretion for teacher behavior in the classroom.[4] Eighty percent of the typical school budget is allocated to human resources—that is, teachers. Change in education means change in teachers. Buildings, schedules, materials, curriculum formats, and other changes should not be ignored, but need to be considered in perspective with change in people. Further, in the final analysis, it is what the teacher decides to do day-by-day with youngsters in the classroom that really matters and that needs to be the focus of change. If we fail to reach this daily encounter, we have dealt only with structural change, not internalized change. To be sure, structural changes are those which can be commanded, are highly visible, and can be implemented with relative vigor and efficiency. We can close a traditional elementary school today and open it three weeks later as a progressive British Infant School or Open Education School. We can throw out the desks and chairs and bring in orange crates, tables, bean bags, and rugs. We can knock down a wall or two and create open space. We can replace the one-teacher–thirty-children arrangement with a team of three teachers asuming responsibility for 100 first-, second-, and third-grade youngsters, all family grouped. We can set up activity areas emphasizing science, language, drama, woodworking, cooking, math, and the like. We can throw out the expensive equipment purchased from commercial firms and bring in an assortment of natural or homemade material. Finally, we can attend a workshop on the role of the teacher in open education so that we might have a model to imitate. We now have an open classroom, or at least what might look like an open classroom to the casual observer. If one stops and lingers, however, one is likely to find that, while the structural arrangements of the classroom have changed dramatically, teachers and administrators have not. They may still see youngsters in the same way; they may still be working under the same assumptions; and for all intents and purposes their behavior and their effect on youngsters may vary little from previous modes. In this example, we have successfully implemented substantial structural change, but not internalized change, and have gained little in the process.

TEACHERS' SOURCES OF CHANGE IDEAS

Any change of lasting quality in schools is basically a grass-roots and informal process.[5] It seems clear that teachers look to other teachers as im-

[4] Theodore Sizer, "Educational Reform: Speculations from Retrospection," *Notre Dame Journal of Education,* Vol. 4, No. 1 (1973), 49–57.

[5] A classic sociometric study of diffusion of innovation among physicians suggests the potency of informal approaches may be a universal characteristic of change in organizations. In this study, trusted professional and social contacts are more important sources of innovation than more official technical sources. James Coleman, Elihu Katz, and Herbert Menzel, "The Diffusion of an Innovation Among Physicians," *Sociometry,* Vol. 20, No. 4, (December 1957), 253–270.

portant models for change. Other teachers possess two important characteristics—trust and credibility.[6]

The advisory system of supervision is based on trust and credibility.
Advisers typically claim no identification with the official school establishment in regard to district vested interests or to evaluation; accept teachers
as they are and work toward goals identified by teachers; and work alongside
the teacher with children in actual teaching. As one teacher describes working
with an adviser,

> Her [the adviser's] way of working is the best way I learn. She'll come in
> the room—look around—then maybe discuss things with me a few minutes.
> Then she'll sit down and work with some children, and she'll talk in a *very
> loud voice* so I can hear without having to stop what I'm doing. I literally
> learned how to talk and work with children in new ways from listening to her.

Table 9-1 summarizes data from two studies—one of teachers in four
urban elementary schools in Canada, and the other of teachers in 10 elementary schools in Chicago. In each case teachers were asked to indicate who
they go to for help and for sources of new ideas and insights. Further, they
were asked to indicate which sources were most reliable.

TABLE 9-1. Sources of help and ideas.

1. SOURCES OF HELP

Sometimes teachers run into problems in curriculum or methods.
When that occurs, they can go for help to several sources. Rank the following
sources in the order in which they provide help to you.

Response	*Haller Study*		
	N	%	Avr. Rank
Principal	14	30.4	2.07
Central office specialists	9	19.6	2.62
School inspectors	0	0	3.55
Other teachers in the school	23	50.0	1.76

[6] Anne Bussis, Edward Chittenden, and Marianne Amarel, "Teacher Perspective as
Change to an Open Approach." Paper presented to American Education Research Association, New Orleans, March 1, 1973.

Response	Keenan Study		
	N	%	Avr. Rank
Principal	15	7.7	2.12
District area and central office specialists and supervisors	8	4.1	2.40
Other teachers in the school	81	41.7	1.35
In-service training	17	8.7	1.67
Books and magazines in field of education	52	26.3	1.32
College and university courses	25	12.8	1.86

2. SOURCES OF IDEAS

A teacher may get ideas and insights about teaching and learning from many sources. Rank the following sources in the order in which they have been most useful to you.

Response	Haller Study		
	N	%	Avr. Rank
In-service courses given by the school system	11	24.4	2.91
Informal conversations with colleagues	14	31.1	2.89
Books and magazines in the field of education	7	15.2	3.20
College and university courses in education	10	22.7	4.21
Meetings in the district	1	2.2	4.13
Immediate superior	3	6.5	4.60
Inspectors and other central office personnel	0	0	5.57

Response	Keenan Study		
	N	%	Avr. Rank
Principal	7	3.6	2.51
District area and central office specialists and supervisors	8	4.1	2.54
Other teachers in the school	67	34.8	1.41
In-service training	26	13.4	1.56
Books and magazines in field of education	53	27.1	1.29
College and university courses	34	17.4	1.74

3. PERCEPTIONS OF RELIABILITY

Suppose an unfamiliar teaching idea were being advocated by each of the sources listed below. For it to be really worth your while to try the idea out, which of these sources would seem most reliable?

Response	Haller Study		
	N	%	Avr. Rank
An elementary school principal	8	17.8	2.93
An article by a respected professor of education	3	6.8	3.93
A colleague teaching same grade	19	43.2	2.30
An inspector	4	8.9	3.73
A widely quoted textbook	3	6.8	3.32
An educational research journal	8	17.8	3.39

Response	Keenan Study		
	N	%	Avr. Rank
Principal	26	14.0	2.14
District area and central office specialists and supervisors	21	11.0	2.03
Other teachers in the school	55	29.0	1.49
In-service training	37	19.7	1.63
Books and magazines in field of education	28	14.8	1.65
College and university courses	24	12.8	2.03

Note: Table 9-1 is constructed from data which appears in Emil J. Haller, *Strategies for Change* (Toronto: Ontario Institute for Studies in Education, Department of Educational Administration, 1968); and Charles Keenan, *Channels for Change: A Survey of Teachers in Chicago Elementary Schools*. Ed. D. Dissertation (Urbana: University of Illinois, Department of Educational Administration, 1974). The questions are from Haller's study.

In both studies the overwhelming choice of teachers for all three questions is other teachers. Teachers go to other teachers for help and for sources of new ideas, and they believe in each other. Principals are not viewed by teachers in these studies as strong sources of change—an indication that perhaps their efforts would be more strongly felt if they emphasized supportive and facilitative rather than directive change roles. Central office directors and supervisors fare poorly in both studies—an indication that perhaps these roles have shifted from the face-to-face concerns of teachers to the bureaucratic concerns of curriculum administration. Books and magazines do fairly well for Chicago teachers as important sources of ideas for change. Keenan suspects that teachers included illustrative curriculum guides, unit outlines, handbooks, manuals of descriptive teaching ideas, and other practical materials in this category. The change ideas presented in this chapter start with the teacher and rely heavily on the teacher to assume responsibility for his own personal development and for instructional improvement.

Some Theoretical Considerations

Perhaps the most useful theoretical statement about change which starts with teachers is that of Chris Argyris in his development of a theory of intervention.[7] Argyris identifies three basic requirements for any successful intervention activity, and these requirements in turn become the primary task of the interventionist. In his words,

> One condition which seems so basic as to be defined axiomatic is the generation of *valid information*. Without valid information it would be difficult for the client to learn and for the interventionist to help.
>
> A second condition almost as basic flows from our assumption that intervention activity, no matter what its substantive interest and objectives, should be so designed and executed that the client system maintains its discreteness and autonomy. Thus *free, informed choice* is also a necessary process in effective intervention activity.
>
> Finally, if the client system is assumed to be ongoing (that is, existing over time), the clients require strengthening to maintain their autonomy not only vis-à-vis the interventionist but also vis-à-vis other systems. This means that their commitment to learning and change has to be more than temporary. It has to be so strong that it can be transferred to relationships other than those with the interventionist and can do so (eventually) without the help of the interventionist. The third basic process for an intervention activity is therefore the client's *internal commitment* to the choices made.
>
> In summary, valid information, free choice, and internal commitment are considered integral parts of any intervention activity, no matter what the substantive objectives are (for example, developing a management performance evaluation scheme, reducing intergroup rivalries, increasing the degree of trust among individuals, redesigning budgetary systems, or redesigning work). These three processes are called the primary intervention tasks.[8]

The role of an outsider who intervenes in an ongoing system in order to facilitate change awareness and perhaps change itself is somewhat different from that of principals, supervisors, or advisers, who are members of the system. Nevertheless, valid information, free and informed choice, and internal

---

[7] Particularly important to this discussion is Chris Argyris, *Intervention Theory and Method: A Behavioral Science View* (Reading, Mass.: Addison-Wesley, 1970). See also his *Integrating the Individual and the Organization* (New York: John Wiley and Sons, 1964); and *Organization and Innovation* (Homewood, Ill.: Irwin, 1965).

[8] Argyris, *Intervention Theory and Method,* pp. 16–17.

commitment are key concerns of principals as they work to bring about change. The task is admittedly more difficult in some respects for an insider because of the "water under the bridge" of his past performance, attitudes, and behavior, which often results in teachers' and principals' holding mutually rigid and often defensive perceptions of each other. Another difference between the outside interventionist and the principal is that valid information, free and informed choice, and internal commitment need to be viewed as part of the total culture of the school, rather than as steps in intervention. They are really dynamic dimensions which interact continuously with each other. That is, valid information leads to free and informed choice which increases the "validity" and quantity of valid information, both of which result in internal commitment. Internal commitment in turn helps generate valid information, and so on, as the cycle continues.

GENERATING VALID AND USEFUL INFORMATION

Valid and useful information is fundamental to understanding and dealing with problems which teachers and schools face. Reasonably accurate and nonevaluative information about what is actually going on is valid information. Such information helps to describe the factors which comprise problems, feelings associated with these problems, and how these factors and feelings relate to each other and to other parts of the total classroom or school. Objectives we value and goals and purposes which we have in mind are further examples of valid information. A comparison of this "real" and "ideal" information often provides us with a third set of valid information— distinctions between where we are and where we would like to be.

We have tried to generate useful samples of valid information. The learning-and-knowledge assumptions inventory, the teacher-student influence grid, the principal's-assumptions inventory, the role-expectation checklist, and the leadership questionnaire are examples of valid-information-seeking devices. All of these would be most helpful in generating valid and useful information for a group of teachers and administrators working to develop a new teacher evaluation procedure, interested in improving communication procedures, or trying to replace a system of suspicion with one of trust.

Usually valid and useful information consists of facts, hard data, and other forms of cognitive information. By and large, we have been reasonably expert at generating such rational information. But, because the major problems facing schools and most other modern organizations interested in changing are people problems, such information is not enough. Many teachers, for example, seem well aware of the importance of individualizing instruction for children, but may resist continuous progress or informal approaches to education because of fear they will lose control of a group of children engaged in learning at different rates or engaged in different activities. Or perhaps they are worried about failing if they tried this new approach, or are concerned about what others in the school would think of the noise level and clutter in their classrooms.

Often the most important valid information which needs to be generated deals with the feelings, assumptions, fears, values, defenses, and worries that each of us has to some degree. One important block to generating valid information is the tendency for people working in formal organizations to engage in role playing. The major roles are those of teacher, principal, supervisor, and student. The problem with role playing in schools is that one often behaves more like an actor than himself—his behavior becomes inauthentic. A teacher may behave as he feels he needs to behave in order to preserve the teacher's role, rather than in a way which seems most suited for the learning encounter at hand. Teachers are supposed to know the answer; therefore, we must not place ourselves in positions where youngsters can find out how little we know. Teachers hide from other teachers and from principals behind role masks. Principals are often guilty of role playing in their interaction with teachers and parents. The more emphasis a school places on status, position, authority, hierarchy, role rights and prerogatives, rules and regulations, and channels and procedures, the more likely that human behavior will approximate a certain artificiality we describe as role playing. That is, the reason for behavior is the preservation of the role system rather than helping the school respond more humanly and achieve its educational objectives.

The generation of valid information is a long and difficult task. This effort is often facilitated by obtaining outside help from a professional interventionist. In any event, valid information requires a commitment from the principal to be open and frank about his opinions and feelings in a way that helps others to be open and frank. This is quite different from being "honest" —that is, saying exactly what you think regardless of the situation and of how other people feel. The principal will probably need to take the initiative in generating valid information and, as small successes begin to accumulate, valid information will become the responsibility of everyone. Valid information can be judged by the extent to which people are gaining nonevaluative feedback; are expressing their own feelings and permitting others to express ideas, feelings, and values; are showing openness to new ideas, feelings, and values; and are experimenting and taking risks with new ideas and values.[9]

FREE AND INFORMED CHOICE

Free choice in our context is not simply the right to choose or not to choose without the benefit of valid information. Our reference is to responsible, free, and informed choice that results from examining a problem from

---

[9] Argyris, *Intervention Theory and Method*, p. 66.

its cognitive and affective dimensions and then freely choosing a course of action or nonaction. The principle of free and informed choice looks to motivation from within as a means to accomplishing internalized change.

> A choice is free to the extent the members can make their selection for a course of action with minimal internal defensiveness; can define the path (or paths) by which the intended consequence is to be achieved; can relate the choice to their central needs; and can build into their choices a realistic and challenging level of aspiration. Free choice therefore implies that the members are able to explore as many alternatives as they consider significant and select those that are central to their needs.
>
> Why must the choice be related to the central needs and why must the level of aspiration be realistic and challenging? May people not choose freely unrealistic or unchallenging objectives? Yes, they may do so in the short run, but not for long if they will want to have free and informed choice. A freely chosen course of action means that the action must be based on an accurate analysis of the situation and not on the biases or defenses of the decision makers. We know, from the level of aspiration studies, that choices which are too high or too low, which are too difficult or not difficult enough will tend to lead to psychological failure. Psychological failure will lead to increased defensiveness, increased failure, and decreased self-acceptance on the part of the members experiencing the failure. These conditions, in turn, will tend to lead to distorted perceptions by the members making the choices. Moreover, the defensive members may unintentionally create a climate where the members of surrounding and interrelated systems will tend to provide carefully censored information. Choices made under these conditions are neither informed nor free.[10]

Some teachers may want to give up responsibility for free and informed choice—indeed, the burden of free and informed choice may be too much for them. Such teachers may want to be left alone and may gladly have others make decisions for them. If forced into choosing "freely," they may choose no change, or try to please those in authority by accepting changes they advocate. It is important to remember that accepting a change and internalizing a change are not the same. When one accepts a change, one merely adopts the manifestations of change; when a change is internalized, it becomes incorporated into a person's attitude and value system as well as into his repertoire of behavior.

Free and informed choice does not come easy for people who have had little experience at it. Indeed, principals may need to help teachers, and teachers may need to help each other to feel comfortable with and competent in exercising free and informed choice. This applies as well to youngsters in classrooms. The extent to which an activity-oriented or informal approach to elementary classroom teaching and living is successful may depend upon the teacher's ability to help youngsters learn to exercise free and informed choice.

[10] Argyris, *Intervention Theory and Method*, pp. 19–20.

This behavior does not come naturally to teachers or youngsters who have lived for a period of time in a school where free and informed choice is discouraged.

It is obvious that free and informed choice cannot be practiced all of the time and in reference to all of the decisions which the school faces. Often teachers may not have the appropriate background to meet the informed requirement, or may not be interested in becoming informed enough to make a free and informed choice. Certain school functions which teachers consider strictly administrative, such as bus scheduling, maintenance problems, purchasing routines, and the like, may be examples.

BUILDING INTERNAL COMMITMENT TO CHANGE

Internal commitment is a result of free and informed choice and may be the single most important contributor to school effectiveness. In earlier chapters, we described the importance of the school's people variables or human organization which in a sense mediates or absorbs the effects of the school's organizational structure, management system, and manifestations of administrative behavior such as leadership styles, distribution of power, status and authority, planning procedures, communication systems, and decision-making philosophy. These school management inputs do not have a very strong direct effect on the extent to which a school is successful. Rather it is the effect of these variables on teachers and students that seems to be the essential link to school effectiveness. Internal commitment is basic to this link.

> Internal commitment means the course of action or choice that has been internalized by each member so that he experiences a high degree of ownership and has a feeling of responsibility about the choice and its implications. Internal commitment means that the individual has reached the point where he is acting on the choice because it fulfills his own needs and sense of responsibility, as well as those of the system.
>
> The individual who is internally committed is acting primarily under the influence of his own forces and not induced forces. The individual (or any unity) feels a minimal degree of dependence upon others for the action. It implies that he has obtained and processed valid information and that he has made an informed and free choice. Under these conditions there is a high probability that the individual's commitment will remain strong over time (even with reduction of external rewards) or under stress, or when the course of action is challenged by others. It also implies that the individual is continually open to reexamination of his position because he believes in taking action based upon valid information.[11]

The principle of internal commitment has long been subscribed to by most educators as an important condition of learning for students. Teachers

[11] Argyris, *Intervention Theory and Method,* p. 20.

work hard to build this commitment by motivating students through attractive classrooms, teacher-pupil planning, interesting demonstrations and field trips, audiovisual techniques, and an assortment of methods and approaches (some rigged, some authentic) to student participation. Some of these methods are more successful than others depending upon the extent to which they provide for the generation of valid information and free and informed choice.

Bringing About Change

Effective schools are those where teachers, students, administrators, and other workers are engaged in problem solving, decision making, and implementation. As organizations, schools engage in these processes as they work to achieve their goals, to maintain themselves internally as human systems, and to adapt to and interact with their relevant external environment.[12]

In Figure 9-1 we show the relationship between the essential processes of the school and the principal's role as a change helper and environmentalist. Our goal is changing the school from an XA to a YB way of life as described in Chapter 7. In this effort, individuals and groups of teachers are engaged continuously in problem solving, decision making, and implementing their decisions. The principal, supervisor, and adviser help by generating valid information, free and informed choice, and internal commitment. Teachers function similarly as they help youngsters engage in problem solving and making and implementing decisions.

There are certain ethical principles with which any change helper and environmentalist must be concerned.[13] If he ignores these principles, he may find himself engaged in a brand of social engineering known as manipulation. These ethical principles are collaboration, education, experimentation, and task orientation.[14] The first of these principles, collaboration, requires that those involved in change form a partnership with each being aware of the intentions of others. Giving attention to the educational-process principle requires that the change helper and environmentalist work to free others from depending upon him. He is concerned not only with the substantive problems which people face but with helping them deal more adequately with problems in general without his help or with less help than previously. He considers change to be experimental and works to help others resist the temptation to freeze change into the system forever. Ideally, changes are discarded when no longer useful. He has a task-oriented, rather than a self-oriented, perspective

---

[12] Argyris, *Intervention Theory and Method,* p. 36.

[13] Kenneth D. Beene, "Democratic Ethics and Social Engineering," *Progressive Education,* Vol. 27, No. 7 (May 1949), 204.

[14] For a discussion of these and other value questions associated with change, see: Thomas J. Sergiovanni and Robert J. Starratt, *Emerging Patterns of Supervision: Human Perspectives* (New York: McGraw-Hill, 1971), pp. 160–169.

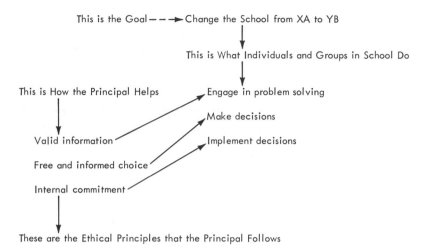

This is the Goal — — ➤ Change the School from XA to YB

This is What Individuals and Groups in School Do

This is How the Principal Helps   Engage in problem solving

Make decisions

Valid information   Implement decisions

Free and informed choice

Internal commitment

These are the Ethical Principles that the Principal Follows

a) Uses a collaborative process

b) Gives attention to educational – process goals

c) Considers change experimental

d) Has a task as opposed to self – perspective

FIGURE 9-1.   Bringing about change when the commitment of teachers is needed.

in the sense that, although he may stand to gain in status, prestige, money, and so on, as successful changes are implemented in the schools, he promotes change for the benefit of the schools rather than for his own self-gain.

SOME IMPORTANT EXCEPTIONS

We have been describing the "long way" to bring about change in schools, one that relies heavily on valid information and free and informed choice. This approach is very expensive in time, money, and human talent and energy, but implementation of change based on internal commitment is the expected outcome and often *but not always* is worth the price. Not all change in schools requires internal commitment from teachers for successful and sustained implementation. Using the long way when it is not necessary is not only a waste of human and material resources, but may actually be an irritant to teachers. Some changes are simply not worth one's getting involved, other changes are of little interest or concern, and still others require specialized or technical knowledge for meaningful involvement.

As an example, teachers are not likely to be terribly interested in and may even resent being involved in many of the routine, managerial aspects of running the school. Often the solutions to such problems are routine, the problems are of little interest to teachers, or active participation requires special knowledge or skills which teachers do not have and may not care about. Further, such changes can probably be accepted or implemented without internal commitment of teachers. The principal's accuracy in estimating the extent to which these conditions exist in a given situation can be increased by having available valid information with reference to how teachers feel about these matters and the expectations they hold for his role.

SOME PRACTICAL CONSIDERATIONS

The problems of bringing about change in elementary schools should be different from those of larger, more formal, specialized, and complex organizations, such as comprehensive high schools, city hospitals, universities, and industrial organizations. Elementary schools should be more like informal organizations and, therefore, characterized by closer relationships among people, less task specialization, open parent-community interaction and exchange, flexibility, and less reliance on position, status hierarchy, and rank among students, teachers, parents, and administrators. If this is not the case, then the elementary school may be too large (over 400 to 600 students), and one should consider relatively autonomous family grouping or schools-within-school plans as possible means to overcome the problem of size. If size is not the problem, then perhaps principals are looking in the wrong places (the high school, central office, or business corporation) for models of organization and administration.

Principals of elementary schools which approximate informal organizations will be more successful in bringing about change if they rely more on behavioral approaches than on seeking political, organizational, and hierarchial solutions to change. The problems of bringing about change in elementary schools may be different, but this does not lessen their importance. "Resistance to change," "change comes hard," and "conservatism," are terms frequently and bitterly highlighted by principals, supervisors, and advisers as they discuss teachers and change. It is important to have some understanding of just what is being resisted. Most teachers do not resist changes in teaching method, school organization, educational technology, and curriculum development and implementation as such. What they resist are changes in the human relationships which usually accompany these more technical changes.[15]

It may be that we have greatly overestimated the extent to which educators are resistant to change. Haller finds that 60 percent of his sample (N = 47) of Canadian elementary school teachers favor more new practices,

---

[15] Paul R. Lawrence, "How to Deal with Resistance to Change," *Harvard Business Review*, Vol. 32, No. 3, (May–June 1954), pp. 49–57.

and 5 percent want fewer new practices. Keenan finds that 78 percent and 12 percent of his sample of Chicago teachers ($N = 201$) are similarly inclined. Using the same question with 114 "Small City," Illinois, principals and supervisors, we find 59 percent favoring more new practices and 10 percent favoring fewer new practices.[16]

Change problems are not primarily related to rationality but to people's feelings. Rationality refers to the extent to which a change is well conceived educationally and implemented according to a logical plan. Typically, change strategies which rely exclusively on rationality are not successful. True, as Lionberger suggests, developing *awareness* to a new idea, product, or practice; *interest* by actively seeking extensive information about the idea to determine its usefulness and applicability; *evaluation* by weighing and sifting information and evidence in the light of existing conditions characteristic of the school; *trial* whereby ideas are tentatively tried out and evaluated; and *adoption* or full implementation of the practice into the ongoing operation of the school are logical and important steps to bringing about technical change.[17] Technical change, however, is only part of the problem, for successful implementation relies on social change—change in human relationships which typically accompany technical change.

PLANNING FOR CHANGE

The first reaction that one often has to any proposed change is "How will this affect me?" A teacher's first concern when approached with the prospect of family grouping, for example, is not the educational efficacy of the idea, but:

"How will my relationship with the children change?"

"How will my view of myself change?"

"How will my authority and influence change?"

"How will the amount of work I do change?"

"How will my relationship with teachers, parents, and administration change?"

"Will I be more or less successful as a teacher?"

"Who will be the team or unit teacher?"

All of these concerns are legitimate and deserve answers. Unless the first set of concerns, the human concerns, are adequately resolved, answers to educational questions or job concerns are only likely to raise new questions and

[16] Haller, *Strategies for Change;* and Keenan, *Receptivity to Change.*

[17] Herbert Lionberger, *Adoption of New Ideas and Practices* (Ames: Iowa State University Press, 1960), pp. 3–4.

to increase skepticism. It is natural for healthy people to be concerned with how changes will affect them, their work, and relations with others, and one is less likely to adequately evaluate the educational efficacy of a change when troubled by these human concerns.

W. J. Reddin has conveniently grouped the ways in which people are affected by change at work. These appear in the form of questions which comprise a change-reaction checklist as shown in Table 9-2.

Individuals and groups facing a proposed change should examine each of these questions. Those questions which seem important in increasing acceptance of change should be marked with a plus (+); those important in increasing resistance to change should be marked with a minus (−). Using the example

TABLE 9-2. Reddin's Change-Reaction Checklist.

Self

(S-1)	How will my advancement possibilities change?
(S-2)	How will my salary change?
(S-3)	How will my future with this company change?
(S-4)	How will my view of myself change?
(S-5)	How will my formal authority change?
(S-6)	How will my informal influence change?
(S-7)	How will my view of my prior values change?
(S-8)	How will my ability to predict the future change?
(S-9)	How will my status change?

Work

(W-1)	How will the amount of work I do change?
(W-2)	How will my interest in the work change?
(W-3)	How will the importance of my work change?
(W-4)	How will the challenge of the work change?
(W-5)	How will the work pressures change?
(W-6)	How will the skill demands on me change?
(W-7)	How will my physical surroundings change?
(W-8)	How will my hours of work change?

Others

(O-1)	How will my relationship with my co-workers change?
(O-2)	How will my relationships with my superior change?
(O-3)	How will my relationships with my subordinates change?
(O-4)	How will what my family thinks of me change?

From W. J. Reddin, *Managerial Effectiveness* (New York: McGraw-Hill, 1970), p. 163.

of family grouping, a group of primary teachers might mark a plus next to questions S-4, S-9, W-3, and W-4. That is, they may see family grouping as enhancing images that they have of themselves as teachers, as affording them more status and prestige, and as providing them with an opportunity to engage in more important and challenging work. Questions which they might check as being important in increasing their resistance to family grouping could include S-1, S-8, W-1 and W-8. One person, for example, might be concerned about not being chosen team or unit teacher, thus lessening his chances of moving into administration. Others find the ambiguities about their future roles as team members uncomfortable. Further, a general concern might exist about the amount and difficulty of work that this plan will require. An important early step in planning for change is bringing to the surface these human concerns. The change-reaction checklist is not an inclusive list and may need modification given individual circumstances.

Once questions which apply have been checked with a plus or minus, it may be helpful to develop a "force-field diagram" which more clearly shows the nature and intensity of driving and restraining forces affecting change. Force-field analysis is a method advocated by the distinguished psychologist Kurt Lewin as a means to understanding and planning for change.[18]

Lewin assumes that change takes place when an imbalance occurs between the sum of driving forces and the sum of restraining forces. This imbalance unfreezes the present pattern or equilibrium that exists in the situation. When driving forces become strong enough to overcome restraining forces, change takes place. When restraining forces are sufficiently reduced or weakened, change takes place.

The force-field diagram illustrated in Figure 9-2 contains the driving and restraining forces previously discussed in our example relating to family grouping. Each of the forces has been given a weight which identifies it as strong, medium, or weak in influence.

Driving Forces		*Weight*
S-4	How will my view of myself change?	medium
S-9	How will my status change?	medium
W-3	How will the importance of my work change?	weak
W-4	How will the challenge of the work change?	weak

Restraining Forces		*Weight*
S-1	How will my advancement possibilities change?	medium
S-8	How will my ability to predict the future change?	medium
W-1	How will the amount of work I do change?	strong
W-8	How will my hours of work change?	strong

[18] Kurt Lewin, *Field Theory in Social Science* (New York: Harper & Row, 1951).

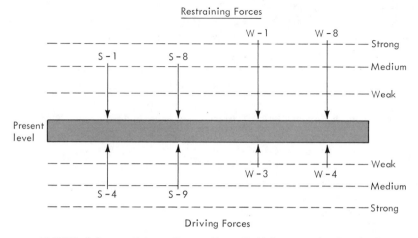

FIGURE 9-2.   Driving Forces: Force-Field Diagram for Family Grouping.

The forces are represented in Figure 9-2 as arrows; the length of the arrow indicates the strength of influence for each force.

Figure 9-2 suggests that restraining forces are exerting a more powerful influence on this group of primary teachers considering family grouping. At this point, the change is likely to be successfully resisted. According to this group's perception of the situation, gains in self-image and status seem equally balanced by concern about advancement possibilities and working as a team member. Further strong concerns about increases in work loads readily override benefits seen in the work's becoming more important and challenging. Change is not likely to occur in the situation unless estimation of the worth of importance and challenge is increased, new benefits are found and added to the driving forces, concern relating to increases in the amount of work are found unwarranted and corrected, and some of the unknowns about the functioning of teaching teams become known.

Using the change-reaction checklists and building force-field diagrams are not going to solve our problems associated with change. This is clearly not their purpose. They can, however, help to open the door to what is on people's minds as they are faced with change. They are methods in generating valid and useful information.

10

Motivating
Teachers to Work

PRINCIPALS AND SUPERVISORS are acquainted with concepts of motivation as they apply to youngsters. Well-motivated youngsters are those who require less supervision and who willingly work to accomplish learning goals. They accept learning goals as personal goals. Further, they seem to enjoy their work, are more loyal to the school, and are more committed to educational activities in general. For them, learning is more like play than work. Indeed, willingly engaging in hard work and enjoying it are trademarks of well-motivated youngsters. By contrast, poorly motivated youngsters seem disinterested and unresponsive. With sufficient prodding, clear instruction, structured learning situations, and close supervision by the teacher, such youngsters are able to do a reasonably satisfactory job. For the poorly motivated youngster, schooling is dull, and schoolwork is seen as a painful necessity.

Principals and supervisors are quick to point out that the motivational condition of elementary school youngsters is largely a function of school

137

philosophy, teacher attitudes, and styles of teaching. Poor motivation is not an inherent condition in youngsters, but is rather a symptom of school, teacher, and educational program problems. It is probably true that some few youngsters are impossible to motivate within the limitations of our present knowledge about youngsters and schooling. However, large numbers of poorly motivated youngsters are indications that the school is not performing adequately.

The emphasis which principals and supervisors give to motivation of youngsters is important and commendable. No less important, however, is the application of these same concepts to the adults who are employed in the school. If we are serious about providing the most effective environment we can for youngsters engaged in living and learning, the highly motivated teacher becomes a high-priority concern of principals and supervisors. Further, the evidence is mounting that significant changes in school effectiveness will not come about quite so much as a result of increasing teachers' salaries (merit or otherwise), decreasing class size, introducing new teaching materials, beefing up the academic training or certification credentials of teachers, reducing the work load, introducing clerical assistants, using performance contracts, and the like.[1] These all contribute a certain amount to effectiveness, but their potency cannot compare with powerful social-psychological variables such as internal commitment and motivation to work. Simply stated, quality education and effective elementary schools are primarily a function of competent administrators, supervisors, and teachers who are internally committed and motivated to work. In this chapter we provide a practical approach to motivation to work. This approach is based on a decade of research and practice in industry and is gaining increased acceptance in education.[2]

Investing in Work

A basic principle in motivation theory is that people invest themselves in work in order to obtain desired returns or rewards. Examples of that investment are time, physical energy, mental energy, creativity, knowledge, skill, enthusiasm, and effort. Returns or rewards can take a variety of tangible

[1] Frederick Mosteller and Daniel P. Moynihan (eds.), *On Equality of Educational Opportunity: Papers Deriving from the Harvard University Faculty Seminar on the Coleman Report* (New York: Random House, 1972).

[2] See, for example: Frederick Herzberg, Bernard Mausner, and Barbara Snyderman, *The Motivation to Work* (New York: John Wiley and Sons, 1959); Saul Gellerman, *Motivation and Productivity* (Washington, D.C.: The American Management Association, 1963); and M. Scott Myers, *Every Employee a Manager* (New York: McGraw-Hill, 1970). For applications to education, see: Thomas J. Sergiovanni and Robert J. Starratt, *Emerging Patterns of Supervision: Human Perspectives* (New York: McGraw-Hill, 1971), Ch. 8; Thomas J. Sergiovanni and Fred D. Carver, *The New School Executive: A Theory of Administration* (New York: Dodd, Mead, 1973), Chs. 4–7.

and intangible forms including money, respect, comfort, a sense of accomplishment, social acceptance, and security. It is useful to categorize expression of investment in work as being of two types: first, a *participation* investment and, second, a *performance* investment.

The participation investment is required of all teachers and includes all that is necessary for the teacher to obtain and maintain satisfactory membership in the school. Meeting classes, preparing lesson plans, obtaining satisfactory-to-good evaluations from supervisors, following school rules and regulations, attending required meetings, bearing one's fair share of committee responsibility, projecting an appropriate image to the public—in short, giving a fair day's work for a fair day's pay. Teachers not willing to make the participatory investment in work find themselves unacceptable to administrators and other teachers. On the other hand, one cannot command teachers to give more of themselves—to go beyond the participatory investment. In return for the participatory investment, teachers are provided with such benefits as salary, retirement provisions, fair supervision, good human relations, and security. In a sense, we are describing the traditional legal work relationship between employer and employee. We can think of no great institution in our society and no great achievements that have resulted from merely the traditional legal work relationship. Greatness has always been a result of employers' and employees' exceeding the limits of this relationship.

The performance investment exceeds the limits of the traditional legal work relationship. Here, teachers give far more than one can "reasonably expect," and in return they are provided with rewards that permit them to enjoy deep satisfaction with their work and themselves. When we speak of motivation to work, we speak of providing incentives that evoke the performance investment from teachers. It is important to distinguish between the kinds of return or rewards which evoke each of these investments. One does not exceed the limits of the traditional legal work relationship for more rewards of the same kind. One does not buy the second investment with more money, privileges, easier and better working conditions, and improved human relationships. These are important incentives as we shall see, but their potency is limited. In the next section we examine the motivation-hygiene theory. The principles of this theory should help us to better understand participatory investments and performance investments at work.

THE MOTIVATION-HYGIENE THEORY

All of the paragraphs which appear below are descriptions of important features of the motivation-hygiene theory. They are stated first in an attempt to sketch out the nature, scope, and potency of the theory. Their description is followed by an analysis of theoretical and research findings that provide the origins of the theory.

1. There are certain conditions in work that teachers expect to enjoy. If these conditions are present in sufficient quantity, teachers will perform only adequately. If these conditions are not present in sufficient quantity, teachers will be dissatisfied, and work performance will suffer.

2. The conditions in work which teachers expect as part of the traditional legal work relationship are called *hygienic factors*. Their absence results in teacher dissatisfaction and poor performance. Their presence maintains the traditional legal work relationship, but does not motivate performance.

3. The factors which contribute to teachers' exceeding the traditional work relationship are called *motivators*. The absence of motivators does not result in dissatisfaction and does not endanger the traditional work relationship.

4. Motivational factors and hygienic factors are different. Motivation to work is not a result of increasing hygienic factors.

5. Hygienic factors are associated with the conditions of work and are extrinsic in nature. Examples are money, benefits, fair supervision, and a feeling of belonging. Motivational factors are associated with work itself and are intrinsic in nature. Examples are recognition, achievement, and increased responsibility.

6. Hygienic factors are important, for their neglect creates problems in the work environment. These problems can result in dissatisfaction and lowered performance. Taking care of the hygienic factors prevents trouble, but these factors are not potent enough to motivate people to work.

7. Hygienic factors meet man's need to avoid unpleasantness and hardship. Motivational factors serve man's uniquely human need for psychological growth.

8. Satisfaction at work is not a motivator of performance *per se*, but results from quality performance. Administrators and supervisors should not use satisfaction as a method of motivating teachers, but as a goal that teachers seek and that is best obtained through meaningful work.

9. Administrators and supervisors who use job satisfaction to motivate teachers are practicing human relations. This has not been proven to be an effective approach. Human relations emphasize the hygienic factors.

10. Administrators and supervisors who consider job satisfaction as a goal that teachers seek through accomplishing meaningful work and who focus on enhancing the meaningful view of work and the ability of teachers to accomplish this work are practicing human-resource

development. This has been proven to be an effective approach. Human-resource development emphasizes the motivational factors.

11. The human-relations approach approximates XB patterns of management, and the human-resource-development approach approximates YB patterns of management as described in Chapter 5.

12. True, not all teachers can be expected to respond to the motivation-hygiene theory, but most can.

In summary, the theory stipulates that people at work have two distinct sets of needs. One set of needs is best met by hygienic factors. In exchange for these factors, one is prepared to make the participatory investment—to give a fair day's work. If hygienic factors are neglected, dissatisfaction occurs, and one's performance on the job decreases below an acceptable level. Another set of needs is best met by the motivational factors which are not automatically part of the job, but which can be built into most jobs, particularly those found in elementary schools. In return for the motivational factors, one is prepared to make the performance investment, to exceed the limits of the traditional legal work relationship. If the motivational factors are neglected, one does not become dissatisfied, but one's performance does not exceed that typically described as a fair day's work for a fair day's pay.

MASLOW'S THEORY OF HUMAN NEEDS

The distinguished psychologist, Abraham Maslow,[3] developed a useful framework for sorting and categorizing basic human needs such as air, water, food, protection, love, sex, respect, success, and influence. These needs are sorted into a five-level taxonomy arranged in hierarchical order of prepotency. The prepotency feature is of particular significance to the taxonomy, for it specifies that needs at the lower levels of the hierarchy need to be reasonably satisfied before one is interested in needs at the next higher level. The five need levels, according to Maslow, are physiological, security, social, esteem, and self-actualization. Figure 10-1 shows a slightly altered needs hierarchy that eliminates physiological needs and adds autonomy needs. This alteration seems particularly appropriate in view of the facts that presently physiological needs seem guaranteed and that workers seem to express considerable interest in control and autonomy.

Figure 10-1 shows the needs hierarchy arranged in triangular form and in the form of a bar graph. To illustrate the prepotency feature, assume that a particular teacher is working at the social-need level of the hierarchy. That is, his present concern is to obtain and maintain acceptance by other teachers. This teacher is not likely to be concerned with esteem, autonomy, and self-

[3] Abraham H. Maslow, *Motivation and Productivity* (New York: Harper and Brothers, 1954).

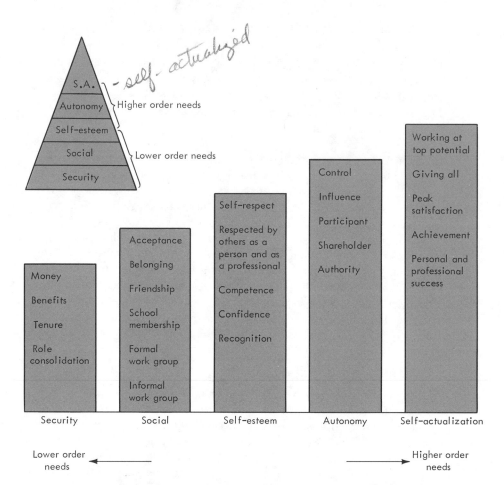

FIGURE 10-1.   The Needs Hierarchy. Lower order needs are associated with hygienic work needs and provide the base for identifying hygienic factors. Higher order needs are associated with motivational work needs and provide the base for identifying motivational factors.

actualization while he is working for acceptance. He will abandon his interest in acceptance, however, if security, an even lower order need, is seriously threatened. As this need becomes reasonably satisfied, he begins to focus on the next higher need, which is self-esteem.

Elementary school principals, supervisors, and advisers need to know teachers' positions in the hierarchy. The level of prepotency for teachers in general and for individual teachers is important, for it makes no sense to motivate at the autonomy level if teachers are insecure, or to emphasize security needs when people need and seek autonomy. Principals who overestimate the operating need levels of teachers might "scare them off." Emphasizing responsibility and participatory decision making with teachers who are concerned about their own capabilities can be as ineffective as underestimating operating need levels. Teachers are usually denied meaningful satisfaction at work when need levels are underestimated. One's goal may very well be to help teachers operate at the autonomy or self-actualization level, but one must start wherever individuals happen to be on the needs hierarchy.

Studies completed in 1966 and 1969 seem to suggest that esteem is the level of need operation of greatest concern to educators in general.[4] Large deficiencies were also reported for autonomy and self-actualization needs, and the importance of these needs should increase as gains are made in the esteem area. Security and social needs seem reasonably met.

The lower order needs of security, social acceptance, and to some extent the more material manifestations of esteem such as title and position are clearly extrinsic in nature. These are the things schools give in order to obtain the participatory investment of a fair day's work. To a certain extent, teachers take rewards of this kind for granted. After all, everyone is entitled to a decent salary, job security, a friendly work environment, and job stature. These are things one gets by joining a school faculty and are not earned by hard work after employment. These needs are associated with the hygienic factors. The higher order needs of self-concept development, feelings of competency, autonomy, and deep satisfaction are needs which are best met through actual performance of work. These rewards are not taken for granted, but are earned as a result of effort and successful achievement. These needs are associated with the motivation factors.

THE MOTIVATION-HYGIENE FACTORS

We have established that hygienic factors are those largely extrinsic in nature and associated with our lower order needs and that motivational factors are largely intrinsic in nature and associated with our higher order needs. Now let us examine the factors themselves.

Motivation-hygiene theory results from the research of Frederick Herzberg.[5] The model for his research is an interview method whereby workers are asked to describe job events associated with satisfaction and dissatisfaction at work. Further, the effects of these feelings and events on one's performance at work are examined. Dozens of studies have been conducted using

[4] Francis M. Trusty and Thomas J. Sergiovanni, "Perceived Need Deficiencies of Teachers and Administrators: A Proposal for Restricting Teacher Roles," *Educational Administration Quarterly*, Vol. 2, No. 3, (Autumn 1966), 165–180; and Fred D. Carver and Thomas J. Sergiovanni, "Complexity, Adaptability and Job Satisfaction in High Schools: An Axiomatic Theory Applied," *Journal of Educational Administration*, Vol. 9, No. 1 (1971), 10–31.

[5] Herzberg et al., *The Motivation to Work*.

this approach with a variety of workers, from scientists to assembly-line workers, in a number of countries.[6]

In the majority of cases, studies reveal that traditional linear notions regarding satisfaction and dissatisfaction at work are in need of modification. Traditionally, it has been assumed that if a cause of dissatisfaction is identified, elimination of this cause results in job satisfaction and motivated workers. Teachers unhappy with school policies, the kind of supervision they are getting, money matters, and class scheduling will move to a state of satisfaction and motivation if these deficiencies are remedied. Motivation-hygiene studies by and large show that this is not the case. Remedying the deficiencies that cause dissatisfaction brings a person up to a level of minimum performance that includes the absence of dissatisfaction. Satisfaction and motivation are the results of a separate set of factors. The factors associated with satisfaction, but not dissatisfaction, are called motivators because of their ability to stimulate performance. The factors associated with dissatisfaction, but not satisfaction, are called hygienic because of their ability to cause trouble if neglected. In Herzberg's words,

> The Motivation-Hygiene theory of job attitudes began with a depth interview study of over 200 engineers and accountants representing Pittsburgh industry. These interviews probed sequences of events in the work lives of the respondents to determine the factors that were involved in their feeling exceptionally happy and, conversely exceptionally unhappy with their jobs. From a review and an analysis of previous publications in the general area of job attitudes, a two-factor hypothesis was formulated to guide the original investigation. This hypothesis suggested that the factors involved in producing job satisfaction were separate and distinct from the factors that led to job dissatisfaction. Since separate factors needed to be considered depending on whether job satisfaction or job dissatisfaction was involved, it followed that these two feelings were not the obverse of each other. The opposite of job satisfaction would not be job dissatisfaction, but rather *no* job satisfaction; and similarly the opposite of job dissatisfaction is *no* job dissatisfaction—not job satisfaction. The statement of the concept is awkward and may appear at first to be a semantic ruse, but there is more than a play with words when it comes to understanding the behavior of people on jobs. The fact that job satisfaction is made up of two unipolar traits is not a unique occurrence. The difficulty of establishing a zero point in psychology with the procedural necessity of using instead a bench mark (mean of a population) from which to start our measurement has led to the conception that psychological traits are bipolar. Empirical investigations, however, have cast some shadows on the assumptions of bipolarity; one timely example is a study of conformity and nonconformity, where they are shown not to be opposites, but rather two separate unipolar traits.[7]

[6] See, for example, Frederick Herzberg, *Work and the Nature of Man* (New York: World, 1966).

[7] Frederick Herzberg, "The Motivation-Hygiene Concept and Problems of Manpower," *Personnel Administration,* Vol. 27, No. 1 (1964), 3.

In Figure 10-2 Herzberg summarizes 12 investigations testing the motivation-hygiene theory. Workers studied in the different investigations included lower level supervisors, professional women, agricultural administrators, men in management positions, hospital maintenance workers, manufacturing supervisors, nurses, food handlers, military officers, engineers, scientists, housekeepers, teachers, technicians, female factory workers, accountants, Finnish foremen, and Hungarian engineers. Superimposed on Herzberg's summary data is a separate study of teachers.[8]

Achievement, recognition, work itself, responsibility, and advancement are the factors identified by Herzberg as contributing primarily to satisfaction. Their absence tends not to lead to dissatisfaction. These are the motivators—the rewards which one seeks in return for the performance investment.

Policy and administration, supervision, salary, interpersonal relationships, and working conditions are the factors that Herzberg identifies as contributing primarily to dissatisfaction. These are the hygienic factors—conditions which workers expect in return for a fair day's work.

In the separate teacher study, achievement and recognition were identified as the most potent motivators. Responsibility, although a significant motivator, appeared in only 7 percent of the events associated with satisfaction. We do not take advantage of the motivational possibilities of responsibility in education—this factor is relatively standardized for teachers in that responsibility does not vary very much from one teacher to another. Work itself did not appear significantly more often as a contributor to satisfaction. Apparently, elements of the job of teaching as we presently know it are inherently less than satisfying. Among these are routine housekeeping, attendance, milk money, paper work, study hall, lunch duty, and the like. The negative aspects of policeman, clerk, and custodial roles seem to neutralize professional teaching and guidance roles for these professionals. Poor interpersonal relations with students; inadequate, incompetent, insensitive, and close supervision; unfair, rigid, and inflexible school policies and administrative practices; poor interpersonal relations with other teachers and with parents; and incidents in one's personal life were the job factors found to contribute significantly to teachers' dissatisfaction.

Herzberg found in his original study with accountants and engineers [9] that, although recognition and advancement were mentioned most often as motivators, the duration of good feelings associated with these rewards was very short. Work and advancement seemed to have medium effects, but good feelings associated with responsibility lasted more than twice as long as those associated with work and advancement, and more than three times

[8] Thomas J. Sergiovanni, "Factors Which Affect Satisfaction and Dissatisfaction of Teachers," *The Journal of Educational Administration*, Vol. 5, No. 1 (1967), 66–82.
[9] Herzberg et al., *The Motivation to Work*.

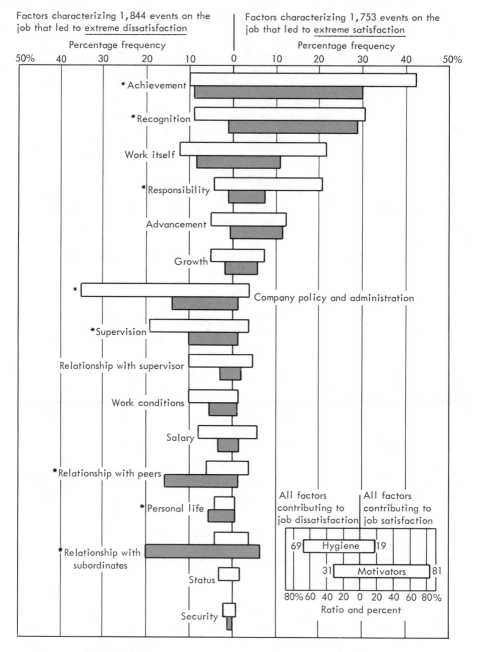

Percentage frequency

Percentage frequency

50% 40 30 20 10 0 10 20 30 40 50%

*Achievement

*Recognition

Work itself

*Responsibility

Advancement

Growth

*   Company policy and administration

*Supervision

Relationship with supervisor

Work conditions

Salary

*Relationship with peers

*Personal life

*Relationship with subordinates

Status

Security

All factors contributing to job dissatisfaction | All factors contributing to job satisfaction

69 Hygiene 19

31 Motivators 81

80% 60 40 20 0 20 40 60 80%

Ratio and percent

FIGURE 10-2.   Herzberg: Factors Affecting Job Attitudes. The shaded bars included with the Herzberg data are the results of a study conducted with the teachers in 1966. The teacher study included 142 dissatisfaction events and 142 satisfaction events. Asterisks identify those factors in the teacher study found to contribute significantly to satisfaction and those found to contribute significantly to dissatisfaction.

From Frederick Herzberg, "One More Time: How Do You Motivate Employees?" *Harvard Business Review,* Vol. 46, No. 4 (1968).

as long as those from achievement and recognition. Negative feelings associated with neglected hygienic factors were generally of short duration.

Teachers as Individuals

The motivation-hygiene theory provides simplified answers to rather complex questions. This is a bold theory which provides broad and general guidelines to principals and supervisors interested in evoking the performance investment from teachers. Its boldness and its broad propositions require intelligent caution as one applies the theory to practice. For example, while the theory suggests that by and large only the satisfiers motivate, it would be wrong to conclude that some people are not motivated by the dissatisfiers. Some individuals are indeed motivated by the dissatisfiers, but under ordinary circumstances it is not natural to be so motivated. The implication is that healthy individuals respond to the motivation-hygiene theory, while those less healthy do not. Further, healthy individuals who are deprived of work satisfactions which come from the motivator factors will seek these satisfactions elsewhere—at home through family membership, hobbies, community activity, sports, and the like. Attention to these aspects of life are important to all of us, but the world of work seems the more natural place for professional workers to find satisfaction for their needs of esteem, competence, achievement, autonomy, and self-actualization.

Teachers who seem more interested in hygienic factors than motivational factors can be categorized as follows: (1) those who have the potential for motivation seeking, but are frustrated by insensitive and closed administrative, supervisory, and organizational policies and practices; (2) those who have the potential for motivation seeking, but who decide to channel this potential into other areas of their lives; and (3) those who do not have the potential for motivation seeking on or off the job. Those in the second and third groups use their jobs as a means to gain or achieve goals not related to the school.

The second group includes many teachers whose goals are buying a second car or a vacation house, supplementing spouse's income to achieve a higher standard of living, putting husband or children through college, and so on. Men in this group often use the teaching occupation as a means to step into another job, such as coaching, counseling, or administration.[10]

[10] Simpson and Simpson maintain that semiprofessional women are far less committed to work careers than are most men of comparable attainments. They note that "a fairly mild economic pressure is often enough, however, to keep them [women] at work. Relatively few of them would face utter destitution if they stopped work. The pressure is more often the desire to maintain a standard of comparative luxury, to help the family move into a larger house, or to save toward the children's college education. . . . Work for women is no longer considered a tragedy; it is an acceptable alternative but it is not the first choice for many."

They further note: "It is true that educated women whose husbands' incomes are

The third group includes individuals who seem fixated at lower need levels. In a sense, they are obsessed with "avoiding" unpleasantness and discomfort to the point that they have not developed the ability to seek satisfaction through the motivators and at higher need levels. Many psychologists regard this obsession as a symptom of poor mental health; if this is the case, then selection procedures should be devised to identify and filter out teachers of this type. Tenured teachers of this type will need to be heavily supervised.

Teachers who have the potential for motivation seeking, but who elect to seek satisfactions of this kind outside of the school, are by and large good teachers who give honest labor in exchange for what they hope to gain from the school. Extraordinary performance is lacking, however, for such teachers do not have a strong commitment to the school and its purposes. Teachers of this kind will be with us for a long time to come, but they cannot be depended upon to substantially upgrade the nation's schools or to display much interest in becoming full partners in the school enterprise, unless they can become attracted to the motivational factors. Teachers interested primarily in hygienic factors, but who have motivational potential, can make significant contributions to the school's work if kindly, but firmly and competently, supervised, or when combined with motivation seekers in schools with differentiated roles and responsibilities for teachers. Hygienically oriented teachers who have the potential for motivation seeking, but are frustrated by the school and its administration, are unfortunate casualties. When we deny teachers motivation expressions, we not only waste valuable human resources, but deny school youngsters important opportunities for self-actualization. In general, hygienically oriented teachers excessively think of their jobs in terms of salary, working conditions, supervision, status, job security, school policies and administration, and social relationships.

THE MOTIVATION-HYGIENE INVENTORY

Attitudes and behaviors displayed by people at work generally reveal their tendencies toward hygiene or motivation seeking. To help you begin to assess your own motivation and hygiene tendencies as well as those of people with whom you work, we present the Motivation-Hygiene Inventory.

The Motivation-Hygiene Inventory is arranged, taken, and scored much like the Assumptions Inventory which appeared in an earlier chapter. Use the

---

high often re-enter the labor force after their children are beyond early childhood, and many of these appear to be motivated by a wish for self expression apart from economic consideration. But the need for self expression which these women say they feel appears to be occasioned more by the boredom of finding themselves with an empty nest rather than by strong identification with the world of work."

Richard L. Simpson and Ida Harper Simpson, "Women and Bureaucracy in the Semi-Professions," in Amitai Etzioni (ed.), *The Semi-Professionals and Their Organization* (New York: Free Press, 1969), pp. 217, 218.

instrument first to assess yourself and then to assess the tendencies of someone with whom you work. Read each set of paired statements and distribute
10 points between each statement (a and b) to reflect the extent to which
each of the statements seems true. If statement a is always true and b never
true, award 10 points to a and none to b. If both statements are equally true,
award each 5 points. You may use any distribution you wish (9-1, 8-2, 4-6,
3-7, and so on), providing that the sum of your distribution equals 10.

The inventory is scored by summing the values which appear in the odd-
numbered blanks to the right of each statement. Scores can range from 0 to
100; higher scores suggest a motivation orientation, and lower scores indicate
a hygiene orientation. Scores ranging from 60 to 80 probably reflect a realistic
balance of interest between motivational factors and hygienic factors with an
emphasis on motivation.[11]

Motivation-Hygiene Inventory

1. a. Emphasizes the nature of tasks, the job itself.   1. _____
   b. Emphasizes the nature of environment, working   2. _____
      conditions associated with the job itself.   10

2. a. Shows primary commitment to the goals of the
      school and the teaching profession and works to
      pursue these goals.   3. _____
   b. Shows primary commitment to private goals or
      extra-school goals and works for rewards from
      the school which will help him to pursue or pur-   4. _____
      chase these goals.   10

3. a. Shows higher tolerance for poor hygienic factors
      in the work environment.   5. _____
   b. Shows intermittent but chronic dissatisfaction
      with aspects of the work environment such as
      salary, supervision, working conditions, sta-
      tus, security, administrative policy, and fellow   6. _____
      workers.   10

4. a. Shows less reaction to improvement of hygienic
      factors.   7. _____
   b. Tends to overreact in satisfaction to hygienic   8. _____
      factors.   10

[11] Scores are apt to be higher on inventories of this type, particularly when used
for self-report purposes, because people have a tendency to respond in socially acceptable
ways. Scores may need to be corrected by subtracting anywhere from 5 to 20 points, depending upon the extent to which one tends to overrespond.

Items which comprise the Motivation-Hygiene Inventory are adapted from Herzberg, *Work and the Nature of Man,* p. 90; and from Sergiovanni and Carver, *The New
School Executive,* Ch. 7.

5. a. Shows milder discontent when hygienic factors
need improvement.   9. _____
   b. Tends to overreact with dissatisfaction when   10. _____
hygienic factors are not improved.   10

6. a. Realizes great satisfaction from accomplish-
ments.   11. _____
   b. Realizes little satisfaction from accomplish-   12. _____
ments.   10

7. a. Genuinely enjoys the kind of work he does.   13. _____
   b. Shows little interest in the kind of and quality of 14. _____
work he does.   10

8. a. Profits personally and professionally from experience.   15. _____
   b. Does not profit personally and professional from 16. _____
experience.   10

9. a. Has positive feelings toward work and life.   17. _____
   b. Seems generally cynical toward work and life.   18. _____
                                                          10

10. a. Has a system of values and beliefs that seems
sincere.   19. _____
    b. Seems prone to cultural noises in the school and
takes positions which are fashionable or which   20. _____
superficially espouse management's philosophy.   10

11

Staff Development: An Alternative to In-Service Education

THE TRADITIONAL APPROACH to staff improvement in schools is through that well-known mechanism called in-service education. Administrators seem well aware of the importance of in-service education, as are school boards and officers of state governments. The net results of this awareness are state-mandated institute days and an assortment of workshops and activities endorsed by school boards and articulated by well-meaning local school administrators and supervisors.

It is also well known that present in-service education practices are not considered very effective and have not been met with enthusiasm by teachers.[1]

---

[1] Ben Harris and Wailand Bessent, *In-Service Education: A Guide to Better Practice* (Englewood Cliffs, N.J.: Prentice-Hall, 1969), pp. 1–10. Henry J. Hermanowicz, "The Pluralistic World of Beginning Teachers," in *The World of Beginning Teachers* (Washington, D.C.: National Commission on Teacher Education and Professional Standards, National Education Association, 1966), pp. 16–25.

Some of the reasons for such negative reactions are that in-service education programs are often (1) too formal and bureaucratic, (2) viewed as administrative responsibilities and teacher duties, and (3) too centralized with a high degree of dysfunctional administrataive planning and scheduling.

The effect of highly centralized formal programs that reflect a high degree of administrative responsibility for planning, scheduling, and implementation is that the emphasis shifts from education to program. Often, a successful program is one that meets legal requirements and is executed smoothly, efficiently, and according to schedule. Further, typical in-service education programs are often characterized by activities that are selected and programs that are developed without serious consideration of the purposes of such activities and programs, and without serious consideration of the needs of teachers. We are not proposing that typical in-service education programs be abandoned; they have their place, as limited as it may be. We are proposing, however, that they be drastically curtailed and that they be replaced by staff development approaches, programs, and activities.

What is the difference between staff development and in-service education? Staff development is *not* something the school does to the teacher, rather it is something the teacher does for himself. While staff development is growth oriented, in-service education assumes a deficiency in the teacher and presupposes a set of appropriate ideas, skills, and methods which need developing. By focusing on these ideas, skills, and methods, in-service education works to reduce the teacher's range of alternatives—indeed, to bring about conformity. Staff development does not assume a deficiency in the teacher, but rather assumes a need for people at work to grow and develop on the job. Rather than reducing the range of alternatives, staff development works to increase this range.

We have observed that teacher growth over the years is less a function of polishing existing teaching skills or of keeping up with the latest teaching developments (these are the foci of typical in-service education programs), and more a function of a teacher's changing as a person—of seeing himself, the school, the curriculum, and students differently. It is this sort of change that is the essence of staff development.

Our approach to staff development in elementary schools is twofold. On the one hand, we advocate an informal and continuous approach based on developing a climate for growth and on enriching the teaching job. On the other hand, we refer to more specific and deliberate attempts by the principal to initiate and facilitate staff development programs. The two go hand in hand, for staff development is not something that can be turned on and off to meet the whims of a planned program; and informal, less explicit staff development approaches are often shaped up, legitimized, and shared through formal programs.

A Climate for Growth

Individual growth of teachers is related to the nature and quality of organizational life permitted in the school. The leadership style of the principal, the distribution of power and authority, organizational structure and procedures, the general level of spirit and support which exists among teachers, and the degree of commitment and motivation to work can be serious impediments or powerful facilitators of staff growth and development.

We have referred to these dimensions in previous chapters. We concluded that an optimal climate for growth in a school is one characterized by high flexibility in people and organization, the sharing of ideas and information, acceptance, encouragement and mutual support, clear goals and a sense of mission, a reasonable amount of individual autonomy, freedom from undue interference, and a sense of cohesiveness and morale. We also noted that if teachers feel unsafe, mistrust each other, find the school organization rigid, feel a lack of educational leadership from the principal, have no sense of direction, find few opportunities for communicating with each other, feel powerless and overburdened by trivial organizational and administrative demands, they are likely to retreat to the safety of their classrooms, hiding from others and from themselves, or manifest open hostility toward change.[2] It is worth mentioning these climate factors again for the most ambitious and logically conceived staff development program has little chance for success in a school with a climate that discourages growth and rewards the status quo.

STAFF DEVELOPMENT THROUGH JOB ENRICHMENT

One important condition related to the overall climate of the school is the extent to which the job itself provides opportunities for growth and development over and above formal staff development programs. The more growth opportunities that exist in the job itself, the richer the job. As we attempt to build growth opportunities into jobs, we are engaged in job enrichment.

The concept of job enrichment for adults varies little from that of enrichment for students in elementary school classrooms. Job enrichment is linked conceptually to the motivation-hygiene theory described in Chapter 10 and is one strategy for implementing this important theory. Enriching the job is a way to motivate people not only to work harder and enjoy it, but to grow and develop personally and professionally.

[2] See, for example: Matthew Miles, "Planned Change and Organizational Health: Figure and Ground," in *Change Processes in the Public School* (Eugene: University of Oregon, Center for the Advanced Study of Educational Administration, 1965), pp. 11–34; and Andrew Halpin and Don Croft, *The Organizational Climate of Schools* (Chicago: University of Chicago, Midwest Administration Center, 1963).

motivational?
needs?

For job enrichment in education to be successful, one needs to develop ways that will better allow teachers to pursue motivational needs at work. That is, how can teaching jobs be rearranged and redeveloped so that teachers will have more opportunities to obtain responsibility, achievement, recognition, and personal and professional growth? What can principals and supervisors do to help people meet their motivational needs? Throughout this book, we have suggested ways in which schools and classrooms might be organized in order to enhance the motivational factors. Further, we have attempted to describe a pattern of behavior and a management philosophy which support and encourage the motivational factors. Moreover, since these conditions are equally important to elementary school children, teacher behavior and classroom life need in turn to enhance the motivational factors for children.

Principals, supervisors, and advisers support and encourage the motivational factors by *delegating responsibility* and providing people with freedom to act in an atmosphere of approval; by providing *access to information* and making available whatever information teachers need for successful achievement; by subscribing to *free and informal choice* which permits teachers to act on their own initiative without interference and close supervision, providing that choices made are informed rather than arbitrary; by developing and maintaining an *atmosphere of support and approval* based on confidence and trust in the integrity of teachers; by *involving* teachers as individuals with much to contribute in *identifying and selecting goals, planning,* and *problem solving;* by providing mechanisms to obtain *feedback* about the effectiveness of goal setting, planning, and performance; and by arranging the work of the school so that teachers' talents are *fully utilized,* and their desires and *capacities for growth* are fulfilled. These motivation techniques are not prescriptions which should be uniformly applied to everyone, but goals that administrators and supervisors hold for all and opportunities that are made available with different rates of intensity depending upon the readiness and capability of individuals to respond.

One indication of the amount of enrichment potential that exists in teaching jobs is the amount of influence teachers and students have on what happens in their classrooms.[3] When we speak of teacher and student influence, we refer to the extent to which teachers and students are free to set their own goals and to make educational program, curriculum, scheduling, and other decisions that will help to achieve those goals. Classrooms characterized by high teacher-and-student influence represent a model job enrichment environment. This is the setting that permits teachers and students to enjoy maximum exposure to delegated responsibility; access to information; free and informal choice; an atmosphere of support and approval; involvement in goal setting, planning, and problem solving; feedback; and full utilization of tal-

---

[3] See, for example, our discussion of the Teacher-Student Influence Grid which appears in Chapter 5.

ents. The presence of these motivational factors builds identification and commitment and increases performance of teachers and students. Staff development is built into jobs that are enriched because of the generous presence of the motivational factors. In order to satisfy their motivational needs, teachers learn and grow daily as they function in this setting.

The opposite extreme is represented in settings where most decisions are made outside of the classroom, and teachers find themselves in the degrading role of direction-giver and monitor of a highly structured and rigid educational program. Students, in turn, merely follow directions. The success of such a program does not require that teachers stretch and grow continuously as persons and professionals. Job enrichment possibilities here are negligible for both teacher and student.

Staff Development Programs

Staff development programs are designed to help teachers to increase their capacity for knowing more about their work and to be able to use this know-how so that they can perform without direct supervision. Staff development objectives are usually of four kinds: presenting information of one kind or another; helping teachers understand this information; helping teachers apply this understanding in their teaching; and helping teachers to accept and be committed to these new approaches. The four kinds of objectives are called knowledge, comprehension, application, and value and attitude integration. Introducing teachers to cuisenaire rods suggests knowledge-level objectives. Understanding cuisenaire mathematics and how it is similar to but different from traditional mathematics suggests comprehensive-level objectives. Using cuisenaire rods and cuisenaire mathematics principles effectively in teaching suggests application-level objectives. Becoming committed to cuisenaire mathematics materials as one useful approach to elementary school teaching suggests value-and-attitude-integration objectives.

A sound staff development program is based on the assumption that we can expect teachers to exhibit know-how in relation to their work, to demonstate this know-how, to perform without excessive supervision, and to continue to grow personally and professionally. At the same time, the school has an obligation to provide opportunities for teachers to increase these capabilities. No one approach or set of objectives can adequately help teachers improve in all four dimensions. Therefore, a sound staff development program will give attention to all four types of objectives.

Good teachers vary their methods depending upon what they hope to accomplish. Staff development programs, too, need to be designed in relation to at least a general sense of purpose and, when appropriate, rather specific objectives. We identify and describe three general approaches to staff development, each appropriate or not depending upon the general class of objectives to be obtained. The three approaches are traditional, laboratory, and informal. Each of the approaches is related to general staff development objectives in Figure 11-1.

Staff development objectives are shown at the top of the figure with approaches to staff development at the left. Traditional approaches seem best suited for knowledge and comprehension-type objectives. Laboratory approaches seem best suited for application objectives and for some comprehensive and value-and-attitude-integration objectives. Informal approaches have very high potential for being able to serve all four kinds of objectives, though they are more suitable for application and value and attitude integration and less suited for knowledge-type objectives. Informal approaches, because of their potency in serving value-and-attitude-integration objectives, seem particularly suitable for developing the will-grow dimension of teacher effectiveness as well as the will-do and can-do dimensions.

Traditional approaches are generally more structured and are designed to meet rather specific objectives. Informal approaches are very low in structure and rely on discovery and exploration techniques. Often objectives are not predetermined, but are assessed after the fact. Laboratory approaches are moderately structured with predetermined directions which permit a reasonable amount of flexibility. A similar relationship exists for participation and involvement of teachers with traditional approaches, providing minimal, informal maximum, and laboratory intermediate participation and involvement. The more structured the program and the more it emphasizes knowledge-type

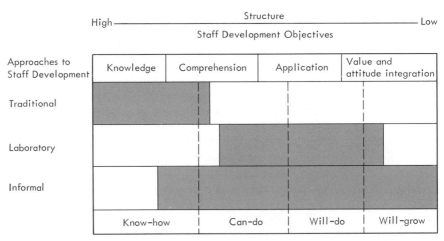

FIGURE 11-1.   Approaches to staff development.

objections, the more it resembles our traditional conception of in-service education.

TRADITIONAL APPROACHES

Traditional approaches to staff development are well known to teachers and administrators and need little elaboration. They seem best suited when a staff development problem can be defined as a deficit in knowledge of some kind. Usually, traditional approaches are accompanied by rather clear objectives and rely on conventional, though well-executed, instruction. Teachers generally assume passive roles and are exposed to logically structured programs or activities. Techniques most often used are lecture, illustrated lecture, demonstration, and observation often followed by guided discussion activities.

Traditional approaches seem well suited for routine information updating of latest books, techniques, principles, and ideas relating to one's work. It is not assumed that a particular group is considering adopting something new, but is only learning more about it. As objectives change from learning to understanding, to applying, to integrating into one's repertoire of behavior, approaches will need to change if staff development is to be effective. If one judges objectives of staff development programs in elementary schools today by approaches commonly used, then one must conclude that elementary school professionals have an insatiable appetite for knowledge, but are not interested in doing very much with this knowledge.

THE LABORATORY APPROACH

The laboratory approach is implicitly and explicitly demonstrated as an important aspect of this book. The approach is explicitly illustrated in the form of the Teacher-Student Influence Grid, the Assumptions about Learning and Knowledge Inventory, the Assumptions Inventory, the Leadership Style and Role Expectation Exercises, and the Motivation-Hygiene Inventory which appeared in earlier chapters. Implicitly it is hoped that college classes and elementary school faculties will work through the book testing its assumptions, values, ideas, and suggestions against their own and those of others with whom they work.

The laboratory approach usually has the following characteristics:

1. The participant is actively involved in contributing data, solving a problem, or conducting an analysis.
2. The activity generally requires study of an actual situation, a real problem, or uses live data, either self-volunteered or from observation of others.

3. Quantifiable data are produced, or impressions are systematically catalogued to reveal the nature of responses of participants.

4. Feedback is provided to permit each participant to compare his reaction with those of others.

5. Data or impressions are discussed and analyzed to develop generalizations and implications for practice.[4]

The involvement of participants in laboratory approaches to staff development is high, though activities are somewhat structured. Generally, outcomes are not clearly identifiable or specifically stated, but participants and leaders have a sense of direction and are working toward general goals. Laboratory approaches are particularly suitable for achieving comprehension, applications, and some value-and-attitude-integration objectives.

INFORMAL APPROACHES

Perhaps the most innovative and provocative approaches to staff development are those which rely on exploration and discovery by teachers. It is assumed that by providing elementary school teachers with a rich environment loaded with teaching materials, media, books, and devices and with lots of encouragement and support from principals and supervisors as well as each other, teachers will interact with this environment and with each other through exploration and discovery. For many, exploration and discovery help teachers to find themselves, to unleash their creativity, to learn more about their own capabilities as people and teachers at the same time as they pick up new teaching ideas, activities, and methods.[5] Furthermore, they have an opportunity to experience the same feelings that children do when similarly exposed to an enriched learning environment.

In distinguishing the most useful approaches to staff development from the least useful, Thelen notes that in the most useful "one finds intensity of personal involvement, immediate consequences for classroom practice, stimulation and ego support by meaningful associates in the situation and initiating by teacher rather than outsider." [6] Informal approaches seem best able to meet these criteria.

Consider, for example, approaches that an outside consultant or inside expert might take in helping teachers use arts and crafts as a more manifest part of teaching language arts, science, and social studies. One approach might be for the expert to give a talk to the teacher on using arts and crafts. This

---

[4] Adapted from Harris and Bessent, *In-Service Education*, p. 45. These authors present a number of detailed activities that illustrate one form of the laboratory method.

[5] See, for example: Stephen K. Bailey, "Teacher's Centers: A British First," *Phi Delta Kappan*, Vol. 53, No. 3 (1971), 146–149. Allan Muskopf and Joy Moss, "An Integrated Day Workshop," *The Elementary School Journal*, Vol. 71, No. 6 (1971), 314–320.

[6] Herbert Thelen, "A Cultural Approach to In-Service Education," in Louis Rubin (ed.), *Improving In-Service Education* (Boston: Allyn and Bacon, 1971), pp. 72–73.

is a traditional approach aimed at the knowledge level. A second approach might be to demonstrate how to make a wigwam with ice-cream sticks and tree bark as part of the expert's talk. A third approach might be to provide groups of teachers with tree bark and ice-cream sticks and talk them through as they construct wigwams as part of the expert's talk. A fourth approach might be to group teachers around tables and provide them with an assortment of materials (cork, clay, sticks, bark, thread spools, string, packing foam, TV dinner trays, egg cartons, coat hangers, paper, wire, and so on). Instead of talking to them, they might be asked to spend the next two hours constructing as many things as they can which could be used to teach a concept or idea in language arts, science, or social studies. For each teacher invention, the group might list as many possible uses as they can. A record could be kept on index cards of what was made, how it was made, and of its possible uses in teaching and learning. This is an informal approach aimed not only at the knowledge level, but at the application and attitudinal-change levels. This last approach has far more potential for helping teachers to be more effective in using arts and crafts in their teaching than methods that require relatively passive teacher involvement.

Joseph Hassett and Arline Weisberg provide an example of the informal staff development approach based on the concept of teachers' exploring "turn-on" agents. The description includes suggestions for using turn-on agents in the classroom.

> A fourth-grade teacher has arranged her room so that she has space for three interest areas. After observing her children, she has decided upon model cars, sand, and fabrics as possible turn-on agents. Her second task is to investigate these materials herself and to brainstorm all the learning experiences she can imagine. This process of brainstorming is one of the most valuable tools in the use of this method. As you work with a material such as sand, let your mind associate freely with all the possibilities involving sand. No matter how farfetched or ridiculous some of them may sound, make note of all the possibilities. Then group your possibilities into areas of exploration; some will be discarded as improbable, some as too sophisticated for the grade level, while others will lend themselves to grouping or clusters. These groupings or clusters are leads to the kinds of questions you will ask, the kinds of suggestions you will make, and the kinds of supplementary materials you will select. Practice brainstorming. It is a valuable activity for any kind of teaching.
>
> This brainstorming and elimination process enables the teacher to anticipate the problems, to prepare other materials to group with the turn-on agent, and to prepare questions and activity cards to guide those children who need a great deal of direction. This final chart, which we call a flow chart, is only a guide, not a rigid plan. Some of the flow areas will be discarded as uninteresting or unsuitable to the age level of the children. Some children may go off in a totally unanticipated direction, and the teacher will have to expand her thinking to include their needs. The flow chart also enables the teacher to provide for books, an integral part of each interest area.[7]

[7] Joseph D. Hassett and Arline Weisberg, *Open Education Alternatives Within Our Tradition* (Englewood Cliffs, N.J.: Prentice-Hall, 1972), p. 34.

An example of a flowchart based on match-box cars as a turn-on agent appears in Figure 11-2.

In this example, a teacher has worked alone in exploring model cars as a possible turn-on agent. This exploration continues as the teacher observes

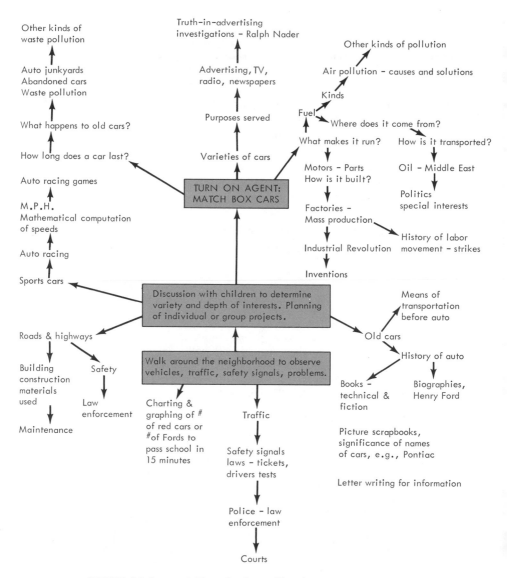

FIGURE 11-2.   A Turn-On Agent Flowchart.

From Joseph P. Hassett and Arline Weisberg, *Open Education Alternatives Within Our Tradition* (Englewood Cliffs, N.J.: Prentice-Hall, 1972), p. 36.

and records student reactions. An anticipated turn-on chart is developed and then revised in terms of student reactions. The development of anticipated turn-on charts by groups of teachers involved in manipulating materials and in sharing ideas about these materials will probably result in more learning for teachers and better teaching for students than if teachers "turn on" alone. This is an excellent way to develop curriculum materials and guides as well as building confidence and understanding.

Another example of informal staff development approaches is teachers' going on school or neighborhood treasure hunts. The object is to discover as many useful materials as one can and to brainstorm as many ways as possible for using these materials in teaching. Nature hunts, rock hunts, junkyard visits, and the like, can be similarly conducted. The use of interest areas, cuisenaire mathematics, cardboard carpentry, live animals, outside work areas, arts and crafts, slide rules, student research projects, drama, independent study, and so forth, seems more likely to occur as teachers not only know about but understand such resources through direct exploratory and discovery experience.

Staff Development Is a Responsibility of Teachers

The approach to staff development one uses depends upon its suitability in achieving staff development purposes. Faculties will need to analyze their position in relation to knowing about, understanding, using, and being committed to certain ideas, activities, programs, and trends presently effecting elementary education in the United States.

One reason for widespread dissatisfaction with typical in-service education programs is that they are viewed as formal administrative and supervisory responsibilities. In a sense they are, but successful programs seem dependent upon teachers' sharing more significantly in this responsibility. The direction, scope, nature, content, and timing of staff development programs are responsibilities best assumed by teachers. Administrative and supervisory responsibilities are qualitative and process ones that, in addition to providing psychological and material encouragement and support, focus on generating valid and useful information about school and classroom problems, providing for free and informed teacher choice, and building identification and commitment to the concept of staff development as well as to the content and substance of staff development programs.

12

More than School-Community Relations

PATTERNS OF SCHOOL-COMMUNITY relations often take the form of a planned public relations program. This approach views participation of the community in school affairs as a privilege rather than a right and is geared to providing a best-foot-forward image through a program of controlled information. "The natural intent of PR is to control the communication in such a way that the best is emphasized. It is also a natural part of PR for encouraging participation of the client, but in ways acceptable to the school." [1]

Acceptable ways typically include a PTA where parents assume at best superficial roles in relation to the school. Open house, education week, teacher days, Christmas programs, and other events are examples of controlled information and guided participation by which the school carefully plans and presents its Sunday face to the public. "Under a successful school PR pro-

---

[1] Mario Fantini, "Community Participation: Many Faces, Many Directions," *Educational Leadership,* Vol. 29, No. 8 (1972), 677.

gram, the parent is made to *feel* that the school has things under control, that the parent can *feel* confident that the child is in good hands. If parents and other community residents feel confident, there is usually little reason for any other kind of participation." [2] Increasingly, the PR approach is becoming a less viable approach to school-community relations for two reasons. In the first place, PR is not working very well. People are less apt to buy what the school neatly packages and sells. Educational equivalents to Ralph Nader have made the public increasingly suspicious of the often glib PR approach. In the second place, the PR approach denies parents the right to become full partners in the schools—a condition of increasing importance for educational effectiveness. True, some communities are still willing to settle for participation on the school's terms, but this number is decreasing.

In this chapter, we advocate partnership rather than participation. This position can be justified on a number of social, philosophical, and ethical grounds, but the fact is that partnership results in better education for children as well as in increased community development. Partnership is simply more effective than participation.

We begin with an examination of the extended elementary school concept, a natural way to build partnership for school and community. A mother-centered, as opposed to a school-centered or child-centered, approach to early childhood education is proposed as an integral part of the extended elementary school. We conclude the chapter with an examination of three approaches to community participation—all of which suggest new roles and functions for the elementary school and its principal.

The Extended Elementary School

Elementary education has traditionally (albeit, arbitrarily), been considered as including three separate phases: preprimary or below first grade; primary or grades 1, 2, and 3; and upper elementary or intermediate which includes grades 4, 5, and 6. The introduction of middle schools which encompass grades 6, 7, and 8 causes some variation, but such schools are not common. "Early childhood education" is often used to describe programs below grade 1, and "elementary education" to encompass grades 1 through 6.

EARLY CHILDHOOD EDUCATION

Two recent reports on early childhood education are examples of indications that there is a widespread need for the extension of early childhood

---

[2] Fantini, "Community Participation," p. 677, italics ours. Fantini is describing, not advocating, PR in this statement.

education well beyond the kindergarten programs offered by many schools.[3] For example, McLure speaks of parent education for mothers beginning with the birth and perhaps even the conception of their infants; research and experimental programs to study the development of children; nursery school programs for children of ages 3 and 4; day-care programs for children of working mothers; and special education programs for those with exceptional difficulties.[4]

The often-quoted work of Benjamin Bloom provides a convincing argument for extending the responsibility, influence, and concern of the elementary school. He notes that over one-half of one's intellectual development at age 17 takes place before one enters kindergarten.[5] Further, large numbers of mentally retarded youngsters can be attributed to maternal malnutrition during pregnancy. Still other children, because of limited language development or limited language ability in standard English, often appear dull to teachers and are classified as slow learners or mentally retarded.

> The first racial analysis of California's 65,000 mentally retarded school children disclosed in January (1970) found that 2.14 percent of all the Spanish-surnamed children and an even higher proportion—3.6 percent—of all the Negro children have been funneled into classes for the noneducable so classified. . . . Over half of those Spanish-surnamed and Negro children in mentally-retarded classrooms in California probably have the ability to be in regular classrooms but have been mis-classified.[6]

The condition of a person's life from the moment of conception to his formal appearance in the school contributes very heavily to his ability and readiness to function adequately as a student. Presently, schools are expending enormous resources in providing remedial help to youngsters who seem to have learning problems. Special reading teachers, slow-learning teachers, measurement specialists, expensive machinery and curriculum packages, very low student-teacher ratios, school psychologists, social workers, speech specialists, special rooms, and so on, demand a large share of the resources of the schools. These resources are misdirected, not in the sense that a strategy of remedial education should stop, but in the sense that the condition is self-perpetuating unless remedial programs are combined with a strategy of preventive education.

[3] William P. McLure and Audra May Pence, *Early Childhood and Basic Elementary and Secondary Education Needs, Programs, Demands, Costs* (Urbana: University of Illinois, National Educational Finance Project, Special Report No. 1, Bureau of Educational Research, 1970); and *Early Childhood Development Alternatives for Program Implementation in the States*. A report of the Education Commission of the States, Denver, June 1971.

[4] McLure and Pence, *Early Childhood . . .* , p. 11.

[5] Benjamin S. Bloom, *Stability and Change in Human Characteristics* (New York: John Wiley and Sons, 1964), p. 64.

[6] *Early Childhood Development Alternatives for Program Implementation in the States*, p. 78. See also Rodger Hurley, *Poverty and Mental Retardation: A Casual Relationship* (New York: Random House, 1969).

A preventive education strategy is one that works to enrich a child's life from conception through infancy and early childhood. Preventive education includes psychological and intellectual enrichment as well as nutrition and health services. Providing a mother of a one-month-old child with a mobile to place over her child's crib seems like such a small thing, as does the introduction of blocks, records, and other materials in the home. Yet these often contribute significantly in preparing a child to learn to read. It makes little sense to spend large sums of money on expensive remedial equipment and specialized personnel while ignoring the major sources of remedial learning problems. We estimate that three out of four learning problems which exist among rural and urban youngsters—particularly the racial and ethnic minorities and the poor—could be prevented by enriching the children's preschool environment beginning with conception. A 25- to 50-percent reduction in learning problems probably can be expected in the predominantly white, more affluent small towns and suburbs as a result of enriching the preschool environment. Most experts concerned with childhood education do not recommend that schools develop formal classroom programs for children under age 3 or 4, but do propose that schools develop links with the home and provide services to the family so that parents are better able to assume responsibilities for the physical and psychological health as well as the informal education of their children.

We have no illusions about the feasibility and practicality of the elementary school principal's single-handedly developing and launching a preventive education program by extending downward the influence of the elementary school on a massive basis. Much can be done, however, to hammer these themes home to central office administrators, school boards, and influential members of the community. Further, with some ingenuity and lots of hard work and concern, most elementary schools can work effectively in preventive education on an informal basis. Indeed, many of the newer patterns of organization which utilize families of youngsters and teams of teachers break the traditional one-teacher-to-25-or-30-youngsters sort of accountability. These new patterns often permit one or two teachers to devote more time in preventive activities in the community. Specialists such as reading teachers; nurses; grade level supervisors; music, home economics, and arts and crafts teachers; librarians; and others must also avoid restricting themselves to only in-school matters, for their unique skills are often most useful in enriching the lives of preschool children.

WHAT THE SCHOOL CAN DO

The elementary school can only do so much in implementing the extended school concept without official support from the school bureaucracy, governmental agencies, and the like, and without substantial financial assistance. True, principals need to lobby long and hard for this support and assistance. In the meantime, administrators, supervisors, faculty, and interested parents need to stretch their imaginations and resources to find ways to extend the influence of the school to the home. One place to start is with parents of children already in the school. By engaging these parents as respected partners with something of value to contribute to the school, one establishes a manifest link into other components of the community.

The following represents a small list of ideas which are inexpensive, require little or no approval from the central school bureaucracy, and if properly developed can eventually be operated almost exclusively by parents. These ideas are meant only to help a faculty or class get started. As a school gets started in discussing or implementing any one of them, a number of alternate approaches and ideas will emerge, but getting started is the toughest task. These ideas require only three ingredients for success—resourcefulness, commitment, and just a touch of good luck.

1. *A walk-home program.* Walking youngsters home occasionally provides teachers and administrators with an opportunity to be seen in the neighborhood and to meet parents on their own ground.

2. *A walk-to-school program.* Encouraging parents to walk children to school can be helpful particularly if parents are met outside by teachers and administrators and are welcomed to the school. Youngsters should then be encouraged to invite parents into the school to see what they are doing. A variation for "drive in" parents can be arranged.

3. *Community field trips.* Making frequent, even routine, trips to the grocery store, public service buildings, local clinic or hospital, bus depot, and other local sites often helps. Such excursions help parents to see the possibilities of using the neighborhood as a learning resource and help to break the stereotype that learning takes place only in schools. Further, formal and informal community contacts which usually accompany field trips build support for the school.

4. *A parent-helper program.* Using parents in the classroom as *full-fledged* helpers can provide enormous benefits for parent, child, teacher, school, and community. We are not speaking of the stereotyped paid paraprofessional, though a small salary could be of help to parents in financial need. The restricted duties of the stereotyped paraprofessional or teacher's aide often win her the title of classroom maid, scorn from the regular teacher, and a low self-image. This second-class status for parents in schools needs to be changed. Principals interested in developing a parent-helper program might look to the cooperative nursery school for ideas.

5. *A baby-sitting program.* A successful parent-helper program often

hinges on whether it can be combined with some provision for baby-sitting in the school. Often parents are not able to arrange for or to afford baby-sitting at home while they come to school. Further, the presence of preschoolers in the school can provide school professionals with an opportunity to demonstrate ways in which parents might work with and care for youngsters at home. A number of educational possibilities for regular school youngsters can also result from the presence of preschoolers.

6. *A toy-lending library.* The development of a toy-lending library where an assortment of toys with potential educational value are collected, catalogued, and made available to parents for use at home with infants and young children has enormous potential. Toys might include mobiles; puzzles; kits containing scissors with patches of paper and fabric; blocks; push and pull toys; wagons and trucks; doll houses; water and sand toys. Fisher-Price and Playskool toys are examples of moderately priced preschool toys available commercially. Just before Christmas is a good time to launch a drive for collecting used but usable toys with developmental value. Goodwill Industries and the Salvation Army are excellent sources of inexpensive used toys. Calling the toy manager at the department and discount stores after Christmas and periodically throughout the year often brings a windfall of new and nearly new toys of educational value.

7. *Guidance in toy use.* A toy-lending library is only as good as its program directed at parents which helps them to see examples of how toys might be used to help enrich the child's psychological and intellectual life. Parents and teachers might be available to demonstrate to a borrower possibilities which toys have for providing this enrichment. Naturally, records, books, and preschool musical instruments would also be available for borrowing. A couple of inexpensive phonographs from a garage sale or thrift shop and perhaps a surplus tape recorder could also be made available to parents for home use.

8. *Toy-construction workshops.* Phase 3 in the establishment of a toy-lending library might include toy-construction workshops where parents make puppets, flannel boards, cardboard clocks, counting devices, and the like, and discuss with other parents the ways in which these devices might be used at home.

9. *A community bulletin board.* Creating a community information exchange in some part of the school often fulfills a neighborhood need as well as drawing parents into the school. Some bulletin board space or office space could be provided for "lost and found," "for

sale," "job wanted," and other kinds of notices of importance to community members. This gets parents into the school to see the library, youngsters at work, and other features of the school which may be of help to them.

10. *Using the written word.* Begging, borrowing, or buying space in neighborhood papers (Pennysavers, block newspapers, church papers) can also be of help in communicating with the school community. Becoming acquainted with area employers and utilizing their facilities (bulletin boards, plant newspapers, memos) are other possibilities for communicating with the public. In addition to communicating school and neighborhood news and events, some helpful tips for better home and family living might be included. Try printing a weekly list of sample menus that are inexpensive, nutritious, and easy to prepare. Develop the list in cooperation with local food merchants so that the week's sale items can be included in the menus. Get nutritional advice from the high school home economics teacher.

11. *Adult education programs.* Adult education programs are often helpful not only in serving adult needs of the community but as a means of communication. In addition to vocationally oriented and hobby-oriented programs, some communities benefit most from image-boosting and self-esteem-oriented programs. "Inexpensive makeup tips," "dressing well on a budget," "home repair," "finding a job," "hair-styling ideas," and "physical fitness" are topics often of interest. It is important to remember that one's relationship with others (particularly family members) matures and improves as one's self-esteem is enhanced. If no formal staff is available for programs of this kind, look to the natural talents of the teachers in the school. Can the fourth-grade teacher be freed for two hours on Wednesdays to put on a workshop for mothers on infant care and feeding? Perhaps the kindergarten teacher can give some tips on beauty aids and self-care for a couple of hours on Monday mornings. What about that teacher with a natural green thumb? Can he be covered (by combining classes, using parent helpers, and so on) for a time once a week to offer tips on house plant care and on growing vegetables? Needs of parents in more affluent communities are, of course, different, but equally important in regard to enriching the lives of youngsters. Crisis intervention, transactional analysis, and other psychological support programs, "winning the rat race" seminars, child-rearing programs which, for example, focus on the whys and unanticipated consequences of stress and strain on children could all be helpful.

Formal Programs for Preschoolers

Informal approaches to preventive education can make a substantial difference in later school effectiveness. As these programs become successful, the likelihood of formal support and assistance will increase. But formal programs are not substitutes for informal approaches; they are only additional options in developing effective preventive education.

Head Start programs are examples of more formal attempts to help preschoolers. Head Start programs are a result of federal legislation aimed at providing early experiences to promote the development of children from low-income families. Guidelines for Head Start specify parental involvement, but since the programs are child centered and held in day-care centers, schools, and other locations away from the home, professional and paraprofessional teachers tend to dominate while parents usually assume passive roles. Only a handful of Head Start programs have been considered effective,[7] though effectiveness seems less attributed to the curriculum or teaching approach used than to whether parents were involved in helping themselves as well as their children. As Karnes states the case,

> It seems that a basic reason for the failure of preschool programming for children from low-income families resides more in the narrowness of the definition of education than in the nature of specific curricula, the care with which they are implemented, and the competencies of the professional personnel. This narrow definition prevents the involvement of parents in the instruction of the child and the reinforcement of learnings, both in the classroom and at home. It is too much to expect that experiences provided in the classroom alone can offset the detrimental effects of the total environment of the child. Thus, early education that is intended to alter substantially the attudes and abilities of the young child must encompass his entire environment. Since the most important influences on the young child are his family members, it is only logical to enlist their aid in promoting his optimal development.[8]

A MOTHER-CENTERED APPROACH

Karnes's work suggests that mother-centered programs are more effective than child-centered or school-centered programs. By "mother centered"

---

[7] See, for example, Carl Bereiter and Ziegfried Engelmann, *Teaching Disadvantaged Children in the Preschool* (Englewood Cliffs, N.J.: Prentice-Hall, 1966); Merle Karnes, "Research and Development Program on Preschool Disadvantaged Children," Vol. 1, Final Report (Urbana, Ill.: U.S. Department of Health, Education and Welfare, Office of Education, May 1969); and D. Weikart, "Longitudinal Results of the Ypsilanti Perry Preschool Project," Final Report (Ypsilanti, Mich.: U.S. Department of Health, Education and Welfare, Office of Education, August 1970).

[8] Merle Karnes, Reid Zehrbach, and James Teska, "A New Professional Role in Early Childhood Education," *Interchange*, Vol. 2, No. 2 (1971), 89.

we mean helping the mother to help the child at home. Mothers can be taught to be as effective as professionals in providing intellectual enrichment to preschool youngsters.[9] Further, mothers are better able to provide the necessary psychological support and nurturance which must accompany intellectual enrichment for very young children.

Two brief descriptions of programs developed by Karnes are provided below. Both programs are mother centered. The first program was aimed at using professional teachers to train mothers to work more effectively with their three- and four-year-old children.[10] The purpose of the first program, a pilot project that lasted only 12 weeks, was to help low-income mothers become more effective in stimulating the intellectual and linguistic development of their three- and four-year-old children. Thirty black children from a "disadvantaged" neighborhood were included in the project. The children were pretested and assigned randomly to experimental and control groups.

Mothers of the children in the experimental group participated in 12 weekly two-hour sessions conducted by experienced professional preschool teachers. Mothers were paid $1.50 for each session they attended, but received no pay for working and playing with children at home.

At the beginning of each work session, parents made educational games from inexpensive or free materials that they used during the following week with their child in the home setting. Examples of such materials were a sock puppet; lotto and matching games; counting books made from pictures obtained from magazines; counting games made from household articles; using an egg carton for sorting; classifying games made by pasting pictures of such items as clothing or furniture on cards; a homemade flannel board for use in reading stories and in teaching number concepts.

In addition to making educational games, mothers learned songs and finger plays. A lending library of books, puzzles, and toys was available where mothers could check out materials for use with their child. Teachers stressed the importance of using materials that provided language stimulation. Special emphasis was placed on helping children label objects and express themselves in complete sentences using standard English. The visual and auditory discrimination skills, good work habits, improved attention span, and listening skills essential for subsequent school learning were fostered through the planned activities.

Teachers and mothers planned meetings cooperatively. Mothers were encouraged to discuss successes and failures with the instructional materials

---

[9] Karnes found that preschool children, some taught by mothers and others by teen-aged girls (both received training and guidance from professionals), did not differ significantly from those taught exclusively by professional teachers using the same approach. The curriculum was an ambitious one which included language development, basic number concepts, vocabulary and classification skills, a kitchen science unit, and self-concept development. Karnes et al., "A New Professional Role in Early Childhood Education," p. 93.

[10] For further details, see Merle Karnes, W. Studley, W. Wright, and A. Hodgins, "An Approach for Working with Mothers of Disadvantaged Children," *Merrill-Palmer Quarterly,* Vol. 14, No. 2 (1968), 174–184.

used during the previous week. Individual differences among children were particularly noted.

The average attendance of the mothers was high; absences tended to be for valid reasons. When a mother did not attend a meeting, other mothers made materials for her. The next day the teacher took the learning activities developed during the meeting, as well as toys, books, and puzzles from the lending library, to the mother who had been absent.[11]

At the end of 12 weeks, children in the experimental group showed a six-and-one-half-months' gain in mental age as compared with only three months' gain for children in the control group. Further, children in the experimental group demonstrated significantly greater gains in psycholinguistic functioning, making an eight-months' gain in language progress in three months.

The first program suggests that mothers can be effective in helping youngsters at home as a result of training by a professional teacher. The second program we describe shows that mothers who have had training can in turn be effective in training other mothers to work and play effectively with children at home.[12]

Since children from low-income homes typically manifest developmental deficiencies by the age of four, intervention must be initiated prior to this age. Because it is difficult to teach the very young child in a classroom setting, intervention in the home is the logical approach. The mother, then, seems to be in the best position to provide the consistent and frequent training necessary to alter significantly the experiences of the child. The efforts of this project were directed toward enhancing the mother's skills in stimulating the development of her child.

To implement this program, a variety of techniques were used to involve and train mothers. Basic to the program were a series of activities structured to bring the mother into a positive learning relationship with her child. During weekly meetings mothers were instructed in the use of a sequential curriculum designed to stimulate the child's cognitive and language development using teaching strategies that emphasized positive reinforcement. In addition, a portion of each weekly meeting was devoted to mother-centered activities with goals designed to foster a sense of personal worth and dignity. One result of these meetings was that the mothers acquired and demonstrated new competences to improve their status in the community as well as in the home.

The first hour of the weekly meeting was devoted to mother-centered topics selected by the group. Child discipline, birth control, and responsibilities for voting are examples of such topics. Articles were sometimes distributed for reading prior to the discussion sessions. Field trips to a nursery school and to the public library were included in the program as were viewing of films.

[11] Karnes et al., "A New Professional Role in Early Childhood Education," p. 97.

[12] For further details, see Merle Karnes, J. Teska, A. Hodgins, and E. Badger, "Educational Intervention at Home by Mothers of Disadvantaged Children," *Child Development,* Vol. 41, No. 4 (1970), 925–935.

The second half of the weekly meeting was child-centered. Toys were one medium used to foster improved teaching strategies for stimulating intellectual and language development. The professional leader demonstrated teaching strategies for using toys, for reading books, and for helping the child complete puzzles. The leader stressed key words that the mothers were to encourage their children to use. Each mother was provided with a child's table and chair and a laundry basket to use as storage for the toys, books, and puzzles supplied by the program.[13]

Professional staff members assumed major responsibility the first year. The second year approximated the first year, except that note taking during meetings, program planning, group leadership, and home visits were shared by mothers. Further, more advanced concepts were introduced such as visual perception and discrimination and motor coordination.

The mother-centered activities during the second year predominantly focused on community involvement. Mothers interacted more during the weekly discussions. They were more responsive to speakers and expressed greater willingness to take a major role in presenting materials at the group meetings. Their interest in community involvement was reflected in increased participation in the community. For example, four mothers took the responsibility for recruiting summer Head Start children. One mother was hired as a Head Start teacher. Two of the mothers were speakers at a Head Start meeting. A number were in attendance at public meetings held to discuss developments that had implications for the poor.[14]

Children of parents in this program showed a mean IQ 16 points higher than those in a control group. Further, psycholinguistic functioning was approximately six months higher. These programs are described to show that mother-centered programs do indeed work, and parental involvement as a means to intervene into the home may be the necessary ingredient that determines success of preschool programs. We are of the opinion that the nature of the curriculum itself—whether the Karnes approach, Bereiter-Engelmann methods, or Piagetian approaches—is not nearly as important in determining success as is the degree of parental involvement. Our own inclination is toward Piagetian approaches with high parental involvement.

As the evidence supporting mother-centered approaches to preschool education accumulates, the federal government is seeking options in addition to the Head Start and Day-Care Center models.[15] One idea which is taking shape among policy developers at the federal level is called "Home Start." This idea advocates, as we do, the use of the home as a learning center. Home Start may provide a viable means of obtaining national support for promoting the extended elementry school concept.

[13] Karnes et al., "A New Professional Role in Early Childhood Education," p. 98.
[14] Karnes et al., "A New Professional Role in Early Childhood Education," p. 99.
[15] It is important that "additional options" be emphasized. The day-care concept is an important one which provides a healthy environment for youngsters of working mothers.

Approaches to Community Participation

We have defined school-community relations as something more than a system of controlled information called public relations. We have advocated a school-community partnership based on the premise of mutual need, help, and support. The elementary school has much to offer the community particularly in the preventive education area through family enrichment. Community members represent a wealth of human resources to be made available to the school. Through active parent participation in the school and its educational program, it is possible, for example, to reduce teacher-student ratios from 30 to 1 to 10 to 1, 5 to 1, or to any other desired ratio.

Sociologists, social workers, and community organization experts often speak of three approaches to community participation, change, and intervention by influential community members such as school principals. These approaches are known as *locality development, social planning,* and *social action.* Our discussions so far in this chapter have described the principal as being engaged in locality development. He is likely to find himself relying heavily on locality development because of difficulty of access to social planning and of bureaucratic norms that often deprive him of a social action role. Each of the three approaches to community participation is examined in following sections. Our position in regard to effective community participation is that principals are naturally engaged in locality development, need to work themselves into positions which provide them access to social planning, and may out of necessity "go for broke"—that is, engage in social action.

Locality development assumes that community change results from broad participation at the local community level. Features of locality development include democratic procedures, voluntary cooperation, self-help, development and reliance on indigenous leadership, and interest in educational objectives. Social planning relies less on lay community participation and more on specialized or professional cooperation and planning. Such problems as delinquency, drugs, social problems, mental health, recreation, traffic, housing, and education are considered by those with appropriate technical knowledge with the object being the development of a cooperative but professional plan for community development. Social action assumes that a disadvantaged segment of the school community is in need of organization, so that it may more adequately make demands on the larger community for increased attention, resources, and treatment.[16]

Table 12-1 compares the three approaches to community participation

[16] For details in regard to locality development see, for example: William Biddle and Loureide Biddle, *The Community Development Process: The Rediscovery of Local Initiative* (New York: Holt, Rinehart and Winston, 1965). For social planning, see: Robert Morris and Robert Binstock, *Feasible Planning for Social Change* (New York: Columbia University Press, 1966). For social action, see: Saul Alinsky, *Reveille for Radicals* (Chicago: University of Chicago Press, 1964).

open to principals on the basis of a number of dimensions including goals, assumptions, change strategies, roles, and power relationships.

LOCALITY DEVELOPMENT

Locality development is the approach typically used by principals and supervisors as they engage in community participation. Locality development relies heavily on self-help strategies and works to tap and develop the human resources of the community. It is assumed that with some guidance, help, and direction, the community will be able to help itself. Change processes rely on broad participation of all school-community members. The principal's role is that of a facilitator, encourager, and catalyst to help the community get started. Locality development assumes that as community capabilities in-

TABLE 12-1. Three Models of Community Organization Practice According to Selected Practice Variables.

	Model A (Locality Development)	Model B (Social Planning)	Model C (Social Action)
1. Goal categories of community action	Self-help; community capacity and integration (process goals)	Problem-solving with regard to substantive community problems (task goals)	Shifting of power relationships and resources; basic institutional change (task or process goals)
2. Assumptions concerning community structure and problem conditions	Community eclipsed, anomie; lack of relationships and democratic problem-solving capacities: static traditional community	Substantive social problems: mental and physical health, housing, recreation	Disadvantaged populations, social injustice, deprivation, inequity
3. Basic change strategy	Broad cross section of people involved in determining and solving their own problems	Fact-gathering about problems and decisions on the most rational course of action	Crystallization of issues and organization of people to take action against enemy targets
4. Characteristic change tactics and techniques	Consensus: communication among community groups and interests; group discussion	Consensus or conflict	Conflict or contest: confrontation, direct action, negotiation

TABLE 12-1. Three Models of Community Organization Practice According to Selected Practice Variables. **(cont.)**

	Model A (Locality Development)	Model B (Social Planning)	Model C (Social Action)
5. Salient practitioner roles	Enabler-catalyst, coordinator; teacher of problem-solving skills and ethical values	Fact-gathering and analyst, program implementer, facilitator	Activist-advocate: agitator, broker, negotiator, partisan
6. Medium of change	Manipulation of small task-oriented groups	Manipulation of formal organizations and of data	Manipulation of mass organizations and political processes
7. Orientation toward power structure(s)	Members of power structure as collaborators in a common venture	Power structure as employers and sponsors	Power structure as external target of action: oppressors to be coerced or overturned
8. Boundary definition of the community client system or constituency	Total geographic community	Total community or community segment (including "functional" community)	Community segment
9. Assumptions regarding interests of community subparts	Common interests or reconcilable differences	Interests reconcilable or in conflict	Conflicting interests which are not easily reconcilable: scarce resources
10. Conception of the public interest	Rationalist-unitary	Idealist-unitary	Realist-individualist
11. Conception of the client population or constituency	Citizens	Consumers	Victims
12. Conception of client role	Participants in interactional problem-solving process	Consumers or recipients	Employers, constituents, members
13. Agency type	Settlement houses, overseas community development: Peace Corps, Friends Service Committee	Welfare council, city planning board, federal bureaucracy	Alinsky, civil rights, black power, New Left, welfare rights, cause and social movement groups, trade unions

TABLE 12-1. Three Models of Community Organization Practice According to Selected Practice Variables. **(cont.)**

	Model A (Locality Development)	Model B (Social Planning)	Model C (Social Action)
14. Practice positions	Village worker, neighborhood worker, consultant to community development team, agricultural extension worker	Planning division head, planner	Local organizer
15. Professional analogues	Adult educator, nonclinical group worker, group dynamics professional, agricultural extension worker	Demographer, social survey specialist, public administrator, hospital planning specialist	Labor organizer, civil rights worker, welfare rights organizer

From Jack Rothman, "Three Models of Community Organization Practice," National Conference on Social Welfare, *Social Work Practice 1968*. New York: Columbia University Press, 1968, copyright 1968, National Conference on Social Welfare.

crease, parents will assume more of the responsibility for developing and implementing school-community programs.

SOCIAL PLANNING

Social planning assumes that problems faced by the community require the technical resources of highly skilled professionals to develop strategies for solution. True, the strategies may be implemented through locality development, but broad strategies are developed or general solutions are proposed by professionals. Those involved in social planning usually include politicians in municipal government; civil servants in housing, zoning, sanitation, traffic, and other governmental offices; park and recreation officials; the courts; law enforcement agencies; social welfare departments; urban planning groups; and health officials. Other groups often included in social planning are private volunteer agencies (boys' clubs, YMCA) and local business groups such as the Chamber of Commerce.

Educators have not been influential enough in cracking this social planning group though their input can help considerably in helping social planners to be more effective in community development. Further, it is becoming increasingly obvious that an effective K-6 elementary school program depends heavily upon an effective preventive education program for preschoolers as well as regular school-community interaction and support. These in turn are dependent upon support and cooperation from those normally involved in community social planning.

SOCIAL ACTION

Principals normally are not directly involved in social action forms of community participation, though informally they may lend support and encouragement to other individuals and groups so involved. If principals find the social planning avenue closed to them and the problems they face hopelessly unsolvable through locality development, then social action may be the only option left. The risks are high, for although social action can be a useful way to improve community conditions, public and semipublic officials such as teachers, principals, assemblymen, and religious leaders rarely survive the controversy that usually accompanies this approach. With the consequences fully in mind, and if conditions warrant such action, this may be the route principals should take to bring about change.

Social action assumes a group of have-nots who are being deprived of power and attention from a group of haves. Goals of social action include the shifting of power, resources, and loci of decision making from the haves (usually the larger community) to the have-nots (usually a specific school community).

> The community is conceived of as being composed of a hierarchy of privilege and power, with the existence of clusters of deprived populations suffering from disadvantage or social injustice. The basic change strategy involves crystallizing issues and organizing indigenous populations to take action on their own behalf against enemy targets. Change tactics often include conflict techniques, such as confrontation and direct action—rallies, marches, boycotts (as well as "hard-nosed" bargaining). The practitioner functions in the role of activist, agitator, broker, negotiator, and partisan. He is skilled in the manipulation of mass organizations and political processes. Power structures are viewed as an external target of action—oppressors or exploiters who need to be limited or removed. The client group or constituency is a given community segment at disadvantage (blacks, the poor, workers). It is assumed that interests among related parties are at conflict or not easily reconcilable since those who possess power, resources, and prestige are reluctant to relinquish or share them. The conception of the public interest is realist-individualist. Clients are viewed as victims of various forces and interests in the society, and their role is that of employer or constituents with regard to the practitioner, as well as participants in mass action and pressure group activities.[17]

[17] Jack Rothman, "Three Models of Community Organization Practice," The National Conference on Social Welfare, *Social Work Practice 1968* (New York: Columbia University Press, 1968), p. 35.

At this point it might be useful for readers to catalogue instances and circumstances where one approach to community participation seems more appropriate or effective than another. It is important to take into account unanticipated consequences, for each of the approaches seeks to end the isolation of the school from the community. One advantage of our present policy of isolation is that, although the school is less effective, the principal has fewer headaches, and the school remains safe and static. The approaches to community participation we have described are ways in which the principal might more effectively intervene in the community. But, intervention is a two-way process. As the school becomes more influential in the community, the community in turn becomes more influential in the school. Locality development invites the influence of grass-roots populism from community members; social policy invites the influence of competing bureaucracies and allied professionals; and social action invites the influence of militant groups. We are of the opinion that this influence will benefit the school, provided the school has equal access to the community and is a partner instead of a victim.

V

Getting to the Heart of Curriculum Matters

13

The Need for Elementary School Program Development

IN PREVIOUS CHAPTERS, we have advocated a leadership role for principals that is intended to produce a climate for the growth of all involved in the program and operation of the elementary school—children, staff members, and parents alike. The main assumption that this role is founded on is that school and classroom settings that promote individual initiative and problem solving are most likely to nurture the fullest possible realization of human potential for all concerned.

In this section, we are concerned with the instructional program. We consider the instructional program to be the heart of the elementary school and the main focus of the principals' leadership, decision-making, and staff development activities. Our concern is, therefore, with strengthening the principal's role as an educational leader, as a colleague of teachers, and as a facilitator of inquiry into the instructional process. This means, as Robert Schaefer has suggested,[1] gradually shifting from the present system of "execu-

[1] Robert J. Schaefer, *The School as a Center of Inquiry* (New York: Harper & Row, 1967).

tive authority which characterizes American education—hierarchical flow from the top down" to a system of "colleague authority" where principals would participate in many decisions related to staff development and curriculum improvement on the basis of demonstrated expertise as scholars and teachers, rather than on the basis of assigned position.

Few would disagree that the elementary school exists mainly to foster the development of children by providing them with educational experiences to which most would not otherwise have access. It is the everyday teaching-learning encounters in and around the classrooms that school is all about. Disagreement arises over what kinds of encounters are most educative and over what roles for principals, teachers, and students are most appropriate for bringing these encounters about. It is all too easy for school staff members to get so involved with covering particular subject matter, keeping children busy in the classroom, maintaining order in the halls and playgrounds, and carrying out other administrative-custodial functions that there is little or no time and energy left for examining the program of instruction and working to improve it; so it tends to get taken for granted.

The chapters in this section are intended to provide some guidelines for bringing and keeping staff efforts on center. This chapter deals with the problems involved in adapting the standard elementary school curriculum to important differences in students, teachers, and community settings. Succeeding chapters include suggestions for ways of rethinking school subjects, adopting a more comprehensive view of human development and the conditions under which it takes place, developing an "open classroom" format in order to implement these fresh views of knowledge and human development, and carrying on continuing in-service professional staff development activities as an integral part of the school day. The theme that runs through all six chapters in this section is the role of the principal as educational leader.

Problems to Tackle

Many unsolved problems of the elementary school instructional program can be subsumed in the quest for ways to organize the personnel, material resources, and activities of the schools so that three main elements are integrated in meaningful fashion: the *students,* their daily lives, the ways they learn or come to know; the *social milieu,* the forces that influence individual, group, and institutional behavior; and the large and rapidly mushrooming store of man's *knowledge.* For the elementary school principal and his teachers, the main questions have to do with how the instructional program with its array of school subjects and teaching-learning activities fits in with all the other encounters which children have that help to shape the course of their development. How can the teaching of the three R's and other subjects be made to work for our students so that they not only achieve and continue on to higher levels of schooling, but also come to function adaptively, creatively, and happily in their child and adult life roles? What are we to do in the face of mounting claims that the differences in school programs that we have devised in recent years make little difference in the lives, or even the school achievements, of many of the children we serve? [2] How can we respond to the popular critics of the schools in ways that define their problems in terms which are susceptible to practical solutions?

THE NONADAPTIVE CURRICULUM

The most important current problem facing educators is the inability of our instructional programs to adapt successfully to the educational needs of children who are not achieving or otherwise not being fulfilled in these programs as they are operating today. Many of the children in question are the ones to whom we have given the general label of "disadvantaged." They are found in Appalachia, on the reservations assigned to our Native Americans, and in migrant worker camps, as well as in the inner cities. But these are not the only ones that the schools have failed. There is also a good deal of dissatisfaction with the ways in which elementary school programs are functioning for many "mainstream" children—those we often term "average," as well as the "exceptional" ones, such as the gifted and the handicapped.[3] Broadly described, the difficulties range from general disaffection on the part of many students and parents to poor achievement in one or more subject areas, from lack of student motivation and interest to acute breaches of discipline, and from the lack of real understanding in knowledge areas such as mathematics and reading (and some which are not school subjects, such as self-knowledge) to a lack of real preparedness for subsequent stages of education and development.

To say that such problems signal the need for sweeping reform and reconstruction of the school systems, or even the "deschooling" of society, is to exaggerate their magnitude—unless, of course, we educators continue to be defensive rather than self-critical and fail to take the initiative in getting to the roots of these problems. Not all students in any given classroom, community, or subculture have such problems. Nor do all teachers. Some teachers already do quite well with children that others fail to reach. However, it is equally extravagant to act as if nothing were wrong with our elementary

2 See, for example: Christopher Jencks et al., *Inequality: A Reassessment of the Effect of Family and Schooling in America* (New York: Basic Books, 1972), and the studies upon which they draw.

3 See, for example: Alice Miel et al., *The Shortchanged Children of Suburbia* (New York: Institute of Human Relations Press, 1967); and Urie Bronfenbrenner, "The Split-Level American Family," *Saturday Review* (October 7, 1967), 60–66.

schools—that we have no problems that things like more money, smaller classes, or better home backgrounds of students could not remedy.

THE PERSISTENT STANDARD CURRICULUM

All the rhetoric and special projects of the past few decades notwithstanding, there has for most of this century been one nearly standardized national curriculum in the elementary schools of this country. The core of this curriculum has been the traditional three R's—reading, writing, and arithmetic—accompanied by various combinations of other subjects including science, social studies, health, art, music, and physical education. There are, of course, some local and regional variations, and there have been some important changes in the ways in which classroom activities have been carried on over the past 60 or 70 years, but by and large the school subjects and most of the teaching methods have been fairly constant across both space and time. Thus, it is possible to visit many different schools from Maine to California and not really be sure which state or region one were in as far as most of the content and methods of instruction are concerned—right down to the arrangements of furniture and wall displays, the instructional materials, and the techniques of control or discipline used by teachers.

Does this sound hard to believe? Well, exactly what has changed since 1900, or just within the past 20 years? Make an inventory of your own school district or building. The materials of instruction have become much more numerous, varied, colorful, and expensive. In some classrooms, advanced understanding of human learning and mellowed attitudes toward children as people have made for more comfortable, warmer human relationships among children and between children and adults. There have also been changes in the names employed for school subjects (together with other shifts in terminology): reading and writing in combination with speaking and listening are now called language arts, arithmetic has become mathematics or "the new math," general science which dates back to the 1930s has become "the new science," and social studies are now called social sciences, having previously been labeled according to separate areas such as history, geography, and civics. In addition, there has been some regular updating of content in many subject areas to reflect new events, discoveries, and interests as well as the adding and subtracting of subject areas from time to time.

Concurrently, the role of the principal has grown and been transformed from that of principal teacher to an administrative-organizational specialist who typically shows very little direct concern for teaching. Indeed, while many principals concern themselves with management and organization in efforts to improve the efficiency of the school, the curriculum is shaped—often quite independently—by teachers, publishers, and state education authorities.

ATTEMPTS AT CURRICULUM CHANGE

In subsequent chapters, ways of getting to the heart of the curriculum and bringing about educationally significant change will be suggested. First, it is useful to review some of the ways in which curriculum development has been carried on that have kept it on the periphery. In the 1920s, for example, a good deal of effort went into analyzing the specific skills needed by adults in our society and trying to match school inputs to the training of such skills, a sort of educational version of the time-motion studies in industry and not unlike our current tendency to overemphasize behavioral objectives. During the 1930s, the heyday of "the progressive school," there was a good deal of interest in making school programs more relevant for more children. We went, in effect, having in earlier days been "subject-centered," from being "society-centered" to being "child-centered," without making much of a dent in the standard curriculum.

As World War II approached, the educational lexicon contained such phrases as "activity programs," "integrated subjects," "the whole child," and "life-adjustment education." Following World War II, we came full circle again. The first postwar round of attempts to improve education focused on making revisions in the school subjects. Because of pressures from a number of different sources, the 1950s saw a flurry of activities involving scholars from a number of colleges and universities, working in some cases with teachers and other professional educators, who began to try to overhaul the subject matter content, organization, and teaching of a number of school subjects. Among other developments of the 1950s were extensions of communications technology, such as instructional television and language laboratories; administrative and organizational arrangements, such as team teaching and various ways of grouping students; programmed instruction and changes in the grade level placement of various school subjects, such as foreign language in the elementary school and algebra in grades 7 and 8. Most of these changes had their concomitants in the design and equipment of school plants and in the production of instructional materials and equipment. The results included whole arrays of innovations from new math and science to cluster or pod classrooms, modular scheduling and continuous progress, and individualized instruction.

As part of this whole process, the federal government began to take an increasingly active role in public education, first through the National Defense Education Act (the "Sputnik Bill"), which concentrated in particular on mathematics, science, and foreign language teaching, and later through the Elementary and Secondary Education Act, still with us at this writing, which was designed primarily to help schools meet the needs of "disadvantaged" students. This was also a period characterized by unprecedented interest and activity by a number of major foundations. Unfortunately, most of the funds and efforts expended did not bring about hoped-for reforms and solutions to the problems inherent in the standard curriculum. And it seems unlikely that the current stress on accountability, policy planning and budget systems, performance contracts, behavioral objectives, and career education is going to alter the situation.

The situation that we are in at all levels of education is this: the repertoire of approaches and methods for curriculum development is not potent enough to reach to the heart of the curriculum and effect significant change. It does not include means that are powerful enough to overcome the status quo, the interlocking sets of assumptions about human development and knowledge, methods and materials for teaching, and aims and expectations for achievement that make up the standard curriculum and the standard ways in which we carry on teacher education and curriculum development. Most of what we have tried falls into one or more of the following administrative-organizational categories:

1. Grouping students and/or staff in various different combinations:
    ability grouping, vertical grouping, achievement level grouping
    team teaching, departmentalization by subjects, combining subjects
    large group, small group, individual instruction, or tutoring
    racially or ethnically segregated or desegregated

2. Packaging of materials and content:
    revising and rearranging textbooks, programmed instruction
    subjects placed in differing sequences, at different grade levels
    subjects added or deleted
    subjects offered separately or combined ("fused," or "integrated," or departmentalized)
    textbooks and materials series, sets, kits, and entire programs offered by publishers
    single or multimedia materials

3. School organization:
    kindergarten through grade 8 in one building
    primary (K–3), and intermediate (4–6), or middle school (4 or 5 through 8)
    self-contained classrooms, clusters, modules, pods

4. Curriculum development activities:
    committees to revise syllabi and courses of study
    committees to review and select published textbooks and series
    after-school meetings, workshops, conferences with speakers—by grade level, school-wide, by subjects
    college and university course work and degree programs with courses in both methods and subject matter content
    certification requirements set at the state or local level with required subjects and other standards

It is not our intention to belittle the curriculum development efforts of the past and present. However, we are concerned that so much of the money and effort that has been expended to date has not resulted in more successful adaptations of the elementary curriculum to important differences in students, their home backgrounds, and their communities. The significant curriculum innovations of the past, as important as they may have been for sustaining the schooling enterprise, have not sufficiently affected the quality of the interactions that take place between teachers and students, and between students and the stuff of their world.

There are a number of reasons why bringing about change in the heart of the curriculum is very difficult. In order to provide some perspective, we have listed a number of these reasons.

First, children are raised by the whole community—in many ways, the whole society—and the school is only part of the community. Because children attend school for such a long time, school staff members have gradually become responsible for more and more aspects of children's lives. This has led to a good deal of confusion concerning just what the teacher's role and the principal's role should be vis à vis the roles of parents and others in the community.

Second, and related to the first point, is the problem of measuring educational outputs and inputs and thus obtaining reliable feedback on the differential effects of various kinds of program elements or variations. This problem is compounded by the fact that many effects of school experience do not show up until years later and are hard to trace back to any particular phase of schooling.

Third, schools as institutions have developed their own subcultures which are relatively self-sustaining and which develop effective defenses against outside intrusions. This means, among other things, that it is quite difficult for school people to be really self-critical, for to be so is to leave themselves vulnerable to outside attacks. This also results in the separation between the world of the school and classroom, on the one hand, and the wider world in which children and their families live, on the other—especially when schools are made to feel that they must select for inclusion in the curriculum only content that is considered noncontroversial and that can easily be packaged for classroom use. All too often, the world as represented in schoolbooks is so different from the world of children's everyday experience outside school that it is easy to see why some become alienated or bored.

Fourth, teachers are not sufficiently challenged as professionals, they are not inducted into professional colleagueship with other teachers and principals, even though many are better educated than those who outrank them in the school administrataive hierarchy. As Robert Schaefer suggests,

> Under present circumstances, vigorous, alive, intelligent, and socially committed young people often find schools lonely and intellectually barren places.

The social norm which now prevails is to treat one's fellow teachers, new or experienced, in a friendly but nonintervening manner. There are few opportunities for serious discussion, and the lack of a developed, specialized vocabulary and meaningful set of pedagogical concepts makes the professional communication which does occur nebulous and imprecise. Teacher education programs rarely prepare teachers for powerful and continuing professional association, but ordinarily aspire only to readying the neophyte for the here and now demands of the job.[4]

Fifth, because of the complexity of a school's operation and the nature of its relationships to the community, it is easy for the administrative-leadership functions to become entirely focused on matters other than those that directly support the teacher-learning process. One example of this can be seen in the extent to which principals have become representatives of "management" who are responsible to a central office, a school board, and a public, while teachers have become "labor," organized in unions to bargain for the most part over salaries, working conditions, and fringe benefits, rather than over matters of more strictly professional concern. The split in the professional ranks has made it difficult for principals to provide leadership for continuing program improvement, since they are so often found in the roles of judge and foreman rather than professional colleague and leader. Schaefer suggests that:

> Administrators who wish to retain some shared association in the instructional efforts of a school—and not only as managers who sit on the other side of the bargaining table—must learn to forgo some of their traditional prerogatives. . . .
> If there is to be fruitful inquiry in the schools, . . . administrators can perform no higher function than to facilitate it. To do so will require the deliberate and self-conscious reduction of executive authority and the nurturing of free scholar-teachers.[5]

Sixth, and most important of all, is the fact that professionals and laymen alike tend to oversimplify the curriculum and staff development process. This is demonstrated by the extent to which we seek single, short-term, and "new" solutions to old and complex problems: the adoption of *a* reading method, the writing of "behavioral objectives," a shift to team teaching or nongraded classrooms, the setting-up of "smorgasbord" programs or "free" schools, or even the "deschooling" of society. Daniel Griffiths recently analyzed the work of such popular critics of the schools as John Holt, Ivan Illich, and Charles Silberman and concluded that their critiques lacked the standards that must accompany criticism and scholarship, showed "an overwhelming faith in a single solution for a complex problem," and were heedless of the

---

[4] Robert J. Schaefer, "The School as a Center of Inquiry," *Perspectives on Education* (Teachers College, Columbia University), Vol. 1, No. 1 (Fall 1967), 9–16.

[5] Schaefer, "The School as a Center of Inquiry," p. 12.

realities that affect individuals involved in schooling and the place of schools in the real world. However, he goes on to ask:

> But where are the professionals? Why have they been silent? Several, hard at work, have incorporated many of the suggestions of the critics into their own programs. In fact some have gone beyond the critics in their zeal for innovation. But professional educators have neither defended defensible positions—like institutionalized public education—nor have they moved to overcome the shortcomings of the critics by developing standards for appropriate and ongoing criticism of educational practices. Not only is criticism a proper role for educators, it is part of their professional obligation.[6]

This situation is further illustrated by the assumption that, once trained in preservice programs, teachers should be able to perform adequately with no further help, except perhaps occasional workshops and in-service or extension courses outside of school hours. There is little or no time built into the teacher's job for continuing professional growth activities.

Some Guiding Principles

The conditions just described are parts of the background. Some of them are dealt with at greater length elsewhere in this book. In the foreground of the next five chapters are the following assumptions about what it will take to make the elementary school program flexible enough to be adapted to individual differences in children, teachers, and communities, yet focused enough to maintain high standards of professional performance and student achievement.

First, whatever may be printed in textbooks and syllabi, the functional curriculum, the one that actually operates and affects children, exists in the minds and the everyday behavior of teachers and other people with whom children have close contact. This means that curriculum development should take place at the local classroom and school level. Curricula cannot be improved significantly through the production of instructional materials that are packaged in publishing houses and central education agencies—unless such materials are designed to effectively teach teachers and principals as much or more than students.

Second, in order for local curriculum development to be carried out successfully, it must follow guiding principles that are sufficiently potent to keep educators focused on matters of central consequence to children's development and to provide clear standards of quality against which to measure results. The principles described in Chapters 14 and 16 are derived from

---

[6] Daniel E. Griffiths, "Can Critics Change the Schools?" *New York University Education Quarterly*, Vol. 4, No. 1 (Fall 1972), 1.

the assumption that human knowledge—including how it is best acquired by children and how it relates to their overall growth and development—is the stock and trade of the schools. An important key to professional growth and program improvement, therefore, lies in the continuing study of the "ways of knowing" and human developmental processes and conditions as these relate to the lives of children who are growing up in a complex world. The main objectives of such study would be to reconstruct the school subjects so that they become more like the knowledge disciplines whose names they often bear, and to develop an understanding of human development and learning that is comprehensive enough to apply to a wider range of different kinds of children, activities, and settings. It is not enough for educators merely to ask scholars what knowledge content should be included in the curriculum and then to ask psychologists how to present it to children so that they might best "master" it. Rather, teachers and principals must continually work at applying the methods and standards of human inquiry to the everyday tasks involved in living and working with children.

Third, in order for this professional staff and program development to take place, it must become an integral part of the working school day and year rather than something carried on only after school hours or on weekends and during vacation time. This can be accomplished, in part, if teachers are not expected to be the sole custodians of children during the full length of every school day, and in part by operating classrooms and other activity areas so that teachers can learn and grow along with their students, and principals along with teachers.

Finally, the elementary school principal needs to become more of a fellow student, teacher, student of teachers, and teacher of teachers. The top-priority administrative duties should be those which best facilitate the functioning of the staff as a kind of community of scholars and teachers.

There is no simple way to bring about significant educational reform; it will require long, hard work at all levels. No national or state commission or project is going to be able to produce a new and better curriculum; this will require concerted and continuous action at every local school and classroom level—with, of course, help from other levels, including universities, state departments of education, professional organizations, and government agencies. And professional educators are not going to be able to bring about needed reform entirely on their own, just within the walls of the schools; many institutions already involved in the making of educational policies and the shaping of the course of children's development will have to join in the effort. But we educators can play a much more influential part than we have in recent decades, if we can focus our attention and energies on the heart of the curriculum: the role of human knowledge in human development and being.

14

School Subjects
and the Knowledge
Disciplines

THE VISION of elementary school reform brought about through innovative approaches to educational leadership that has been conjured up in previous chapters is not new. The problem has been to find the proper handles on the various elements that make up a school program that would enable us to rearrange and reshape them in fruitful ways, in ways that would enable us to retain what is most important to children's development while changing or adding or deleting less central items. We have typically failed to challenge long-standing assumptions and habits and have then been left to wonder why we could not effect the kinds of changes we hoped for. Our situation is somewhat analogous to that faced by those would-be, pre–Wright brothers inventors of the airplane, who may well have been thwarted in their efforts by the fact that they assumed that the power plant for their contraption would have to be a steam engine with its poor weight-to-horsepower ratio.

It does not seem too far-fetched to assume that many "free" schools and many school faculties where the principal served as the facilitator of faculty decision making failed to bring about desired changes in the school curriculum because they took one or more of the program elements for granted rather than challenging and, when necessary, reconstructing or replacing it. The program element that needs challenging is the content of the curriculum, the form and manner in which human knowledge is introduced to children.

This chapter is intended to encourage principals to lead their faculties in challenging standard assumptions about the nature of human knowledge and how children might best acquire it, to work out reformulations of the various knowledge fields, and thus to prepare for reorganizing the ways in which knowledge is introduced to children. We present one source of guidelines for charting courses to workable local versions of the integrated or "open" curriculum and for keeping cooperative staff work on curriculum development and professional growth efforts on course.

Knowledge in and out of School

When a baby is born, he knows virtually nothing. As he grows older, his gradual acquisition of knowledge, his finding of meaning in the original "booming, buzzing confusion," is influenced and nurtured by his total environment. The young child is taught by many kinds of experiences, planned and unplanned, in and out of formal educational settings. As mentioned in the previous chapter, cultural forces outside the school's purview can greatly influence children's school achievement, even in areas such as reading and mathematics where schools are supposed to provide the major inputs. Many in-school influences exist, moreover, that would not normally be listed as parts of the curriculum.[1] Children can and do learn a lot on their own, and, without direct adult supervision, they can often manage their own affairs quite well, that is, "control" themselves, make decisions, and carry on cooperative group work and play.

The most obvious example of finding order in seeming chaos without benefit of formal instruction is found in the infant's acquisition of speech. This is possible because the infant has constant and direct access to the language being spoken around him and to him, and he gets a good deal of encouragement from his parents, in addition to the fact that comprehending and speaking is directly related to getting many different kinds of needs fulfilled. In the course of everyday living with others, the infant receives continual feedback on the appropriateness of his own outputs and the extent of his own understanding, usually without those with whom he is in communication being aware that they are providing it. This whole process is facilitated by the fact that in every language there are relatively consistent patterns of sounds and intonations, and these are employed over and over again in

[1] Norman V. Overly (ed.), *The Unstudied Curriculum* (Washington, D.C.: Association for Supervision and Curriculum Development, National Education Association, 1970).

reference to concrete objects and events. From these patterns, the young child gradually extracts rules for producing his own speech as well as for understanding the speech of others, although he can neither describe what these rules are nor benefit much from verbal statements of them supplied by others. By school age, most children have already mastered the essential structures of the oral language that is spoken around them at home.

In similar fashion, children develop knowledge of a wide range of other aspects of life in which they are immersed during their waking hours. This knowledge involves many personal and household routines, concepts of self and other, adult and child roles, television, stores and shops, geographic relationships, space and time relationships, and a great deal about the physical properties and functions of objects. As they grow toward school age, children collaborate increasingly with one another in activities such as games, representative play, construction projects, and excursions on their own initiative and with minimal adult supervision. In such situations they are quite capable of leadership, decision making, conflict resolution; in short, they have already developed much of the competency needed to keep group members task-oriented and functioning.

In view of all this, we educators need to ask ourselves why knowledge is handled as it usually is in schools and why more responsibility for managing their own activities is not given over to children instead of being handled by teachers under the heading of control or classroom discipline. Contrast the sort of education that takes place in the examples given above with that offered in the classrooms of typical elementary schools. Children outside of school learn through cycles of listening and observing, copying and modeling, receiving feedback on their own behavior and making adjustments, and by asking questions. They can do all these things in a number of areas at a time and all the while be engaged in activities that are of importance to them. In school, children are presented much the same kinds of content—but didactically, in predetermined sequences, with various areas isolated from each other and from the children's everyday life encounters. While in home and neighborhood, children continually confront problems and test their own solutions, in school they are presented with someone else's answers to problems that they have not raised or defined, but that (they are assured) will be important to them sometime in the future.

We are not suggesting that all education in school is rigid, restricted, and inadequate, while that which takes place outside is all "free" and liberating. If we did not have schools, we would have to invent some equivalent institution for guiding the development of the young. The problem is how to recognize and capitalize on the most educative influences in and out of school, while minimizing the noneducative or miseducative ones. How can we get handles on those materials, settings, and practices that contribute most to children's development as fully functioning human beings and extend them where they exist and introduce them where they are absent? We think that

part of the answer lies in treating human knowledge in the curriculum as being contained in, and developed through, the scholarly disciplines as fields
of inquiry, and not in the form of the school subjects as they presently exist.

School Subjects vs. Disciplines

One of the main barriers to the local development of instructional
programs is to be found in the difference between school subjects and the
knowledge disciplines, and between the producers of knowledge in the many
basic and applied fields and the consumers of knowledge in the schools and
even in colleges and universities where the producers usually work. A school
subject is an educator's attempt to render a field of knowledge such as
mathematics, literature, or history into a pattern of subject matter and activities that can easily and efficiently be presented to children of different
ages and grade levels for mastery. But school language arts is not language
as viewed by psycholinguists (or small children), and reading is somehow kept
separate from writing and literature. Similarly, school mathematics is not
mathematics as mathematicians and some developmental psychologists understand it,[2] and school history is not the historian's history.

Instead, the knowledge involved in school subjects is often like cut
flowers—and sometimes even like artificial ones. Without roots in the soil of
the discipline where it was produced, school knowledge cannot grow and adapt
to changing conditions and to individual differences in children, but must be
kept looking fresh through artificial means. It cannot be transplanted, as it
were, to other soils, or grafted or hybridized; nor can it reproduce itself.
School knowledge must therefore be taken as is, as a sterile, finished product
that will not be suitable for many consumers and not applicable to many
situations.

Disciplined knowledge, related to the discipline in which it is generated,
on the other hand, is like a rooted plant. It can continue to grow and change
and adapt, shedding obsolete leaves and branches along the way and yielding
up seeds from which further knowledge can grow at future times and places.
Disciplined knowledge need not remain as it stands at any particular time
and place, but can be cultivated anew in response to changing needs and
interests.

The most crucial implication of the lack of congruity between school
subjects and knowledge disciplines derives from the fact that subject matter
is taught and learned in school in ways that are qualitatively different from
the ways in which the knowledge that spawned this subject matter was
originally generated. Thus, the content of knowledge, the *product,* is separated

[2] See, for example: Kenneth Lovell, *The Growth of Understanding in Mathematics*
(New York: Holt, Rinehart and Winston, 1971).

from the *process* by which it was produced, so much so that teachers become consumers, or at best distributors, along with their students and, hence, are cut off from the sources of what they teach.

The consequences of this situation should be carefully pondered by principals and their staffs who are interested in significant curriculum improvement and professional self-development. As a guide to such study, additional points of difference between subjects and disciplines have been listed in Table 14-1.

TABLE 14-1. Comparing subjects and disciplines.

School Subjects	*Knowledge Disciplines*
The procedures by which content is "mastered" or acquired by students in the subjects are different from those by which it is acquired by scholars and artists or even small children, as in the case of one's mother tongue. Emphasis is placed upon the verbal presentation of terms, descriptions, definitions, and rules —in short, on knowing *about* rather than knowing. Little differentiation is made in the teaching-learning methods that are employed from subject area to subject area. Subject-matter content is arranged for presentation in a sequence which is different from the sequence in which it was originally developed. The process of education and the process of inquiry and artistic creativity are different.	Children, like scholars, are assumed to have to engage in the construction of knowledge in order to be able to adequately understand what is produced and communicated by others. This construction is carried out in modes that are consistent with the characteristics of each discipline and the developmental levels of the individuals involved. There is a good deal of differentiation of method of inquiry and communication both by discipline and by developmental level of producer or audience. The sequence of acquisition is determined by the order of developmental stages and the processes of inquiry in each field. The process of education is similar to the process of scholarship and artistic creation and criticism.
Subject-matter content is cut off from its sources and subjected to oversimplification and distortion. Isolated facts and figures are often meaningless in the absence of a supporting theoretical framework and generalizations, and verbalized theories and principles are often meaningless in the absence of supporting facts and applications.	Subject matter related to its inquiry sources is harder to misconstrue. The disciplines contain built-in checks and balances: canons of proof, standards of scholarship, ways of testing conclusions or determining the limits of their application in light of relevant evidence, and procedures for judging validity or quality. Certainty is not a necessity; emphasis is on the best understanding possible in light of available knowledge, competence, and stage of development of children. Individual bits of information are given meaning within a supporting framework of concepts, generalizations, and attitudes.

TABLE 14-1. Comparing subjects and disciplines. **(cont.)**

School Subjects	*Knowledge Disciplines*
The ways in which content is selected for school use results in only the most certain and agreed-upon and, therefore, often the most noncontroversial subject matter being included in textbooks and other materials. What is selected must be supported by general (statewide or, often, national) consensus. This means that teachers usually ignore or omit many problems which are of direct and immediate concern to their students and others in the community, because they are considered controversial, because the teacher does not know enough about them, or because they are not included in the course of study or the textbooks which are in use.	Because the way of knowing is of greatest importance in the disciplines, agreement is focused there rather than on particular conclusions. While selected topics or problem areas might be required of all students, what is to be studied is also selected because it illuminates the ways of knowing of one or more disciplines. Local problems do not have to be ignored, for they can be studied from the viewpoints of several disciplines at once. The scope of the curriculum can go far beyond what has previously been printed in textbooks and similar materials.
The separation of subjects from knowledge fields has led to the separation of subject areas from one another.	Similar problems and situations can be studied from the points of view of several fields simultaneously, and fields can be integrated at their natural points of contact.
Defining curriculum content in terms of school subjects does not deal adequately with the problem of rapid increase in man's knowledge or with future changes. Areas not now in the curriculum would have to be made into new subjects in order to be included and thus would take up additional time slots and require the production of new sets of instructional materials. When new subjects are added, existing ones often have to be dropped or severely curtailed. Exclusive focus on products, on conclusions, many of which will soon be obsolete, is not adequate preparation for the future.	Emphasis on the disciplines and their ways of knowing can equip children to understand a wider range of areas with less time and effort, and to keep their knowledge up-to-date in the face of changing conditions and interests. The choice of adding or deleting content can be made much more rationally. Over the years of elementary school and beyond, students can acquire the means for both keeping up with new developments and for pursuing their own interests in topics not specifically introduced by teachers or instructional materials.

THE KNOWLEDGE DISCIPLINES

Every growing child comes into an inheritance of human knowledge that has been cooperatively constructed and shared by people from many nations over many generations. What makes this cooperation and sharing possible is that the means for using symbols to represent, categorize, and interrelate the objects and events of experience has been standardized and made universal through the development of the knowledge disciplines. Each discipline consists of a community of scholars or artists who work together toward bettering our understanding of the dimensions of man's experience within its domain. Although there are many divisions of knowledge based upon unique characteristics of each knowledge field, there are important interrelationships. Not only do some fields cover similar domains, but they often share similar methodologies. In fact, the main function of some of the disciplines (such as history and anthropology) is to synthesize and integrate knowledge from the others.

The main implication of all this for the elementary school curriculum is that, if children are to become better able to share in man's knowledge, they must share in the methods and the categories of the disciplines; that is, they must share in *disciplined* knowledge. It is not enough simply to have experience with various activities and institutions, locations, settings, people, and things; these phenomena must be described and interpreted and communicated about in disciplined ways. Otherwise the knowledge gained is apt to be isolated and incomplete.

An example of disciplined knowledge may be demonstrated through its analogy to the mental image of a town or city that we adults take with us when we move to a new community and try to find our way around. This image, or "map," has been constructed from our prior experience with at least one other town, and it combines in one interrelated framework such concepts as direction (north, uptown, and so on), section of town (residential, commercial, industrial), institutions and agencies (schools, post offices, libraries), and some sort of grid pattern of thoroughfares (streets, tracks, freeways, rivers) and intersections from which various locations may be specified or identified. The more different towns that this map of "town-ness" is based on, the more powerful and adaptable a discipline we have with which to guide our inquiry into the new town's dimensions and render it familiar and meaningful to us. In contrast, a person (especially a young child) not equipped with such a map is severely restricted in his movement about the new town, because he can easily get lost, and he is dependent on others for either taking him places or giving him very specific directions for finding his way around.

In short, disciplined knowledge has three characteristics that are helpful to children who are trying to build understanding in a field, to their teachers who are helping them build it, and to principals and other educational leaders who are trying to help teachers grow professionally. First, disciplined knowledge is *selective*, it guides a student in knowing what to look for, and it helps focus attention on relevant data. Second, it is *integrating* in that it shows how the various parts, the separate pieces of data, fit together to form meaningful patterns of relationships at the same time that it provides a context from which the key concepts of each field derive their meaning. Third, disciplined knowledge is *generative* in that it contains the seeds of further inquiry, ways of recognizing where knowledge is lacking or limited, or where new findings seem to refute older formulations.[3]

In Figure 14-1, the major knowledge disciplines are arrayed in contrast with the standard elementary school subjects. Many of those fields not listed are subdivisions or combinations of those in the figure and can be easily derived. The several disciplines have been arranged in a way that reflects some of their salient characteristics. Those lower in position (with the exception of language) are more specialized and narrow in scope; moving towards the top, the disciplines listed are increasingly integrative and inclusive of those below them. The disciplines toward the left are empirically based, more objective, and deal with more regular and predictable phenomena; those to the right become increasingly subjective and determinant. Certain physical and chemical changes are easily predicted and replicated, for example, while individual behavior is less so, and what is "good" or "beautiful" cannot be reduced to a set of laws or rules and tested empirically.[4] Note, too, that language, or the entire range of representational systems used for communication, is related to all the fields and interacts with each in different ways.

Basing the elementary school curriculum on the disciplines is, of course, no easy matter. There are few places where a principal or his teaching staff can go to find descriptions of the various fields that would be directly applicable to the development of programs for children. Certainly most college and teacher education courses in the various disciplines do not treat content as fields of inquiry. Moreover, it is doubtful that many college faculty members understand their own fields in their most disciplined forms and, therefore, limit their potential use to educators. The following section contains suggestions for ways of describing the disciplines that render them more accessible to teachers and students.

DESCRIBING A DISCIPLINE

Although the existing disciplines may inherently possess the most teachable and learnable paths to human understanding, it is not going to be possible for educators simply to go to various scholars and obtain ready answers to such questions as "What is the nature of your discipline?" or "What are its ways of knowing?" We need to know more specifically what

---

[3] For further reading in this area, see: Philip H. Phenix, *Realms of Meaning* (New York: McGraw-Hill, 1964); A. Harry Passow (ed.), *Curriculum Crossroads* (New York: Teachers College Press, 1962), especially the chapter by Phenix; and F. S. C. Northrop, *The Logic of the Sciences and the Humanities* (New York: Meridian Books, 1959).

[4] See: G. E. Moore, *Principia Ethica* (New York: Cambridge University Press, 1960); and George Santayana, *The Sense of Beauty* (New York: Dover Publications, 1965).

FIGURE 14-1. The knowledge disciplines.

Philosophy and Religion

History

Ethics   Aesthetics   Criticism

Physical Geography   Cultural Anthropology
Geology   Physical Anthropology

NATURAL SCIENCES   BEHAVIORAL SCIENCES   POLICY   HUMANITIES   ARTS
Physics   Social Psychology   SCIENCES   Self-Knowledge   Literature   Graphic
Chemistry   Psychology   Sociology   Economics   Drama   Plastic
Biology   Political   Music
          Science   Performance
          Education

LANGUAGE AND REPRESENTATION   Presentational Forms
Mathematics   graphic symbols,
          drawing, movement,
Ordinary language (prose)   Poetry   gesture, ritual,
Specialized languages of the disciplines   myth, imagery

THE SCHOOL SUBJECTS

General Science   Social Science   Literature   Art
"New Science"   History, Geography, Economics
          Music
Mathematics   Language Arts and Reading   Reading   Dance
Arithmetic   Writing, listening

to ask and how to ask. We need to challenge scholars and artists in ways that will be of maximum help in the planning of instructional activities and materials for use with children.

As an aid to getting started in this task, an outline of the main categories and characteristics of a discipline is presented below. In using the outline, the reader may recognize two familiar aspects of the knowledge disciplines: (1) the *products* of inquiry, and (2) the *methods of inquiry*. These two aspects have often been referred to as "content" and "process" respectively, and are often (albeit, inappropriately, in our view) considered separable from one another. Note, too, that, although there is a good deal of overlap among the disciplines with respect to various dimensions, there are also significant and crucial differences among them. The understanding of these differences is essential to the development of meaning.[5] The discipline categories and characteristics are as follows:

Domain. First of all, each discipline has a describable domain consisting of the specific aspects of human experience it tries to comprehend. Historians describe and interpret past events, anthropologists study man in the broad perspectives of evolution and culture, and political scientists specialize in the distribution of power, especially as it relates to decision making and government. Some domains are subdivided and others joined together. History, psychology, and philosophy, for example, all have their competing "schools," as well as topical subdivisions. On the other hand, some fields have been formed by joining two disciplines together, as in astrophysics, biochemistry, cultural geography, and psycholinguistics.

In the elementary school, the main purpose of language—written or oral—is the communication of shared experience among students and between students and others. Mathematics adds the dimensions of quantity and magnitude to what is experienced and offers a means of describing phenomena through numbers and number relationships. Literature describes humanity—all the possible ways of being human in the widest variety of probable and improbable situations. History involves the reconstruction of the past from its remains in order to yield perspective on and a better understanding of the present. Physical geography describes and explains regions on the surface of the earth and interprets their characteristics in terms of their potential for man's use.[6]

[5] For further treatments of ways of describing disciplines, see: Phenix, *Realms of Meaning;* Joseph J. Schwab, "The Content and Structure of a Discipline," *Educational Record,* Vol. 43, No. 3 (July 1962), 197–205; Northrop, *The Logic of the Sciences and the Humanities;* and Stanley Elam (ed.), *Education and the Structure of Knowledge* (Chicago: Rand McNally, 1964).

[6] For sources of additional descriptions of many of the disciplines, see, for example: Jerome Bruner, *The Process of Education* (Cambridge, Mass.: Harvard University Press, 1960); David L. Elliott, *Curriculum Development and History as Discipline.* Unpub-

Methods of Inquiry. Scholars and artists in each discipline share ways of knowing, or sets of methods with which they produce the characteristic outputs of that field—hypotheses and theorems, books or paintings, performances, or criticism. Historians employ the methods of historiography: locating and analyzing sources, establishing degrees of factuality, arranging events chronologically and interpreting them, and writing down their findings for others to read. Ordinary language is acquired and refined through continuous use: talking and writing to and with others; listening and reading; and getting critical feedback on accuracy, style, and form, clarity of meaning, effectiveness, and aesthetic appeal. Most creative writing involves a good deal of pondering and organizing of ideas (not to mention research and human experience), getting one's ideas down on paper, and editing—often taking the article, poem, or novel through a number of drafts. Literature, art, music, and drama can involve exhibition, performance, and criticism in addition to their creation. Economics and political science involve valuing and policy making as well as the more objective study of human behavior.

The central method of mathematics entails reasoning deductively from postulates (givens) and supporting the assertions one makes with reasons. For the young child, development in mathematics is accomplished through performing mathematical operations on the objects and conditions of the world: counting, measuring, grouping in sets, describing relationships, and representing ideas graphically as well as with numbers and equations. The "scientific method" employed by physicists, chemists, biologists, and behavioral scientists involves, first of all, the description of the phenomena of a given domain—atoms and molecules, chemical or interpersonal interactions, or the structural and functional characteristics of individuals or social groups. Most of this description is accomplished through the use of the specialized prose of each field plus mathematics (including statistics), but metaphor and other forms of imagery, as well as photographs, drawings, and diagrams, are also used.

The explanation of physical, biological, or social phenomena is a complex process involving problem definition, hypothesizing, hypothesis testing, and theory building—though not necessarily in that order, nor in any clear-cut series of steps from problem to solution. Scientific inquiry is made up of imagination and intuitive leaps as well as logical deductions and mathematical formulas.

A most important, and frequently neglected, aspect of each discipline is found in the nature of the symbols, or forms of representation, it employs.

---

lished Doctoral Dissertation (New York: Teachers College, Columbia University, 1963); A. R. King and John A. Brownell, *The Curriculum and the Disciplines of Knowledge* (New York: John Wiley and Sons, 1966); Herbert A. Thelen, *Education and the Human Quest* (New York: Harper & Row, 1960); and Alfred N. Whitehead, *Aims of Education and Other Essays* (New York: Free Press, 1967).

Distinctive kinds of "logic" are to be found both in the concepts and generalizations formed and in the ways in which ideas are represented for recording and communication. Among the representational systems are gesture, ritual, and dance; ordinary language and mathematics; the imagery of simile, metaphor, and myth; the combinations of form, color, texture, and perspective in painting, sculpture, and architecture; the rhythmic, melodic, and harmonic patterns in music; and the dramatic forms of acting and role playing.[7]

The Disciplines and the Elementary School

Obviously, children in the primary grades are not immediately capable of sophisticated inquiry and adult levels of understanding. Their understanding of themselves and their world must be built up gradually over the years of childhood, adolescence, and even adulthood. Nor is it possible to introduce *all* the disciplines in any one year, by the end of the sixth grade, or even by the twelfth grade. Some selection and assignment of priorities, as well as careful sequencing, will need to be carried out. Selection will have to be made on the basis of local goals and objectives for children's development, but the wider the range of disciplines to which children are exposed in some depth, the more full their development can be. Some entire fields and aspects of some others are appropriate for kindergarten and the primary grades; others are best left for the upper grades and even for secondary school and adulthood.

Also, it is not our intention to suggest that textbooks and other instructional materials simply be rewritten to outline the "structures" of the disciplines, in some kind of orderly K–8 sequence, perhaps with chapter headings such as "Domain," "Methods of Inquiry," and the like. The nature of the various fields and their ways of knowing cannot successfully be taught didactically, in predetermined sequences. Instead, they must be learned gradually, through practice, as children carry out their everyday explorations to extend their knowledge and competence. One does not have to be versed in the philosophy of science to carry on scientific inquiry anymore than the young toddler requires grounding in the philosophy of language in order to learn how to talk. Children can be guided in knowing what to look for, and how to look, to see the world from the points of view of the various fields without (at least at first) being able to explain to someone just exactly what it is that they are doing.

But for the adults that are going to do the guiding—parents, teachers,

---

[7] The distinctions referred to here are illuminated by Susanne Langer in her *Philosophy in a New Key* (New York: Mentor Books, 1949).

principals, or others—the situation is different. For these people, a good deal of self-conscious knowing about knowing, the ability to analyze how we come to know, will be necessary. Since it must be obvious that every teacher is not going to become an overnight expert in every discipline (nor even in the handful underlying the present school subjects), there is a long task of professional development for curriculum improvement ahead. Building the kind of understanding of the disciplines and their ways of knowing will take time and effort. In some cases, school faculties may want to "relearn" one field at a time as a group. It certainly makes sense to think of different teachers— and the principal—as specializing in a field or two and having responsibility for introducing it to others on the staff.

In all of this, the principal can have a key role as leader and model. He can help establish the conditions for study and program improvement, work to mobilize needed resources in school and community, and work to interpret and clarify the process to all concerned. These and other activities are discussed in Chapters 17 and 18. In the intervening chapters, another major source of guidelines for curriculum improvement is considered.

15

Human Development
and the
Standard Curriculum

THE KNOWLEDGE DISCIPLINES have been presented in the preceding chapter as a foundation upon which to build curriculum improvement and professional staff development activities. The disciplines, properly tapped, could yield important guidelines for selecting and presenting curriculum content to children. Fruitful utilization of the knowledge fields involves two main tasks: first, developing descriptions of these fields and their ways of knowing in their most educative forms, and, second, working toward an understanding of the course of human development and learning, as it proceeds from early childhood to early adolescence. The principal can participate in these tasks both by facilitating the work of other staff members and by joining in the study of the disciplines in relation to the teaching-learning process.

Development is that process whereby the nearly helpless infant gradually acquires, in a series of stages, the behavior patterns, the competencies, and the physical attributes of the adult. As he develops from infancy, each individual's grasp of the world and his ability to function in it progresses from simple to complex, undifferentiated to differentiated, concrete and mainly sensory-motor-based to abstract and formal, nonverbal to verbal, and egocentric to multicentric. Just how this development takes place and under what conditions is a subject about which there is a good deal of disagreement, but we think that the view of development and the view of learning held by educators make an educationally significant difference. In this chapter, we describe two prevalent views, each of which, if considered alone, we believe to be inadequate. In Chapter 16 we describe a view which includes these two, but which is comprehensive of a wider range of individual approaches and more compatible with our emphasis on the knowledge disciplines. At the end of this chapter is an inventory which serves first to describe and summarize the main features of each of the three views of human development and second, to help clarify one's own assumptions and beliefs.

Educators' Views of Development

The views we hold on development and learning, however implicit they may be, influence the ways in which we work with children and other adults. Teachers have a good deal of influence over the kinds of experiences children have and the ways in which such experiences are used. They exercise this influence in a number of ways: through the selection of materials, the arrangement of settings, their own behavior and the rules and demands they make, and the raising of open-ended questions and the presentation of challenges. There are also more subtle influences brought to bear through the expectations that teachers have for the level of performance of individual children and through the kind of interpersonal climate that is created in the classroom.[1] Our choices of activities are influenced in turn by what we think is best for children, what will contribute most to, or detract least from their developmental progress.

It is, therefore, well for us to be clear on what views we hold so that we can be in a better position to modify or improve them, if necessary. One very useful activity for a school staff to carry out on a continuing basis is the examination, questioning, further testing, development, revision, or even abandonment of views held by its members, along with the practices based on these views.[2] Self-examination is as important for principals and supervisors as it is for teachers, since the ways in which an educational leader works with

[1] See Norman V. Overly (ed.), *The Unstudied Curriculum: Its Impact on Children* (Washington, D.C.: Association for Supervision and Curriculum Development, National Education Association, 1970).

[2] See L. Festinger, *Theory of Cognitive Dissonance* (Chicago: Row, Peterson, 1957); and David E. Berlyne, "Curiosity and Education," in J. D. Krumboltz (ed.), *Learning and the Educational Process* (Chicago: Rand McNally, 1965).

his staff have many close analogies to the ways in which teachers work with children.

As a major step in the process of trying to reach a better understanding of our professional selves and the situations in which we work, we should probe for answers to the following kinds of questions:

1. What is human development? What takes place in an individual when it occurs? How are development and learning related?

2. What is it that develops? What is the nature of the various knowledge areas? How does knowledge in each area relate to overall human behavior and development?

3. What are the main mechanisms or processes involved in development and learning? What contributions are made to these processes by heredity? by environment? What are the sources of motivation and reinforcement? Why do we develop and behave in some ways and not in others? What determines the scope and sequence of development?

4. What relationships are there among the various dimensions of development and behavior: intellectual, affective, perceptual-motor, physical, moral, linguistic?

5. Under what conditions can development in any dimension be facilitated? What should be the main emphases of schooling? What are appropriate adult and child roles in the promotion of development? What is the proper or optimum relationship between formal and informal experiences?

6. Which of the major approaches to elementary education does a particular teacher or staff prefer, and why?

Two Common Views of Development and Learning

Students of human behavior, especially psychologists, have devised a number of different descriptions and explanations of human development and learning.[3] Three main views will be summarized, two in this chapter and one in the next, and examples of teaching practice, or program models, to which

---

[3] The reader will recognize such names as B. F. Skinner, Sidney Bijou and Donald Baer, Robert Gagné, Jean Piaget, Jerome Bruner, Robert White, Albert Bandura and R. H. Walters, and Arnold Gesell, among others. For summaries of some of these views, consult such works as: Alfred L. Baldwin, *Theories of Child Development* (New York: John Wiley and Sons, 1967); Jonas Langer, *Theories of Development* (New York: Holt, Rinehart and Winston, 1969); and Henry W. Maier, *Three Theories of Child Development* (New York: Harper & Row, 1965).

they are related will be presented. The main purpose of presenting these descriptions is to help facilitate movement of school staff members from unsatisfactory aspects of the standard curriculum toward local school programs that are better suited to individual children within the settings in which they are growing up.

The first, View A, underlies most standard practice in elementary schools today. As far as it goes, this view is adequate as a guide for the planning of teacher-learning activities, but it does not go far enough. View B is the basis for many of the so-called free schools and many custodial day-care centers, as well as the more formal "developmental placement" programs. It, too, has some value as a basis for understanding children's development, but is too narrow to stand alone. View C includes elements of both A and B, but goes further than either to provide a more comprehensive and potentially more fruitful perspective.

VIEW A: BEHAVIORAL-ENVIRONMENTAL

In this view, development is seen either as an accumulation of learnings over time, or as the progressive combining of sets of responses with other responses. The simplest unit of development is a stimulus, or cue, coupled with a response (S-R). Responses and patterns of responses which are elicited and reinforced are always thought of in terms of overt behaviors shaped by the environment rather than as mental structures within the individual; hence, the name *behavioral-environmental* is often given to this view. In order to teach a child something, therefore, one can simply wait for desired response patterns to appear and then reinforce them with verbal praise or tangible rewards, or one can communicate or model the desired behavior patterns and reinforce the child's making the appropriate responses. It should be easy to recognize the behavior-modification, operant-conditioning, and programmed-instruction approaches, as well as the standard lessons-and-reward systems based on gold stars, marks, and other forms of approval.

Basically, View A is a straightforward and practical approach which works in the sense that it can be made to account for a good deal of human behavior. The problem is that it neither accounts adequately for all observable learning and development nor suffices as a sole foundation for teaching practice. View A is particularly limited in its applications to teaching and to the design of educational programs and materials. For example, no one kind of reinforcement works for all people in all situations. A reward for one person may be a punishment for another. And yet marks, grades, verbal praise from the teacher, and even tangible rewards such as tokens, candy, and money are often used in indiscriminate ways that ignore possible differences in children and adults. On the other hand, since many kinds of behaviors are being reinforced all the time—often by unidentified reinforcers in the environment—teachers and principals unwittingly sustain and inhibit much student and staff behavior.

Not all those who take View A limit themselves to the responses-followed-by-rewards pattern of the familiar learning experiments. Some see environmental shaping taking place through a variety of sources, including those "ecological" reinforcers that lead men to climb high mountains and small tots to keep attempting flights of stairs, even when they constantly fall down.[4] In addition, those who emphasize "social learning" hold that children shape much of their behavior after that of older models with whom they closely identify. Finally, the conditions under which various kinds of learning may be brought about differ significantly. Robert Gagné reports, for example, that there are five distinct domains of learning, each of which requires a somewhat different approach: motor skills, verbal information, intellectual skills, cognitive strategies, and attitudes.[5] These domains are in turn related to the various disciplines and their ways of knowing in differing degrees and combinations.

In any case, applying View A to school and classroom practice is no easy task, if one accepts all the distinctions and limitations identified by its main proponents. Nevertheless, as far as it goes, this view can offer valuable guides for efforts to improve the curriculum, especially if it helps us to understand that behavior and development of children and adults are influenced through contact with the larger context of the environment and everyday relationships, above and beyond specific lessons and school subjects. We need to be sensitive to the ways in which our own behavior as individuals may be teaching others more than we intend, including things that are contrary to our intentions. And we must be alert to the ways in which the wider environment may be providing stronger cueing and reinforcement for children and teachers than those events that take place in classroom and school. Above all, we need to turn much more of our attention to finding ways of reinforcing the processes of inquiry, the development by each individual of a general knowledge framework, and the acquisition of desirable expectations and attitudes, while putting less stress on specific products and conclusions or narrowly conceived methods and skills. In Gagné's terminology, we need to be concentrating more on the domains of intellectual skills, cognitive strategies, and attitudes in addition to the motor skills and verbal information that now fill so much of the standard curriculum.

But View A, with all its potential, does not go far enough to serve as the sole basis for the planning of curriculum and instruction. It seems clear that

---

[4] See Sidney W. Bijou and Donald M. Baer, *Child Development: A Systematic and Empirical Theory,* Vol. I (New York: Appleton-Century-Crofts, 1961), Ch. 5.

[5] Robert M. Gagné, "Domains of Learning," *Interchange,* Vol. 3, No. 1 (1972), 1–8.

our environment contributes a good deal to the shaping of our behavior. It is also clear that proper training procedures cannot shape every kind of behavior or mold every kind of individual. We need to seek a wider and more comprehensive basis for our work if we are to realize significant reform from our labors.

VIEW B: MATURATIONAL-NATIVIST

Although the preceding approach gives environment, or "nurture," the dominant role in development, View B emphasizes heredity, or "nature." In this approach, the difference between the adult and the child is that the latter has not lived long enough to mature and, therefore, is not ready to do and to understand many of the things that an adult or older child can. As each child grows older, he will develop as a result of the unfolding or maturation of inner structures. Since this unfolding is guided by one's genes, this view is sometimes labeled *maturational-nativist*. Forces in the environment provide opportunities for the individual to learn what he is ready to learn, but they cannot produce readiness.

Outside influences can also affect the rate of development through variations in the conditions under which each individual lives, including the availability of food, shelter, intellectual stimulation, interpersonal security and support, and so forth. To teach under View B means to nurture in much the same fashion as a gardener cultivates a plant. Teaching and child rearing mainly involve providing a warm, hospitable setting in which children can pursue their own interests and needs. Teaching means being prepared to offer instructional materials and other educative resources when children show interest and readiness. Teaching can also mean direct instruction in various subject areas with children placed in homogeneous groups on the basis of readiness tests or developmental scales, but direct instruction that is poorly timed and imposed on an unwilling or unready child will fail to produce growth and may even inhibit such growth.

View B underlies what was perhaps the most familiar approach to nursery school and kindergarten before the advent of "compensatory" preschool programs. At the kindergarten and primary level, its most thoroughgoing application is in the Developmental Placement programs of the Gesell Institute.[6] In these programs, each child's stage of development is regularly and systematically assessed so that he may be placed in situations where the materials, equipment, and adult guidance is designed to match his readiness level. At the intermediate and secondary levels, examples can be found at

---

[6] See Frances L. Ilg and Louise Bates Ames, *School Readiness: Behavior Tests Used at the Gesell Institute* (New York: Harper & Row, 1964); and Cheshire Public Schools, *Handbook for Readiness Teachers* (Cheshire, Conn.: Cheshire Public Schools, 1969).

schools patterned after Summerhill and at many of the so-called free schools
that have been organized in the United States during the last decade or so.
In addition, many who misunderstood John Dewey's ideas produced the
laissez-faire "progressive" schools which have been the butt of so many jokes
and whose originators were taken to task by Dewey in his 1938 volume,
Experience and Education.[7] What is probably the most extremely distorted
interpretation of View B in practice, although more by omission than commission, can often be found in the centers for extended day-care of children
of working parents. In these centers, the staff considers their function to be
strictly custodial rather than educational. A major problem with this view is
that teachers often underestimate the effects of other influences and thus miss
opportunities to enhance and enrich children's development by playing too
passive a role.

As indicated in Figure 15-1, View B is inclusive of practices ranging

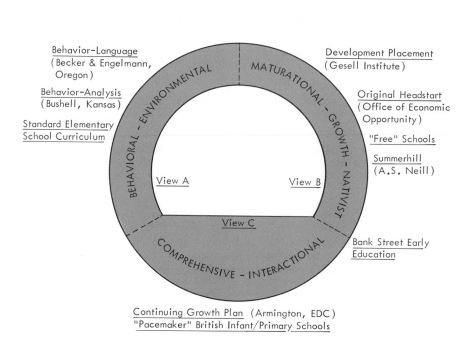

Behavior–Language
(Becker & Engelmann,
Oregon)

Behavior–Analysis
(Bushell, Kansas)

Standard Elementary
School Curriculum

Development Placement
(Gesell Institute)

Original Headstart
(Office of Economic
Opportunity)

"Free" Schools

Summerhill
(A.S. Neill)

Bank Street Early
Education

Continuing Growth Plan (Armington, EDC)
"Pacemaker" British Infant/Primary Schools

FIGURE 15-1.   Three Views of Human Development and Learning. The
three views described in Chapters 15 and 16 have been diagrammed here
to show their relationships to each other and to a number of well-known
program models. For descriptions of most of these and other models, see:
Eleanor E. Maccoby and Miriam Zellner, "Experiments in Primary Education"
(New York: Harcourt Brace Jovanovich, 1970); and Far West Laboratory,
"Early Childhood Information Unit" (New York: Educational Products Information Exchange Institute, 1973).

[7] John Dewey, *Experience and Education* (New York: Collier Books, 1963).

from minimal adult intervention to the systematic and prestructured lessons and activities that are typical of View A. Many developmental placement programs have detailed outlines of equipment and procedures to be used at various stages of development or readiness, although many of the traditional nursery schools and kindergartens try to allow each child as much freedom from adult interference as possible within the limits of available materials, space, and equipment.

If both View A and View B have limitations as the sole basis for planning instruction, then a view drawing upon the strengths of each while adding other important dimensions would be one to which educators might turn for guidance. Figure 15-1 shows diagramatically how View C, Comprehensive-Interactional, can serve this synthesizing and extending function. We describe View C in detail in the next chapter.

Self-Inventory on Views of Development

In order to help further clarify the differences among the three major views of development and to facilitate in-service study and discussion within school staffs, we include as Figure 15-2 an inventory which was developed by the EPIE Institute.[8] This inventory should not be considered as a formal test of one's views, but rather as a means to summarize the main features of each view, and as an aid to clarify one's values and beliefs about development and learning.

The following procedure is suggested for the use of this inventory.

1. Read through all the statements in order to obtain an overview of the trends in each column.

2. Go back to the beginning and check the statements that you agree with most.

3. If your view of development varies for different dimensions of development (language, emotional-affective, psychomotor, and so on), run through the inventory for each one separately. If you find general statements in two columns with which you agree strongly for several dimensions of development, check them both. Then, when you have finished the whole set, review your responses to see whether more or most of your tallies are in one column.

4. Summarize your responses on the tally sheet following the checklist and refer to the references given in Figure 15-1 for descriptions of the program models that correspond to your view.

[8] Educational Products Information Exchange Institute, "Early Childhood Education: How to Select and Evaluate Materials," *Product Report No. 42,* Vol. 5, No. 6 (March 1972), 15–22.

FIGURE 15-2. Where do you stand on human development?

From Educational Products Information Exchange Institute, "Early Childhood Education: How to Select and Evaluate Materials," *Product Report No. 42*, Vol. 5, No. 6 (March 1972), 15–22.

1. What is human development? What is it that takes place in the individual?

A	B	C
☐ Development consists of progressive changes in the observable behavior of an individual as shaped by his environment over time. Basic unit is the stimulus-response (S-R) connection which is maintained by continuing reinforcement from the environment.	☒ Development consists of the unfolding, or maturing, of genetically programmed patterns of behavior which are based on the presence of growing physiological structure.	Development consists of progressive transformations of internal structures which are the basis for individual behavior, and for which observable behavior patterns are outward evidence.
☐ Development is the accumulation of discrete "learnings" over time, or the cumulation of discrete combinations of stimuli and responses, with the responses becoming progressively more complex as the individual achieves higher orders of learning and with the simpler (more basic) patterns being prerequisites for the achievement of higher order response patterns.		☒ Development is the accumulation of discrete "learnings" over time, or the cumulation of discrete combinations of stimuli and responses, with the responses becoming progressively more complex as the individual achieves higher orders of learning and with the simpler (more basic) patterns being prerequisites for the achievement of higher order response patterns.
☐ Development is the progressive reconstruction of general internal structures which form the basis for more specific patterns of behavior or capabilities.		☒ Development is the progressive reconstruction of general internal structures which form the basis for more specific patterns of behavior or capabilities.

2. What is it that develops?

A ☐

Knowledge exists in the external world, and is acquired piece by piece in cumulative fashion. The mind is like a switchboard and storage area (data bank).

B ☐

Much of what we know preexists in the genes at birth and is brought out in successive stages through the maturation of the body with the help of proper environmental nourishment. Specific details of knowledge are also supplied by the environment.

C ☒

Knowledge exists primarily in individual knowers, and must be constructed by each one out of the data of his experience—and goes through successive qualitative transformations (as well as increasing in quantity). The mind is a transformer with storage capacity.

3. What is the nature of school subjects and other areas of knowledge?

A ☐

The disciplines, or subject field, are viewed as authoritative sources of knowledge which must be adapted (simplified and broken into pieces) for transmission to children. Scholar and student employ very different procedures for gaining knowledge.

B ☒

Knowledge fields are largely or partly inborn, so knowledge disciplines engage partly in recording what is already there (e.g., capacity for language) and partly in adding specific details (e.g., the forms of English as opposed to Spanish).

C ☐

Disciplines are viewed as models of ways of knowing about man and the world which children can draw upon in their quest for meaning. Student and scholar differ in degree rather than in kind.

4. *How does knowledge in these areas relate to overall development?*

A	B	C
☐ Main aim of instruction in the knowledge areas is to help the individual get it "right," that is, have his view of the world, way of doing things, correspond as much as possible to the way it "is" (or at least as it is seen by selected authorities).	☐ Aim of instruction is to provide optimum conditions for each individual's knowledge to mature and to take on the specific details of those in his subculture or society.	☒ Aim of instruction is to guide individuals in inquiry and to keep in continual process of transaction with other individuals so that they may share the process of inquiry and construct equivalent views of the world around them.

5. *What are the main mechanisms or processes involved in development?*
  a. *What developmental tasks are required of the individual?*

A	B	C
☐ Stress on perceptual-motor and verbal learning (paired associates—S-R bondings, chains or series, definitions, rules, verbal explanations) to equip individual to deal with the problems of living.	☐ Stress on individual expression and creativity within a context of activity (play for young children) which facilitates the unfolding of knowledge and skills and the addition of specifics.	☒ Stress on finding order and relationships: classification, seriation, generalizations, through the performing of concrete (and later, formal) operations, to help equip the individual with needed cognitive structures.

b. What are the proportional contributions of heredity (genetic code) and environment to development?

A	B	C
☐ Humans are organisms shaped largely by environment within limits set by heredity (as indicated, for example, by IQ scores).	☐ Humans are adaptive organisms with adaptive mechanisms largely programmed into the genes as a result of the process of evolution.	☒ Humans are active organisms continually meeting environmental forces halfway by engaging in adaptive behavior.
☐ Relatively passive learner (with minimal initiative and responsibility) shaped by environmental forces through the mechanism of reinforcement.		☒ Relatively active individual always striving to bring complex environmental stimuli under his control.

c. *What are the sources of motivation and reinforcement?*
Why do we learn certain things and not others?

A	B	C
☐ Mainly passive individuals are motivated to develop through systems of externally supplied reinforcement (rewards, punishment, and other incentives).	☒ Genetically programmed individual grows and matures unless blocked by circumstances in the environment. Warm, accepting setting gives general support for all development.	☐ Active individual is moved to inquire and extend his understanding and skill through recognition of dissonance between his present constructs and new data or inputs from others. Resolution of dissonance is reinforcing.
☐ Reinforcement of learning is possible through knowledge of correct responses, as well as from other sources besides tangible rewards, verbal praise, etc.	☐ Premature demands for performance can be crippling.	☒ Conflicts between individual drives or desires and norms or sanctions of others set up crisis situations which need to be resolved, if individuals are to remain healthy and fully functioning.
☐ Individual is motivated to learn, and reinforced, by similarity of own behavior to and approval by persons with whom he closely identifies.	☐ Conflicts between individual drives or desires and norms or sanctions of others set up crisis situations which need to be resolved, if individuals are to remain healthy and fully functioning.	☒ Individual motivated to learn, and reinforced, by similarity of own behavior to and approval by persons with whom he closely identifies.

d. What determines the scope and sequence of learning and development?

A	B	C
☐ Developmental progress is additive: main difference between younger and older person is that former has simply not had enough time to learn what the older one knows.	☐ Development progresses through a number of genetically determined stages, each of which must be fully completed before one is "ready" for the next.	☐ Development courses through several distinctive stages: e.g., sensory-motor to concrete-operational to formal-operational, or oral-sensory to muscular-anal to locomotive-genital, etc.
☐ Developmental progress is cumulative; simpler and less complex learnings are prerequisite to more difficult and complex; main difference between elementary and advanced is the number of prerequisite stages one has passed through.		☒ Developmental progress is cumulative; simpler and less complex learnings are prerequisite to more difficult and complex; main difference between elementary and advanced is the number of prerequisite stages one has passed through.

6. What relationships are there among the various dimensions of behavior and development: cognitive, affective, linguistic, perceptual-motor, physiological, moral, etc?

A	B	C
☐ There are clear distinctions among intellectual (cognitive), affective (emotional), and physical (perceptual-motor) development and behavior.	☐ It is important for a child to be free of emotional problems in order to develop intellectually (and in other ways).	☒ The cognitive map of an individual is a synthesis of intellectual, affective, and perceptual-motor constructs and functioning. None can be dealt with in isolation.
☐ These dimensions are capable of being isolated from each other for the purposes of instruction.	☐ Emotional-affective (including personality development, self-concept, etc.) is considered the most important focus for child rearing and teaching.	☒ Emotional-affective (including personality development, self-concept, etc.) is considered the most important focus for child rearing and teaching.
☐ Language is both a medium for communication and concomitant with thought, so that training in correct language usage and logical statements is the main avenue for promoting intellectual development.	☐ Language is a medium of communication emerging on a genetically determined schedule and given particular shape by the language environment in which a child is raised.	☒ Ordinary language (speech and writing) is only one of several media for representing phenomena (and thoughts). Language is employed for communication with others and to store and retrieve previously made constructions to and from memory.
	☐ Language must be used sparingly in instruction and always in ways matched to child's level of readiness.	☒ Thought and language arise separately, and thought precedes language statements in cognitive development, although both interact in certain important ways. Language must not be allowed to substitute for other forms of development.

Tally Sheet Summarizing Responses to Questions on Human Development.

	A	B	C
1. What is human development? What is it that takes place in the individual?	☐	☐	☐

2. What is it that develops?

3. What is the nature of school subjects and other areas of knowledge?

4. How does knowledge in these areas relate to overall development?

5. What are the main mechanisms or processes involved in development?

   a) What developmental tasks are required of the individual?

   b) What are the proportional contributions of heredity (genetic code) and environment to development?

   c) What are the sources of motivation and reinforcement? Why do we learn certain things and not others?

   d) What determines the scope and sequence of learning and development?

6. What relationships are there among the various dimensions of behavior and development: cognitive, affective, linguistic, perceptual-motor, physiological, moral, etc.?

	A	B	C
Totals			

The majority of the tallies should fall under one of the three columns, although there may be some "hybrid" combinations. Since View C is in part a synthesis of Views A and B, care should be taken to see whether or not one agrees with the statements in that column rather than with some less extensive combination of the two others.

As the reader may have recognized by now, the estimates of views of development and learning made here should be related to the teacher influence analyses suggested in Chapter 5. Views A, B, and C correspond quite

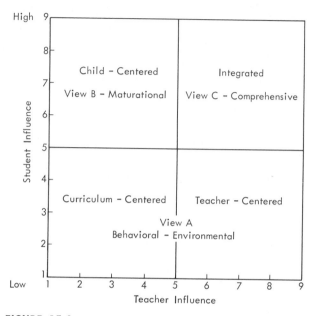

FIGURE 15-3.   Views of development and patterns of teacher-student influence.

directly to the cells in the teacher influence grid (Figure 5-1). This correspondence is shown in Figure 15-3.

In the teacher-centered quadrant, students yield to rather heavy teacher influence and exert relatively little influence on classroom goals, functioning, and operation. On the other hand, the curriculum, subject matter, and textbook are the dominant forces in the curriculum-centered quadrant with students and teachers responsible for few decisions of importance. In each case, as is consistent with View A, students are assumed to be largely reactors to external forces or stimuli provided by the teacher or the curriculum.

In the child-centered quadrant, students are granted much more control and influence over classroom life with teachers assuming facilitative and supporting roles. As is consistent with View B, the child-centered approach is based on the assumption that children develop as a result of unfolding or maturing of inner structures.

In the next chapter, we consider View C—an integrated approach that we feel offers the most complete foundation upon which to build an educational program and to improve classroom teaching in today's elementary schools.

16

A Comprehensive
View of
Human Development

ONE CONSEQUENCE of taking too narrow a view of human behavior and development is that when a particular approach does not work for a child or group of children, we do not know what to do about it. Some common ways of coping with situations in which the approaches we employ do not achieve desired ends include: (1) putting the blame on the children for not being sufficiently ready or motivated, (2) finding fault with the methods in use, and (3) blaming ourselves as practitioners for not being able to adequately carry out the approach in question. In all three cases, narrowness of view can inhibit or prevent refinement and improvement.

In this chapter, we discuss a more comprehensive view of child development than those previously considered. This view is our best estimate of the most promising model of human development for educators, given the present state of our art. However, our discussion is to be considered only a blueprint

221

from which faculty, individual teachers, and principals must construct practical working versions.

View C: Comprehensive-Interactional

Encompassing and transcending the two views described in the preceding chapter is one that synthesizes them in a larger framework. For this reason, View C can be called the *comprehensive-interactional* view. In the perspective of View C, there are five main sets of influences that contribute to shaping the course of human development from birth through adulthood: *maturation,* to which genetic factors make the major contribution; *experience,* where environment supplies the main input; *developmental tasks,* in which the individual takes the initiative and through which he interacts with objects, actions, and relationships within and around himself to promote his own development and adaptation; *consultation,* in which the individual interacts with others who are also engaged in the process of development; and the continuous interaction among all the preceding taking place as the individual strives to maintain *equilibrium* as an integrated person. The main purposes of all this activity are to make order and sense out of the world and render it predictable, and to become increasingly competent in dealing with the persistent life situations which each person has to face throughout his life.

Under View C, the child is seen as a naturally active, seeking, and adapting individual who constructs his own understanding of his world through continual transactions with it. Each child is a developing personality with feelings, emotions, and attitudes, and the complex concept of self is the most important one that develops over the years. In fact, some who hold View C see young children driven to behave as they do by sets of drives or tensions that must be released and channeled in socially acceptable and productive ways.[1] How well a child copes with the many situations he confronts influences how competent he becomes and feels, what attitudes he has toward himself, and the nature of his relationships with others. Indeed, the term "competence" has been used to encompass a number of aspects of development which are often dealt with separately: for example, language, cognition, affect, self-concept, and social and problem-solving skills.[2] The cognitive-intellectual aspects of development are the main mediators and integrators of all the others.

[1] See, for example, Erik H. Erikson, *Childhood and Society* (New York: Norton, 1963).

[2] See Robert W. White, "Competence and the Psycho-sexual Stages of Development," in M. R. Jones (ed.), *Nebraska Symposium on Motivation* (Lincoln: University of Nebraska Press, 1960); and Burton L. White, "An Analysis of Excellent Early Educational Practices: Preliminary Report," *Interchange,* Vol. 2, No. 2, (1971), 71–88.

DEVELOPMENT IN HIERARCHICAL STAGES

An important guide to matching instructional materials and activities to individual children is found in the concept of developmental stage or learning hierarchy. The operations that the infant and young child carry out to advance their own development are mainly sensory-motor in form, but as the child grows older, he becomes increasingly able to carry out internal mental operations. In the newborn infant, the operations or developmental tasks consist of activities such as sucking, grasping, following with the eyes, and vocalizing. As development progresses, each discrete operation is gradually combined with others into increasingly coordinated and complex patterns of relationships. At first, the child knows things by what he can and cannot do to and with them using his senses and his limbs. As time goes on, new operations appear, are coordinated with older ones, and become internalized so that they can be carried on mentally. To facilitate this mental manipulation, many operations are also linked to representational systems in which some things, or actions, can be made to stand for or represent others. Oral language is the most obvious form of representation and mode of communication, especially as the young child begins to use words, but representation is also carried on through imitation, gesture, and make-believe.

The child who enters kindergarten has come a long way. He has all but mastered speech in his mother tongue and may even recognize some printed words. He is well acquainted with the workings of the world immediately around him, and he can carry out many everyday tasks on his own. However, it is important to keep in mind that the young child's knowledge is limited to what he has experienced directly and at first-hand. Most of his understanding is dominated by the way things appear to his senses. His view of the world is largely egocentric and, therefore, he cannot see things the way they look or feel to others. Although the kindergartner can talk about things often in very adultlike ways, the educator has to be careful not to be misled by this verbal facility into thinking that talk can substitute adequately for carrying on direct motor-perceptual manipulation of the objects and events which the child is attempting to understand.

As each child advances through the elementary school years, he gradually becomes more like an adult in his ability to deal with abstractions, to mentally manipulate aspects of his experience, to carry on complex problem-solving activities involving numerous variables, and to understand others' abstract verbal communications. Both the beginning and the end of the elementary school span are marked by transition periods in which profound changes are taking place in the ways in which the child understands the world, changes that are qualitatively more significant than any that will take place for the rest of his life. In the terms coined by one of the chief architects of the comprehensive-developmental view, Jean Piaget, the elementary school years include the major developmental stage of concrete operations, where children can deal logically with events within their experience, and portions of two others, the prelogical stage from which the kindergartner is just emerging and the formal operations stage into which the sixth-grader is rapidly moving.[3]

The main features of the hierarchical-stage perspective on human development are:

1. There is a continuum of distinctive, yet intimately interrelated, stages. At each stage the *dominant* behavior patterns are qualitatively different; that is, each individual's ways of thinking, bases for making moral choices, conceptions of self and others, vary from stage to stage in general, yet behavior more characteristic of higher or lower stages does occur.

2. The stages are hierarchical in the sense that (a) each stage occurs in invariant order from the lowest to the highest, with environmental forces being able to affect the rate of progress, but not the order of stages; (b) each lower stage is prerequisite to the next higher one and must be fulfilled before the individual can advance to the next stage; and (c) each subsequent stage incorporates all the functions of the previous ones at a more complex level. The type of behavior carried on at the lower stage does not disappear, but is transformed into a higher level of functioning and can appear in its original form, too, under the right conditions.

3. Development takes place along a continuum, or spiral, rather than in stair-step fashion; thus, an individual is not only capable of patterns of behavior characteristic of other stages, but does not necessarily operate on the highest level of which he is capable at all times.

4. Progress to higher stages is not inevitable with increase in chronological age: it does not occur through maturation alone, and rates of development can vary widely among individuals and across developmental dimensions and knowledge areas. Developmental progress must be stimulated through active interactions with the people and objects of the world in ways relevant to each stage, dimension, and knowledge area.

5. Although it is possible to change an individual's behavior by directly rewarding specific acts, it is more fruitful in the long run for behavior change to come about as a result of the stagewise extensions and rearrangements of each individual's cognitive map that occur as he continually confronts situations that require such change.

[3] For background reading in this area, see: Hans G. Furth, *Piaget for Teachers* (Englewood Cliffs, N.J.: Prentice-Hall, 1970); and *Piaget and Knowledge* (Englewood Cliffs, N.J.: Prentice-Hall, 1969). See also Molly Brearley and Elizabeth Hitchfield, *A Teacher's Guide to Reading Piaget* (London: Routledge and Kegan Paul, 1966); and Jean Piaget, *The Child and Reality* (New York: Grossman, 1973).

The most important part of the hierarchical framework can be called *general knowledge*. This is the overview and general understanding; the mental roadmap that enables a person to work out in his mind any number of different routes for getting from one idea to another. *Specific knowledge,* on the other hand, consists of particular locations or explicit directions or recipes. General knowledge is the larger framework that interrelates many specifics and facilitates learning and retention. Specific knowledge consists of the pieces, the names of things, verbal rules, definitions, and concept labels. The ability to conceptualize, to form concepts and principles, is considered to be general knowledge, and each concept, particularly each example of a concept, is considered to be specific knowledge.

Specific knowledge is very important; moreover, it is unavoidable since it is around us all the time, and each of us must possess a good deal of it in order to function adequately in everyday life. It is, however, altogether too easy for educators and parents to neglect the development of general knowledge in their anxiety to provide children with specifics. Although much specific knowledge can be transmitted to children through direct training, general knowledge requires different sets of conditions and longer time spans. General knowledge is developed as a result of what Lawrence Kohlberg has called "massive general experience," the continuing everyday encounters with objects and situations which children approach from many different angles, manipulate physically, verbally, and mentally, compare what they see with others, and seek answers to many, many questions.[4] Most of these encounters need to be carried out by children on their own initiative, but there are many ways in which adults can help by providing materials, settings, interpersonal support, and guidance.

IMPLICATIONS FOR ELEMENTARY EDUCATION

There are a number of implications of a hierarchical-developmental perspective for the planning, implementation, and evaluation of instructional programs. We should think of scope and sequence in terms of a spiral that is narrow at the base and becomes increasingly wider and deeper as it moves upward. This spiral symbolizes the child's movement from very limited experience and the ordering and interrelating of that experience at the preschool level to ever-expanding and differentiating ways of knowing about the world. Concepts are not "learned" in their final form for once and for all at any one point in time, but continue to grow and develop as each individual gains more experience and moves upward through successive stages of development in each knowledge area. For example, the concepts "mother" and "bottle" have one set of meanings for the newborn infant, another set of meanings for the toddler, and so on, up to and beyond the time when that same in-

[4] Lawrence Kohlberg and Rochelle Mayer, *Early Education: A Cognitive-Developmental View* (Chicago: Dryden Press, 1973).

dividual has his own children and grandchildren. Similarly, history topics and works of literature cannot be "done" at just one age or grade level. *Winnie the Pooh, The Wind in the Willows,* and *The Little Prince,* to name just three, are stories that can be read again and again and yield new and deeper meanings at each succeeding stage of development. There is often enough content in single events of history for several contemporary historians with various viewpoints, as well as those in succeeding generations, to find plenty of fresh things to say about them.

Another aspect of the hierarchical-stage view pertains to teacher judgments as to whether children are "right," that is, responding appropriately to questions that are posed, problems encountered, or interpersonal situations in which they are involved. "Rightness" is partially a function of the individual's current developmental stage in any given dimension. Thus, the five-year-old who describes space travel in terms of his local rapid transit system, and to whom outer space is anywhere beyond the end of the line (which is as far as he has ever gone), is really quite correct as far as he is able to go. Similarly, the child who is still largely egocentric and, therefore, cannot yet perceive situations from the points of view of other people, should not be chastized for not considering the feelings of others. The appropriateness of a child's behavior cannot be judged exclusively by adult criteria. If a child is expected to say the "right" things and to act in "right" ways, he may show conformity, but not commitment and understanding.

Following View C, a school should be a laboratory where children and adults can confront questions and problems, try out their own methods and approaches to finding answers and solutions, and test their own conclusions. Some of the problems and questions will arise out of those that have already been solved. As old answers are tried out in new situations, discrepancies will appear and the limitations of previous formulations will be revealed. The wise teacher and principal can arrange the environment so that many different kinds of problems can be confronted on a number of different developmental levels.

Basic to View C is the assumption that neither the teacher nor the student can assume a passive role in the life of a classroom. View C is demanding in its intellectual expectations for both student and teacher. To the teacher goes major responsibility for providing a living and concept-rich educational program, and to the student goes major responsibility for getting to the inside of this educational program. Students are not free to chart their own exclusive course as in View B, nor are they required to merely react to the educational program as in View A. In View C, students, teachers, and the disciplines of life become interdependent parts of the school's educational program.

17

Evolving
Open Classrooms

WHAT WE HAVE ATTEMPTED to provide in the chapters just preceding is a theoretical basis for navigating in instructional waters. The navigation aids offered are the knowledge disciplines with their ways of knowing conceived in a hierarchical-developmental perspective and a concept of educational program to replace the standard curriculum with its predetermined scope and sequence of content, its largely didactic and teacher-centered or child-centered methodology, and its overdependence on standardized tests for use in evaluation of pupil progress. The disciplines viewed developmentally can provide a common thread for students, teachers, and principals to follow through the curriculum of the elementary school, thus replacing the standard school subjects.

In these final two chapters, we offer suggestions to teachers and principals for carrying out the long-range tasks of reformulating educational programs while they are in operation. Suggestions provided are based upon actual case studies,[1] but are necessarily summary-composites rather than detailed accounts.

Before proceeding, a word on terminology is necessary. As indicated in Chapter 6, an informal approach to classroom teaching is, in our judgment, most consistent with the kinds of elementary school organization, leadership, and instructional program that are the main themes of this book. In the title of the present chapter the same approach is labeled "open classroom," but others have referred to informal approaches as "integrated."

Whatever they are called, open or informal classrooms are complex and involved operations. Each one is unique, reflecting a particular mix of participants, materials, and settings, and each must evolve from more formal formats over a period of years. There is no such thing as *the* open classroom, and there is no way of producing a full-blown one overnight.[2] Classrooms that appear open to some observers are not; yet there are many classrooms that possess degrees of openness, but go unheralded. The problem facing teachers and principals who are interested in informal approaches to elementary education is how to develop more than the superficial trappings of openness.

Getting Started

The best way to start the process of program redevelopment and in-service growth of staff is with volunteers in schools where a good percentage of the teachers have had at least two years' teaching experience. Some teachers may want to start off slowly by concentrating on single subject areas, or by giving over only small periods of time each day when children are encouraged to pursue independent activities. Others will prefer to "go for broke" and immediately begin to teach their children how to take responsibility for their own learning in all subject areas, as well as engaging in the process of reconceptualizing those knowledge areas. In any case, all involved should be allowed to move with "all deliberate speed," or at a pace that feels most comfortable and manageable to each individual. Teachers who volunteer will be most apt to commit the time and energy needed to make significant progress, and after the first crew gets well underway and builds up some excitement and enthusiasm, others will want to join in. Some arm twisting might be done by the principal and other leaders to urge participation, but any efforts that smack of compulsory involvement are apt to create more resent-

---

[1] Most of the suggestions have been implemented by the staffs of one or more public elementary schools in northern California.

[2] This was Lucy A. Haskell's conclusion after a year of intensive study in England. See *The Pacemaker British Primary Schools: Studies in Innovation and Change in Education*. Unpublished Doctoral Dissertation (Berkeley: University of California, 1971).

ment than creativity. Experienced teachers who have already worked out relaxed ways of living with children can give more time and thought to innovation and study than most beginners who are often still concerned with maintaining control and discipline.

Children and their parents will also need to be involved in the changes that are made. Students not accustomed to acting on their own initiative and taking responsibility for their own conduct will have to learn how. Adult control can be phased out as pupil control takes hold. Parents will need to be helped not only to find ways to participate in the classroom and otherwise to enrich their children's lives, but often just to recognize reading, writing, and mathematics in their new forms, that is, without relying exclusively on textbooks and workbooks to assure them that these areas are being covered. Above all, it is best not to announce at the outset of a curriculum redevelopment effort that the school is embarking upon a special "new" program, whether it is called open, informal, or whatever. The more gradual and ordinary the shift, the better for all concerned. In curriculum reform, evolution works better in the long run than revolution.

CLASSROOM ORGANIZATION PATTERNS

Assuming that a teacher is starting out with a fairly traditional approach to school subjects and teacher-initiated activities, there are a number of organizational arrangements for the classroom that can be employed, either singly or in combination.

1. Learning centers can be organized in which single knowledge areas are represented by various kinds of materials and problems to solve or activities to carry out. These can be tailored to individual students or to levels in the developmental sequence and should be varied enough to accommodate a range of learning styles and individual interests on the part of the children.

2. Individual and small group contracts between students and the teacher can be established, outlining objectives to be pursued and work to be completed over given periods of time in one or more knowledge areas. Contracts work best when they are worked out cooperatively between students and teachers.

3. Individual, small group, or whole class projects can be organized within single knowledge areas or on problems that cut across several areas. These projects can be set up in learning centers or they can involve a wider range of activities and locations including those outside the school and classroom. The duration of such projects can be anywhere from one or two days to more than a month.

4. Individual, small group, or whole class projects can be developed

involving the concurrent study of selected topics or themes from the points of view of a number of disciplines.

5. One or two time periods during each day can be set aside for students to work in a manner different from the traditional way. This can be in single subject areas or a kind of "free activity" period for work on electives such as art, music, movement, and crafts as well as in regular areas such as history, mathematics, and language.

6. The teacher can select one subject or knowledge area to be approached from a direction utilizing teacher-pupil planning, contracts, and projects focused on problems or themes. Sometimes an area that is not a regular part of the standard curriculum makes a good place to start—for example, movement, art, group dynamics, self-knowledge, or music.

There are several keys to reorganizing classroom work. Among them are *cooperative planning* among teachers and students in light of mutually understood aims and objectives; careful *record keeping* by teachers and students of aims, actual activities carried out and materials used, and evaluation results; and allowance for as much *individual initiative* on the part of teachers and students in determining the time, place, and manner of their learning activities as they can currently handle.

Some school staffs have found it helpful to work out a sequential list of objectives for various knowledge areas as specifically as possible covering the entire range of age or grade levels represented at their school. Having such a list can help free teachers from the idea that certain subjects, skills, or levels of development are restricted to certain grade levels. Such a list can also facilitate smooth articulation of student developmental activities and teacher guidance from one grade level or teacher to the next. Most important, such a sequential outline often gives teachers a clear perspective from which to operate in carrying on teacher-pupil planning activities.

The learning center can be viewed as an intermediate step on the road to the organization of more free-wheeling and flexible activities and experiences. As an alternative to textbooks and workbooks, a learning center can offer students a specific place to go within the classroom and specific directions for daily work without the usual restrictions. Each center can offer the teacher a way of evolving individualized activities for students which are valid developmentally and in relation to the ways of knowing of relevant disciplines on a day-to-day or weekly basis without having to produce a whole year's program in advance. Student work contracts are a variation on the learning center idea, since they can detail places to go and resources to tap, thus giving the student the task of assembling materials and ideas he needs, instead of having the teacher collect all the required items for him. Students can help create learning centers and materials for other students to use.

The other side of the aims-and-objectives coin is record keeping and evaluation. Regular records should be kept by both students and teachers. Records are needed of aims and objectives formulated, contracts entered into, learning encounters engaged in, settings and experiences exposed to, and outcomes and results. Each student might, for example, keep a booklet subdivided into knowledge areas and topics in which he can log selected activities, check off developmental milestones as they are passed, carry unfinished work over for future attention, and write up evaluations of various facets of his schoolwork and his own progress. Teachers should keep similar records on students and should compare these records with the ones kept by students from time to time. This evaluation is formative in that it contributes continually to the learning-teaching process. Further, evaluation of this sort encompasses a wider range of aims and objectives than do existing standardized tests and exercises at the end of textbook chapters.

Quality assessments of student progress, concerning materials and procedures used as well as the acquisition of knowledge and competence, can be made by individuals and groups. Techniques that can be employed include observation often using checklists as guides; interviews; reviews by outside agents; criterion-referenced tests; demonstrations such as readings, recitals, and performances; and standardized tests. Evaluation centers, like learning centers, can be set up to guide students and teachers through self-evaluation. Where necessary, these centers could be constructed with the help of resource people possessing needed expertise.

Student initiative and autonomy, as important as they are, cannot be created by teacher fiat; students will need to learn how to take responsibility for promoting their own development. With a good deal of prior structuring, children with little experience can start off by handling small tasks with short time spans and gradually take over more and more responsibility on their own. A teacher might, for example, group her students into three types: "people-to-people" students who have to be under direct adult supervision most of the time; "learning station" students whose days are organized largely around learning station activities; and "autonomous" students who are on their own during those parts of the day when students are carrying out individual and small group activities, but who meet regularly with the teacher to plan and to discuss their work. People-to-people students would be aware that they could move up to working in centers on their own and, ultimately, to independent functioning as they acquire the necessary competence and are able to accept the necessary responsibility.

INSTRUCTIONAL VEHICLES

In the open classroom, the structure of activities is derived in large part from the knowledge disciplines viewed developmentally rather than from predetermined sequences of subject matter to be presented in series of lessons. Still, it is important to identify organizational vehicles in the instructional program that can serve to help students to clearly see their progress. Instead of merely trying to fulfill expectations of a teacher on a day-to-day basis, each student should have a goal-oriented role over which he has a good deal of control.

Three general kinds of vehicles can be employed to fulfill the function of carrying students through their various stages of development: knowledge area formats, projects, and community problems.

Knowledge Area Formats. For the most part, ways of introducing students to the knowledge disciplines should be developed by individual teachers and local school staffs using resource persons and materials from the various fields as needed. There are, however, a number of sets or series of *focusing materials* already on the market that can be put to creative and productive use by classroom teachers. Examples of these include materials available from the Science Curriculum Improvement Study (SCIS); the American Academy for the Advancement of Science (AAAS), "Science: A Process Approach"; the Elementary Science Study (ESS) science programs; the Nuffield Foundation Mathematics Project in mathematics; "Man: A Course of Study" from the Educational Development Center (EDC); and the Lawrence Senesh economics materials, "Our Working World."

Knowledge area formats such as these can be employed with large groups, small groups, or individual students. Each can be utilized in a learning center and through student contracts for work to be completed at each individual's own pace over given periods of time. In the hands of the classroom teacher, these formats also lend themselves to the promotion of a good deal of student and teacher initiative and autonomy, as well as to the use of many resources beyond the sets themselves, the school, and the classroom. In many ways, the packaged kits and the units suggested in some of the professional books can serve as means for making a transition from a standard school subject program to a more discipline-centered and developmental one. This can work especially well if teachers and principals themselves engage in many of the activities suggested for students and thus learn along with their students about the knowledge areas involved and how each illuminates typical human situations. Crucial to the use of such highly organized curriculum materials is the preservation of discretion for teachers. Such materials should not be considered as teacher substitutes, but as aides or tools to be adjusted, adapted, and tinkered with by professionals at work.

Problem Areas and Projects. Activities that center on problem areas, project themes, or other kinds of recurring topics make up another format for structuring the program of the open classroom. Such approaches were much more familiar to American educators during the 1930s than they have been since the end of World War II, but the recent interest in the British Primary

Schools has brought about a revival of project and activity methods. What is involved in this format is the organization of children's school activities, including their studies in the knowledge areas, around topics, themes, and problems. Some of these are taken up regularly at given grade levels, others only when they are of current importance. Topics can cover such areas as "transportation," "horses," "Indians," or "man's tools." Contemporary problems might include pollution, the population explosion, war, or poverty. Younger children can deal best with problems that focus on family, school, neighborhood, and other familiar experience areas. Projects may center on exploring questions through research and experimentation leading to the sharing of findings, or on the production of a play or film requiring background research and the development of technical skills, on the planning of a picnic or bazaar, or on the working-out of interpersonal relationships or group processes within the classroom.

Projects and similar activities often serve as vehicles for independently carrying students through a series of days and even weeks. This in turn can free the teacher to circulate about the room to help individuals and groups when needed and to make sure that everyone has the resources needed. Teachers also are able to leave the classroom for short periods to take selected students on trips, to help arrange for use of resources elsewhere in the building, or to confer with parents and colleagues. During the teacher's absence, many older children will be able to carry on alone, while classrooms with younger children can be successfully supervised by parent volunteers or the principal and other members of the administrative staff. A school library or Instructional Materials Center also makes a good second classroom in which students may work without the direct and constant supervision of their own teacher.

Community Problems and Projects. Activities in which students engage can also involve adults outside of school—parents, government employees, elected officials, business and professional people, members of service agencies, or other teachers and scholars. Students can be involved in out-of-school, but school-related, enterprises for brief periods of time or up to a period of several months. The problems that activities focus upon can be many and varied with some being very practical "how-to" skill-building ventures and others directly related to one or more disciplines involving concept building, research, and problem-solving. Children might clear a vacant lot and equip it for a playground, raise money to buy equipment for a nature center or conservation project, or just find out about how things work by studying the operations of a supermarket, a post office, a manufacturing plant, a farm or ranch, or a hospital. In each case, the adults involved could participate in helping the children to understand what was going on, what roles were taken by various people, and how various functions interrelated. It is even possible to have "satellite centers" around the community to which children might go on selected days, or for periods of a week or more at a time, to study some aspect of the community or wider environment before coming back to their regular classroom to sum up and report their findings.

Again, the disciplines and their ways of knowing can serve as invaluable guides to making all experiences as educative as possible for all concerned. The principal, of course, would have a key role in seeing that the many parts of the extended school campus fit together, as well as in being the chief teacher and scholar in selected knowledge areas.

INSTRUCTIONAL MATERIALS

Instructional materials and equipment play a central role in the structuring of children's activities. In the open classroom where there is minimal dependence on preselected and presequenced mass-produced materials such as textbooks and workbooks for the patterning of activity, the kinds and quality of materials to which children are exposed need to be carefully selected. In fact, all instructional materials, whether produced locally or commercially, should be regularly subjected to systematic *curriculum design analyses* and *learner verification*.[3] Learner verification studies are designed to determine in what ways, and how well, specific materials actually function with various kinds of students. A curriculum design analysis contributes to the understanding of the materials' content with respect to four main categories: aims and objectives, scope and sequence of content, methods of teaching and learning, and evaluation. Learner verification is carried on only to a very limited extent by the commercial producers of educational materials, and yet their products are enormously influential in structuring the day-to-day and hour-to-hour learning activities in which school children engage. One recent study found that in Texas children spent 75 percent of their classroom time and 90 percent of their homework time with textbooks and textbook-related materials.[4]

The hard reality behind all of this is that the great majority of the instructional materials on the market are not developed in direct interaction with potential users, nor are they user-tested and then revised in light of user feedback. For the most part, materials are promoted by their commercial producers rather than learner-verified, and the little field testing that is carried out usually leads to the dubious conclusion that the product is fine the way it is.

---

[3] See, for example, "Shifting Educational Realities and the Learner Verification of Instructional Materials" (New York: EPIE Institute, July 1973). The EPIE Institute has worked out, with Maurice Eash of the University of Illinois, Chicago Circle, a "Curriculum Design Analysis" instrument for use in evaluating materials for its *EPIE Product Reports*. Educational Products Information Exchange (EPIE) Institute, 463 West Street, New York, New York 10014.

[4] See Michael Kirst and Decker Walker, "An Analysis of Curriculum Policy Making," *Review of Educational Research*, Vol. 41, No. 5 (1971), 479–509.

The onus is not entirely on the producers, since they could not function as they do without cooperation from school purchasing agents and decision makers, including principals. Recent studies of the "state of the art" of the evaluation and selection of instructional materials have revealed that:

Selectors typically fail to investigate claims made for products by their producers.

Selectors often consider too few options, often selecting from among the first few items offered, either because they are unaware of alternatives or because there is no time to look further.

Selection is often done without regard for special staff training and/or equipment requirements of the materials.

There is a lack of consistency in educator judgment; often principals and administrators are poor judges of the learner effectiveness of materials, and selectors are not in touch with the population of children for whom the selections are being made.

In all too few cases, school districts have banded together to share the cost of analyzing products, to use local expertise in the evaluations, or to analyze the information they may have collected on the functioning and effectiveness of given products.[5]

All of this can be remedied, not only by more local production of materials best suited to local students and situations, but also by teaming up with other schools and school districts to put pressure on producers to carry on continuous learner verification and revision of their materials.

LOCAL PRODUCTION OF INSTRUCTIONAL MATERIALS

In planning for movement toward open classroom formats, many teachers will have to try to take a fresh view of instructional materials and their role in children's development. There is a whole range of items from all sources that can engage children's attention and contribute to their development. One has only to consider the countless everyday objects, from toys to tin cans, kitchen utensils and cereal boxes, to street signs and articles of junk, that provide the grist for children's learning mills. Think of all the potentially educative items that fall in one or more of the following categories:

People, animals, and other living things.

Places, locales, buildings, closed and open spaces.

---

[5] See, for example, Educational Products Information Exchange Institute, *Evaluation Practices Used in the Selection of Educational Material and Equipment* (Albany: Division of Educational Communications, State Department of Education, December 1969).

Patterns of relationships, concept class members, sequences, cause-effect relationships, time, space, interpersonal interactions.

Qualities, such as color, shape, size, and texture (which are external), and feelings (which are internal).

Events, happenings, occasions, situations, predicaments; and actions, processes, procedures, and tasks.

Representations, such as things people say, gestures and facial expressions, imitation and role playing, numbers and mathematical relationships, writing and printing, pictures, diagrams, and models.

These are categories of direct experience with everyday-life phenomena that children can draw upon in their building of knowledge and understanding.

There are differences in point of view about the extent to which one must deal with children's direct experiences in order to promote meaningful development of concepts, generalizations, problem-solving skills, and attitudes. Nevertheless, most authorities would consider it important to expose children to direct contacts with concrete objects and actions at least during the initial stages of any instructional sequence, particularly when the children have not yet acquired the cognitive structures necessary for dealing with phenomena in abstract terms. Therefore, when considering the production and use of instructional materials, it is important to keep in mind the extent to which they are concrete or abstract. See, for example, the scale provided in Figure 17-1.

Summing Up: The Educator's Role

The role of the educator should be to complement and to collaborate with, rather than to try to replace or preempt, what children and the community are already doing. More specifically, the educational agent and especially teachers and principals should see to it that children have access to the following conditions of growth and development:

1. Relevant experience situations, both as part of their everyday life and interests and as contrived instructional situations, the object being to help children become involved in the fullest possible range of disciplines and ways of knowing.

2. Exemplary models of a wide variety of ways of knowing and behaving as a human being; examples of people engaged in roles involving the sciences, literature, the performing arts, and moral choice making; cues to what to look for in the various fields of knowledge; and ways of relating the knowledge fields to one another and to the wholeness and complexity of everyday living.

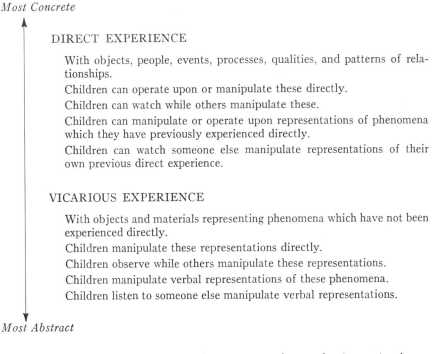

Most Concrete

DIRECT EXPERIENCE

With objects, people, events, processes, qualities, and patterns of relationships.

Children can operate upon or manipulate these directly.

Children can watch while others manipulate these.

Children can manipulate or operate upon representations of phenomena which they have previously experienced directly.

Children can watch someone else manipulate representations of their own previous direct experience.

VICARIOUS EXPERIENCE

With objects and materials representing phenomena which have not been experienced directly.

Children manipulate these representations directly.

Children observe while others manipulate these representations.

Children manipulate verbal representations of these phenomena.

Children listen to someone else manipulate verbal representations.

Most Abstract

FIGURE 17-1.   A scale of experience referents for instructional programs.

Access to various kinds of experience means contact, in more thorough ways than might be usual. Access means opportunities to see, feel, and manipulate first-hand; it means a large measure of individual control over the time, place, and manner of contact; and it means sufficient time to ponder, to try things out, to let ideas "rattle around," to make mistakes and correct them, and to share and consult with others.

The younger the child, the more important it is for him to be able to draw upon data in the setting and time period in which he lives. This means not only acknowledging differences among children in their lives outside of school, but also valuing what each child brings with him and helping him to value it and to build upon it. How he conceives of himself, the dialect he speaks, the nature of his family and the neighborhood in which he lives, all of these represent important springboards to further understanding.

Educators can also provide guidance in:

1. Carrying on the developmental, or learning, tasks, that are at the same time appropriate to the various knowledge disciplines, the

developmental levels of the individuals involved, and the areas of experience and instructional resources which are available.

2. Continually moving back and forth from the relatively complex and interrelated aspects of everyday living to the relatively simple and selected foci of the individual disciplines. Children can, for example, be helped to move from direct encounters with various aspects of the marketplace to classroom reenactments of the producer-to-consumer movement of goods and services, and thence to dealing with such basic economic concepts as producer, consumer, division of labor, money as a medium of exchange, and back again.

Interpersonal support can also be supplied for inquiry, for risk taking and making mistakes, and for being self-critical as well as critical of others. Children and teachers, or anyone delving into new and unfamiliar areas, need settings in which they can be free of the many, complex demands of day-to-day living so that they may have time to study and discuss, ponder and experiment, and reach and test new conclusions. Even in areas of knowledge and in relation to problem areas that do not lend themselves to group instruction, the presence of group support and guidance can be vital. Groups of individuals who meet and work together regularly (although not necessarily every day) can get to know one another well and thus build the foundations for trust and mutual support.

Finally, *flexibility* is needed to permit maximum use of existing resources, while allowing for a range of individual differences in interests, learning styles, levels of development, and temperament. Locales for activities need to be many and varied: sometimes in classrooms and at other times in the school building and the wider community. Groupings need to be flexible, too; children should be able to work alone, in small groups, with children of their own age and older, and with adults. Those who offer guidance and counseling must be chosen as much for what they have to offer to specific children as for their official status as teachers, experts, or administrators. This means the extensive use of parents, older children and youths, adult aides and volunteers, people from different occupations, and scholars from various disciplines. This also means that a wide variety of materials and equipment must be employed. Textbooks and other specifically designed media would not necessarily be excluded, but many items that are locally produced and otherwise made available to children and teachers on a local or regional basis must be included.

18

Staff Development for Curriculum Improvement

IT IS OUR BELIEF that the "curriculum" is community-wide and not
the exclusive property of the schools. No manner of change that takes place
exclusively within the walls of the schools and that involves only students and
school staff will suffice. All educational agents with whom children have contact need to be involved—especially parents. Further, broader reforms in the
society at large are ultimately going to have to take place, including the
virtual elimination of poverty; of discrimination on the basis of sex, race, or
ethnic origins; and the broadening of the bases used for judging individual
worth.

This suggests that the elementary school curriculum cannot simply be
written down and packaged for dissemination to schools across the nation. The
main curriculum development work needs to be carried on by local educators
and students in ways best suited to local situations. Published materials such
as books, films, and other media will be needed, but in themselves are not
sufficient. *Knowledge exists in people, and the school curriculum is in the*

minds of teachers. Both knowledge and curriculum must be built up gradually and continually transformed over long periods of time through the active participation of people. There are no quick and easy formulas and no packages of instant curriculum. Further, there is no real help for the educator who is unwilling or unable to put a good deal of hard work into his own self-development. Ideally, the best instructional materials are those that teach the principals and teachers who use them as much as or more than they teach children.

Needed Directions

Curriculum development comes down to being mostly professional staff development. To change the curriculum is to change teachers' understanding of what they are doing. Changes in instructional materials and equipment can support the process of professional development as can changes in verbal statements of assumptions and objectives, but neither is sufficient in itself. The balance of this chapter examines the role of the school in the overall education of children and provides some specific suggestions for professional staff development activities.

We should seek to understand the process by which such school programs develop, and the general principles guiding developments, not just the final product of program development activities. What the principal should seek to understand are the conditions under which teachers are willing and able to work for reform and the principles that guide such work so that it accumulates over a period of years. How parents and other community members can best be kept in touch with, as well as involved in, the changes that do take place are other important considerations.

SOME ASSUMPTIONS

As we consider the interdependent nature of staff development and curriculum development, our discussion is based on the following assumptions.

1. The major responsibility for decisions about educational program belongs to the professional staff as it consults closely with parents and the broader community. The goal is to develop autonomous school communities that reflect the educational philosophies and goals of teachers, principals, parents, and children.
2. Principals act primarily as educational leaders and as partners with teachers and others in the educational process. They teach, lead curriculum reform, and support the development of others.

3. The curriculum undergoes continual development and evaluation by the school staff in cooperation with others in the community. Professional staff development is built into the educators' regular job. In-service training is emphasized more than preservice preparation.

Two of these assumptions are crucial. First, there must be a good deal of *autonomy* for each school's staff concerning matters of policy, planning, and budget with all staff members sharing key decision-making and instructional activities. This autonomy includes, among other things, the availability of discretionary funds for each teacher's use in purchasing supplies and materials throughout the school year and much flexibility on determining the time, place, and manner of meeting with students. Second, staff and program development means the use of the knowledge disciplines and specialists in child development and learning in new ways. The best-known examples of both of these conditions are currently to be found in the British educational system where headmasters and their staffs are the main loci of control in public-supported education, with the Local Education Authorities (roughly analogous to our school boards) and the Central Advisory Council (something like our state departments of education) playing subsidiary (albeit, important) advisory and supportive roles.

Some Approaches to Staff Development

It is important to find ways of having teachers spend less of their regular working hours as custodians of groups of children. Part of developing the answer lies in working out new ways of being *with* children, that is, fresh teacher-pupil roles. Another part of the answer lies in scheduling and resource use that allow teachers to work with other adults for certain hours within the school day. In this section, we offer some suggestions for ways to promote professional staff development through encouraging and enabling teachers to become part-time scholars and students of the process of education.

Elementary schools should become centers of inquiry and scholarship with a humanistic and developmental emphasis. Provisions for teachers to further their own education should be built into the school day, week, and year, just as we build in provisions for the education of children; the two are indeed intimately related. This means time during the school day will need to be set aside for study seminars, for joint planning and sharing with colleagues, for self-analysis of one's own teaching and learning processes, and for other similar activities, rather than just using the time available at the end of the school day, on weekends, or during the summer. This may also mean eleven-month contracts and perhaps eleven-month school years, with the time for which teachers are paid divided between direct instruction and counseling with students and other professional activities.

One format for carrying out this continuing staff development effort is the seminar or workshop. A basic agenda for such seminars—modified, of course, to suit local needs—might look like this:

1. Using the points of view and inquiry tools of selected disciplines, participants would study everyday situations in school and community. These situations could include individual behavior, perhaps case studies of students, classroom and other group behavior, the school system or building staff and many aspects of the wider community. Part of the time would be spent becoming familiar with ways of knowing and conceptual structures to be employed, and then applying these to the objects of study. The disciplines involved could be those directly related to the school's instructional program and to teaching, or those related to problems involved in working as a staff and in the wider community. In any case, the problems taken up should be those considered important by those involved.

2. The process described above is then repeated employing the same disciplines and ways of knowing, but focusing on other cases both within the same community and in other areas, or employing disciplines not previously brought to bear on the same objects of study. As these studies progress, implications can be drawn from them concerning both further study and applications to programs with children.

3. Either in the course of carrying out the activities suggested above, or as a subsequent step after each round, teachers can work to systematically relate each of the disciplines to other areas of the curriculum and to other disciplines.

4. Another important task which can be the subject of workshop sessions has to do with the reconstruction of professional and lay educational roles and of institutional structures and functions in order to promote individual initiative, open-ended inquiry, and competence in coping with the problems of working cooperatively in child-rearing and teaching activities. This process can be aided through the kinds of studies suggested above, but it involves the day-to-day working-out of interpersonal relationships, as well as major policy-making and strategy sessions.

5. Finally, both as a part of steps 1–3 and as a kind of culminating activity, workshop participants should be given the opportunity to construct materials for classroom use. Such materials might include data banks, verification materials, kits of inquiry tools, and formats

for evaluation and record keeping, as well as tools for studying their own teaching behavior and the teaching-learning process as it takes place in their classrooms.

However the workshop and seminar sessions are organized and scheduled, they should be related as much as possible to the actual work of teaching. Teachers on any given staff will show varying degrees of readiness for making changes in their classroom and other professional roles. Some may feel more comfortable starting with one subject area that is currently under study in a seminar, or with special work in that subject area that is carried out by students only during a special "activity" period once a day or once a week. Other teachers may be ready to begin learning centers in a single subject area and then quickly spread the format to others. In any case, starting with teachers "where they are" is as important as it is with students. The principal will have to use his best-informed judgment in order to individualize his work with teachers as much as possible.

Time to carry on in-service activities is an extremely important factor. Some teachers will be willing to spend many of their afternoons and even evenings and weekends preparing for their work with students and working on their own self-improvement, but this is really too much to expect as a matter of course. Ultimately, time for carrying on staff and program development activities will have to be scheduled as a regular part of the days and weeks of the school year. Such flexible scheduling means depending upon adults at other locations (parents, librarians, special educational agents, various stores and other businesses, volunteers) to act as sponsors for various activities and as helpers responsible for children's safety. There are many possibilities. At the outset, time for professional activities can be found in a number of different ways.

1. Through a weekly "minimum" day in which school either begins late or is dismissed early to give staff members time to work together, with parents, and with other adults. A variation of this is to shorten the school day when most children are present by from thirty minutes to a full hour on all or most days.

2. Special teachers, student teachers, participating parents, and volunteers can all take over classrooms or groups of children in order to free regular teachers for periods of up to an hour or more at a time.

3. Teachers on eleven-month contracts could rotate regularly between working directly with children and carrying on study and leadership activities. Even with nine-month contracts it might be better to put the money that might otherwise be allocated for the salaries of central office supervisors and other nonclassroom personnel into salaries for

additional classroom teachers who could continuously work together and rotate in and out of direct contact with children.

Similar reallocations of funds could be used to buy the services of representatives from the various knowledge disciplines to provide inputs to teachers at selected times during the school year. Instead of giving the traditional college or extension classes which teachers often attend to obtain more credits in a field, these scholars and artists could get teachers involved in the kinds of work they do. Psychologists could, for example, help teachers collect data on the behavior of individual children and interpret those data from the points of view of different schools of learning and development. Similarly, teachers could survey their region in the manner of the physical geographer, the community's history in the manner of the historian, or they could engage in writing, dramatic acting, or painting, together with appropriate forms of artistic criticism. Another line of study that would enrich and facilitate both individual development and cooperative efforts would be in the areas of self-knowledge, interpersonal relationships, and group dynamics. Behavioral scientists could help teachers redevelop their own roles, build competence in value clarification and decision making, and help troubleshoot at the points where problems arise to block progress toward change and reform. An action research design could also be formulated to help provide formative evaluation feedback on the degree to which the procedures being employed are producing the desired results in the classrooms, personally, in the school staff group, and in the wider community. Teachers and others can participate in following this design, interpreting findings, and planning future steps in light of conclusions. In all this the principal has a key role, in line with the principles presented in earlier sections of this book.

SCHOOLING AND EDUCATION

The role of the school in the overall education of children can be summarized under three headings: working directly with children, working with others who deal directly with children, and influencing other contributors to the educational process. For the foreseeable future, at least, the school and its classrooms will continue to be the main loci for formal educational activity. Because they have more direct access to children, teachers are in a position to take responsibility for overseeing and helping to coordinate children's general educational experience. This means that, in addition to providing much of the access, guidance, and support, teachers should carry out the dual function of diagnosis and evaluation, monitoring each child's developmental course across a whole range of disciplines and dimensions of behavior. Teachers should try to keep in touch with the kinds of experiences children are having in the community, what instruction or guidance they are getting in relation to that experience, and what they are making of it—in effect, a kind of master charting of the overall educational encounters of each child.

PARENTS AND OTHER ADULTS

Teachers, principals, and other professional educators can also extend their work to enrich the lives of children by working with parents, older children and youths, and other adults in the community to involve them in the education of students and to aid in coordinating their inputs with those of the schools. More than this, teachers can include others in their on-going in-service training and professional development activities. Professional development does not have to be confined to those areas in which people are actually going to be working with children, but can extend to one's own personal life, to the tackling of problems in one's family, community, and nation.

Index